GREEK HISTORICAL DOCUMENTS:
THE HELLENISTIC PERIOD

SOCIETY OF BIBLICAL LITERATURE
Sources for Biblical Study

edited by
Charles E. Carlston

Number 16

GREEK HISTORICAL DOCUMENTS: THE HELLENISTIC PERIOD

by
Roger S. Bagnall and Peter Derow

SCHOLARS PRESS
Chico, California

GREEK HISTORICAL DOCUMENTS:
THE HELLENISTIC PERIOD

by

Roger S. Bagnall and Peter Derow

Published by
SCHOLARS PRESS
for
The Society of Biblical Literature

Distributed by
SCHOLARS PRESS
101 Salem Street
PO Box 2268
Chico, California 95927

GREEK HISTORICAL DOCUMENTS:
THE HELLENISTIC PERIOD

by
Roger S. Bagnall
and
Peter Derow

DF
235
.A1
B33

Library of Congress Cataloging in Publication Data

Bagnall, Roger S.
   Greek historical documents.

   (Sources for Biblical study ; no. 16)
   Includes bibliographical references and indexes.
   1. Greece—History—Macedonian Hegemony, 323–
281 B.C.—Sources. 2. Greece—History—281 B.C.–146
B.C.—Sources. I. Derow, Peter. II. Title. III. Series.
DF235.A1B33   938'.08   81–5604
ISBN 0–89130–496–7 (pbk.)   AACR2

Printed in the United States of America
1   2   3   4   5   6
Edwards Brothers, Inc.
Ann Arbor, Michigan 48104

To the memory of
C. BRADFORD WELLS

CONTENTS

TABLE OF DOCUMENTS

PREFACE

This volume contains both inscriptions and papyri from the period from the death of Philip II of Macedon in 336 to the end of the Ptolemaic dynasty in 30 B.C. The book does not, unlike its predecessors in the series, contain any literary texts. We regret this all the more in that many of the texts important for the parts of the Hellenistic period where no connected ancient narrative exists are fragmentary and inaccessible to most undergraduates. But the book is already much longer than its companions and we have thought it more important to present the documents.

The volume is intended for use either independently or as a companion for C. Bradford Welles, *Alexander and the Hellenistic World* (Toronto: Hakkert 1970). The present volume largely follows the organization of Welles and includes most of the papyri and inscriptions mentioned by him. The papyri have been prepared by Bagnall and the inscriptions by Derow, although we have each examined the other's section.

The choice of papyri began with a list made by Alan E. Samuel at a time when he hoped to collaborate on this volume himself. When other commitments prevented the realization of this plan, he turned his preliminary collection over to Bagnall, and it has been helpful at many points. Most of the work on the papyri was done during 1972-1974 when Bagnall was in Tallahassee; he owes some useful suggestions to students in his Hellenistic history class there who used the first draft. He was able to remedy many of the deficiencies of the Florida State University Library with funds from a grant from the university's Council on Faculty Research Support, and for this he remains grateful.

The portion of the manuscript concerning papyri was read by Elsa Peterson Gibson, whose comments improved accuracy, intelligibility, and style throughout.

The work on the inscriptions was carried out largely in Toronto between 1973 and 1975 and finished at the Institute for Advanced Study in Princeton, where Derow is extremely grateful to have been invited to spend spring 1976 as a member of the School of Historical Studies. The selection was influenced partly by the desire to include the inscriptions cited by Welles along with many of those frequently referred to in the standard

XV

histories (in English) of the Hellenistic period, and partly also by the desire to provide documents particularly from those periods where non-epigraphical evidence is relatively scarce or fragmentary. To the Office of Research Administration of the University of Toronto Derow would like to express his thanks for two grants-in-aid which helped to facilitate this undertaking, as he would also to Michael M. Sage for bibliographical assistance at an early stage of the project. Many improvements in the inscriptions were effected by Professor M.B. Wallace, who kindly agreed to check the translations.

It can hardly be hoped that further errors have not escaped us in a work of this sort, and we shall be especially thankful to readers who send us corrections and suggestions for an eventual new edition.

This book owes much, directly and indirectly, to the scholarship and wisdom of C. Bradford Welles, our teacher at Yale and Princeton. The tradition of attention to documents which he inherited from Michael Rostovtzeff led him in turn to instill into his students a profound respect for even the humblest of first-hand testimony from the ancient world. This volume is offered to his memory in the hope that through it more students may be able to approach the Hellenistic world directly and to sense the fascination of its remains.

March, 1976   Roger S. Bagnall
                     Department of Greek
                     and Latin
                     Columbia University

                     P.S. Derow
                     Department of Classics
                     University College, Toronto

When circumstances prevented the realization of the original plan of publication by Samuel, Stevens Publishers of Toronto, the Society of Biblical Literature very kindly agreed to take over the volume in their series of 'Sources for Biblical Study.' We are grateful to Professor Charles E. Carlston, the editor, and to the staff of Scholars Press for their care in the final stages of preparation. Except for a few references, the book reflects the state of the manuscript in spring, 1976.

December, 1980

A NOTE ON EDITORIAL PRACTICE AND ABBREVIATIONS

Each document is given a brief introduction, which seeks only to provide a context; any detailed discussion is impossible here. The notes at the end are intended to justify our translation in cases where it relies on a text different from that cited as a source and to explain possibly obscure points not covered in the introduction or in the glossary. The bibliographical notes included with some documents suggest only some works that we have found helpful.

Within the texts, square brackets, ([,]) indicate places in which the damaged original has been restored, while parentheses indicate editorial insertions for the sake of clarity or give the probable sense of an unrestored passage. We have indicated small lacunae for which no restoration is offered by dots (...), longer ones by dashes (———). It should be said that in the case of papyri where a usable English translation already existed we have used it with whatever alterations were needed rather than make an entirely new version. In the case of inscriptions, the versions in Welles' *Royal Correspondence* have been taken over with some changes; for the rest, although English (and other) translations were consulted where available, it seemed on the whole desirable to make new translations. These, it should be said, aim more at being fairly literal than at anything else. The technical and formulaic nature of many official texts makes it difficult to suggest good alternatives to some phrasings.

Names have been transliterated for the most part in a literal Greek-English system. A few well-known people (especially royalty) and places have been given in the traditional Latinized or Anglicized forms. Ptolemy is used for kings and their family, Ptolemaios for commoners. All dates are B.C. unless otherwise noted.

Papyri are cited according to the system described in the *Checklist of Editions of Greek Papyri and Ostraca* (Missoula 1978). The collections of inscriptions cited are the following:

Asylieurkunden = G. Klaffenbach, *Asylieurkunden aus Kos* (Abh. Akad. Wiss. Berlin 1952)

Erythrai = H. Engelmann, R. Merkelbach, *Die Inschriften von Erythrai und Klazomenai* I, II (Bonn 1972, 1973)

I. Délos = *Inscriptions de Délos* (Paris 1926-)

IPE I² = B. Latyschev, *Inscriptiones Antiquae Orae Septentrionalis Ponti Euxini Graecae et Latinae* I, 2nd ed. (Petropolis 1916)

Ilion = P. Frisch, *Die Inschriften von Ilion* (Bonn 1975)

Milet I 3 = A. Rehm, G. Kawerau, *Das Delphinion in Milet* (Berlin 1914)

Moretti = L. Moretti, *Iscrizioni Storiche Ellenistiche* I (Firenze 1967)

OGIS = W. Dittenberger, *Orientis Graecae Inscriptiones Selectae* (Leipzig 1903-05)

Priene = F. Frhr. Hiller von Gaertringen, *Inschriften von Priene* (Berlin 1906)

RC = C.B. Welles, *Royal Correspondence in the Hellenistic Period* (New Haven 1934)

RDGE = R.K. Sherk, *Roman Documents from the Greek East* (Baltimore 1969)

SEG = *Supplementum Epigraphicum Graecum* (Leiden 1923-71)

Staatsverträge = *Die Staatsverträge des Altertums*, vol. III, ed. H.H. Schmitt (München 1969)

*Syll.*³ = W. Dittenberger, *Sylloge Inscriptionum Graecarum*, 3rd ed. (Leipzig 1915-24)

Tod, *GHI* = M.N. Tod, *Greek Historical Inscriptions*, vol. II (Oxford 1948)

Some corrections to papyri are cited from their listing in:

BL = F. Preisigke et al., *Berichtigungsliste der griechischen Papyrusurkunden* (1915-)

I POLITICAL HISTORY

A. Alexander the Great

1. PRIENE HONORS ANTIGONUS

Tod, *GHI* 186 (*Syll.*³ 278)   Summer, 334

Following his victory over the Persians in the cavalry battle at the Granikos River in May of 334, Alexander proceeded south in Asia Minor and, after his arrival at Ephesos, set about the liberation of the Greek cities (Arrian 1.18.1-2; on Alexander's actions and policy here see esp. E. Badian, "Alexander the Great and the Greeks of Asia," *Ancient Society and Institutions, Studies Presented to Victor Ehrenberg* [Oxford 1966] 37-70). To this period (about August, 334) belongs the present decree of the city of Priene (cf. the reference to autonomy in the prescript). Antigonus, later known as the "One-Eyed" (Monophthalmos), served in Alexander's army as commander of the allied contingents until early in 333 when he was appointed satrap of Phrygia (Arrian 1.29.3). From Alexander's death in June, 323 until his own on the field at Ipsos in 301, Antigonus' rôle in the struggles of the successors was a major one (see further nos. 6 and 7). Precisely what he did for Priene in 334 is unknown.

[Resolved] by the *boule* [and the *demos*], on the second of [the month] Metageitnion, at a [regular] assembly, the Prieneans being autonomous, Hippo[krates] being the *prytanis*: to Antigonus, son of Philippos, Macedonian, who has been a benefactor and who is zealous toward the city of the Prieneans, to give to him *proxenia* and citizenship and the right to own land and house, and freedom from taxation on all things pertaining to his own house, except land, and the right of import and export, both in war and in peace, free from plunder and without special treaty, and access to the magistrates and the *demos* of the Prieneans first after the sacred matters; and for these things to belong to him and to his descendants.

2. A LETTER OF ALEXANDER TO THE CHIANS

Tod, *GHI* 192 (*Syll.*³ 283)   332

Early in 333 the island city of Chios, previously governed by a democracy that supported Alexander, was betrayed to Darius' commander Memnon (Arrian 2.1.1;

cf. Diod. 17.29.2). An oligarchy was thereupon established and a number of people, presumably anti-Persian democrats, expelled from the city. In the latter part of 332 the democrats succeeded in turning the city over to Alexander's admiral Hegelochos after a siege (Arrian 3.1.3-4; Curtius 4.5.15-18). It is probably to the period immediately after the recovery of the city by Alexander's forces that this letter belongs. While the prescript indicates that the letter was addressed by Alexander to the Chians, its original form seems to have been altered in the process of transcription at Chios: note the differing forms of reference to Alexander in the third person, the use of what appears to be the royal plural in the provision about the Chian triremes, and the ambiguous "us" (a royal plural, or does it refer to the Chians themselves?) in the last sentence but one.

Deisitheos being the *prytanis*; from King Alexander to [the] *demos* of the Chians. All the exiles from Chios are to return; the form of government in Chios is to be *demos*. Law-drafters are to be chosen, who shall draft and revise the laws, in order that nothing may be contrary to the democracy or the return of the exiles; the results of the revision and drafting are to be referred to Alexander. The Chians are to provide twenty triremes with crews at their own expense, and these are to sail for as long as the rest of the fleet of the Greeks sails with us. Of those who betrayed the city to the barbarians, as many as have already departed are to be exiles from all the cities sharing in the peace[1] and are to be subject to arrest according to the resolution of the Greeks; as many as have been caught are to be taken before and judged in the *synhedrion* of the Greeks.[2] If there is any dispute between those who have returned and those in the city, they are to be judged in this matter before us. Until the Chians are reconciled with one another, there is to be as large a garrison as may be sufficient among them from Alexander the King, and this the Chians are to support.[3]

3. CYRENE SUPPLIES GRAIN TO THE GREEKS

Tod, *GHI* 196   330-326

Early in the 320's Greece labored under a serious shortage of grain (cf. no. 62). Prices rose widely, but such was the fertility of Cyrene in North Africa that it could at the same time distribute grain from a massive surplus (probably at reduced prices rather than free; so Tod, *GHI* II, p. 276). The total listed here is 805,000 *medimnoi* (the equivalent of 1,207,500 Attic *medimnoi*, if the figure is given according to the Aeginetan standard, cf. Tod, loc.cit.), and it went to numerous places in Greece and the islands, as well as to two individuals: Alexander's mother Olympias (a total of 72,600 *medimnoi*) and his sister Cleopatra (50,000).

The priest (is) Sosias, son of Kalliadas. Those to whom the city gave grain, when there was the shortage of grain in Greece: To the Athenians, 100,000 (*medimnoi*); to Olympias, 60,000; to the Argives, 50,000; to the Larisaeans, 50,000; to the Corinthians, 50,000; to Cleopatra, 50,000; to the Rhodians,

30,000; to the Sikyonians, 30,000; to the Meliboians, 20,000; to the Megarians, 20,000; to the T[en]ians, 20,000; to the Lesbians, 15,000; to the Theraeans, 15,000; to the Oitaeans, 15,000; to the Ambrakiots, 15,000; to the Leukadians, 15,000; to the Karystians, 15,000; to Olympias, 12,600; to the Thessalians of Atrax, 10,000; to the Kythnians, 10,000; to the Opountians, 10,000; to the Kydoniates, 10,000; to the Koans, 10,000; to the Parians, 10,000; to the Delphians, 10,000; to the Knossians, 10,000; to the Boeotians of Tanagra, 10,000; to the Akarnanians of Palairos, 10,000; to the Megarians, 10,000; to the Meliboians, 8,500; to the Phliasians, 8,000; to the Hermioneans, 8,000; to the Oitaeans, 6,400; to the Troizenians, 6,000; to the Plataeans, 6,000; to the Keans of Ioulis, 5,000; to the Aiginetans, 5,000; to the Hyrtakinians, 5,000; to the Aiginetans, 5,000; to the Keans of Karthaia, 4,000; to the Kytherans, 3,100; to the Keans, 3,000; to the Illyrians, 3,000; to the Keans of Koresos, 3,000; to the Ambrakiots, 1,500; to the [I]ketyrians, 1,000; to the Knossians, 900.

4. RESTORATION OF EXILES TO TEGEA

Tod, *GHI* 202 (*Syll.*³ 306)   324

In summer 324 Alexander sent Nikanor of Stagira to the Olympic Games with instructions for him to have the victorious herald read out the following communication: "King Alexander to the exiles from the Greek cities: We were not responsible for the fact that you are in exile, but we will be responsible for your return to your own fatherlands. We have written to Antipater about these matters, that he might compel to bring back (their exiles) those cities that do not wish to do so." (Diod. 18.8.4; cf. 17.109.1). On the whole the measure was welcomed, especially by the more than 20,000 exiles present, but it produced immediate discontent at Athens and in Aetolia (Diod. 18.8.6 ff.). It also produced problems in the various cities affected, and the present text gives an indication of how the situation was handled at Tegea. Apparently a previous piece of Tegean legislation had not found complete favor with Alexander, and what we have is a version revised in the light of the statement of principles communicated to the city in the king's *diagramma* referred to at various points in the text.

[——— King Alex]ander [———] the *diagramma*; (it) is to be written as the city has corrected (it) according to the objections raised in the *diagramma*. The exiles who return are to receive the property on their father's side, which was theirs when they went into exile; and as many women as, not having been given in marriage, held property and did not in fact have brothers (are to receive) the property on the mother's side. And if it should happen, in the case of a woman given in marriage, that her brother and his line be extinct, then she shall have the property on the mother's side, and it shall not go to a more distant relation. Regarding houses, each is to have one (house), according to the *diagramma*. If a house has a garden by it, let him not take another (garden); if there is no garden by the house, but there is one up to a distance of a *plethron* away, let him take half of it, as is prescribed in the case of other land. As the price of the houses,[4] let him receive for each house two minas; the tax-assessment on the houses is to be as the city reckons; the tax on the gardens is to be double what is prescribed in the law; the city is to remit the money and not to give a formal receipt either to the exiles or to those previously enjoying citizen-rights at home.[5] Regarding the festivals which the exiles have been missing, the city is to deliberate, and whatever the city decides after deliberation is to be valid and binding. The foreign court is to sit for sixty days. For as many as do not file suit within the sixty days, it is not to be possible for them to have property claims judged in the foreign court,[6] but at all times in the city court. If they discover anything subsequently, (let them bring it to court) in sixty days from the day the court begins to sit; if he does not file suit even within this time, it shall no longer be possible for him to have the matter judged. If any return later, when the foreign court[6] is no longer in session, let him register the property (in question) with the *strategoi* within sixty days; and if the matter is one that requires defense, the court is to be at Mantinea. If he does not file suit within this period, it shall no longer be possible for him to have the matter judged. Regarding the sacred moneys [———] amounts owing, in cases where the city has settled with the goddess[7] let him who is in possession of the property give over half of it to him who has returned, just as the others are to do. As many as have themselves been in debt to the goddess, by way of guarantees or otherwise, if he who is in possession of the property has evidently settled the debt to the goddess, let him give half to the one returning, just as the others are to do, without delay. If he has evidently not paid the goddess back, let him give over half of the property to the one returning, but let him settle the debt from his own half. If he does not wish to settle it, let him give over the whole of the property to the one returning, and let the latter, when has received it, settle the whole debt to the goddess. As many wives or daughters of the exiles as remained at home and married or who went into exile and later married in Tegea and paid for their exemption (from banishment) remaining at home, neither these nor their descendants are to be subject to inquiry about paternal or maternal property, except those who were forcibly exiled subsequently and who are returning on the present occasion, either they themselves or their children — both they and their descendants are to be subject to inquiry about the paternal and maternal property, according to the *diagramma*. I swear by Zeus, Athena, Apollo, Poseidon that I shall bear good-will towards those who have returned whom the city has resolved to receive back, and I shall bear no malice against any of them for anything he may propose after the day on which I swear the oath, nor shall I stand in the way of the safety of those who have returned, neither in [. . .] nor in the public affairs of the city [———] against those who have returned [———] to the city[———] what is written in the *diagramma* about [———] nor shall I give counsel against any one (of them).

5. RESTORATION OF EXILES TO MYTILENE

Tod, *GHI* 201 (*OGIS* 2)   324

This inscription is part of a decree passed by the Lesbian city of Mytilene and containing regulations dealing with the return to the city of exiled citizens. The context is probably the same as that of the similar Tegean enactment of 324 (no. 4), although it has been assigned also to that of Alexander's letter to the Chians (no. 2; see C.B. Welles, *AJA* 42 (1938) 245-260). It is at any rate clear that these measures were directly influenced by communication from Alexander.

[———and let the] *basileis* [favor the one who has returned on the ground that] the one previously [in the] city [is guilty of fraud. But if any of those who have returned] does not abide by these settlements [let him not receive (?)] from the city any property and let him not [enter into possession] of any of those things which those previously in the city granted to him, but let those previously in the city who granted (them) [to him] enter upon possession of these things, and let the *strategoi* [transfer the possessions back] to the one previously in the city [on the ground that] the one who has returned [has not observed the settlement], and let the *basileis* favor [the one] previously [in] the city on the ground that the one [who has returned] is guilty of fraud. And if anyone institutes a lawsuit concerning these things let neither [the *peri*] *dromoi* nor the *diaskopoi* nor any other magistrate bring it to court. [It is to be the concern of] the *strategoi* and the *basileis* and the *pe*[*ridromoi* and] the *disaskopoi* and the [other] magistrates if [everything does not take place] as [has been written] in the [decree; and let them condemn [him who disregards any of the things] written [in the decree], in order that [there may be] no difference between those who have returned and those [previously] in the city, [but] (that) all who have been reconciled [may deal] with one another [without suspicion and] without plotting, and (that they may abide by [the king's answer and] by the settlement in this decree. The *demos* [is to choose as arbitrators] twenty men, ten [from those who have returned] and ten from those previously in the city. Let these [maintain careful watch] and see to it that there shall be no [difference between those] who have returned and those previously in the city; and [they shall act] concerning the disputed possessions [so that those who return] shall, [preferably,] come to terms both with those in the city and with [one another], and, failing this, that they shall be as just as possible, and that all shall abide by the settlements which the king has determined [and by the reconciliation], and shall inhabit the city [and the country] in a state of concord with one another. And concerning possessions, [after] the settlements [have been accepted] as far as possible, and concerning the oath, [which the] citizens [are to swear], concerning all these things where mutual agreement has been achieved, let the men chosen bring (reports) before the [*demos*, and let the *demos*,] when it has heard, deliberate as to what it considers advantageous. [If the *demos* considers the] mutual agreements advantageous, [it is to decree for those who] returned during the prytany of Smithinas [the same as] has been decreed [for the rest]. If there is anything lacking from this decree, [the decision concerning this shall be] with the *boule*. When the decree has been ratified [by the *demos*, the entire] *demos*, on the twentieth of the month [after the sacrifice, is to pray] to the gods that the settlement between those who returned [and those previously] in the city occurs for the safety and happiness [of all the citizens]. [All the public] priests and priestesses are to open the temples and [the *demos* is to come together for prayer.] The sacrifices which the *demos* vowed, when it dispatched [the messengers to] the king, are to be offered on the king's [birthday] every year; present at the sacrifice are to be [the twenty men and the] messengers sent to the king, [the ones from those previously] in the city and the ones from [those who returned.] When the treasurers have had this [decree] inscribed [on a stele———.]

B. The Successors of Alexander (323-276)

6. ANTIGONUS AND SKEPSIS

RC 1 (*OGIS* 5 + II 538) and *OGIS* 6   311

The peace concluded in 311 between Antigonus on the one hand and Cassander, Lysimachus and Ptolemy on the other is known only through this inscription and a brief report in Diodorus (19.105.1). The terms, according to Diodorus, were as follows: "Cassander is to be *strategos* of Europe until the Alexander born of Roxane comes of age; Lysimachus is to be master of Thrace, and Ptolemy of Egypt and the cities bordering on it in Libya and Arabia; Antigonus is to have command over all Asia; the Greeks are to be autonomous." The sequel to this, as Diodorus reports, was the murder by Cassander of Roxane and the young Alexander. With the disappearance of this last recognized royal remnant, "each of those who ruled over peoples or cities maintained hopes of monarchy and held the territory assigned as subject to him as a sort of spear-won kingdom" (Diod. 19.105.4). The terms of the peace itself had effectively put the seal upon the partition of Alexander's empire. For Antigonus the peace represents an enforced denial of any wider ambitions, but by championing the cause of the Greek cities he was able to achieve at the same time something of a diplomatic triumph. This stance was not new to him in 311 (he had proclaimed at Tyre in 315 that all the Greek cities were to be "free, ungarrisoned, and autonomous" [Diod. 19.61.3]), and it is effectively reasserted in the explanation of the negotiations contained in the letter to Skepsis, which was presumably only one of many such sent out to the cities. In the Skepsians' reply, Antigonus' report is enthusiastically welcomed and cult honors are decreed for him.

RC 1

——we exercised [zeal for the] liberty [of the Greeks], making for [this reason] no small concessions and distributing money besides, [and] to further this we sent out Aischylos along [with Dema]rchos. As long as there was agreement [on] this we participated in the conference on the Helle[s-pont],[8] and if certain men had not interfered the matter would then have been settled. [Now also,] when Cassander and Pto[lemy] were conferring about a truce and when Prepelaos and Aristodemos had come to us on the subject, although we saw that some of the demands of Cassander were rather burdensome, still as there was agreement concerning the Greeks we thought it necessary to overlook this in order that the main issue might be settled as soon as possible; for we should have considered it a fine thing if all had been arranged for the Greeks as we wished, but because the negotiation would have been rather long, and because we were anxious that the question of the Greeks should be settled in our lifetime,⁹ we thought it necessary not to let details endanger the settlement of the principal issue. What zeal we have shown in these matters will I think be evident to you and to all others from the arrangements themselves. After the dealings with Cassander and Lysimachus had been completed, to conclude which they had sent Prepelaos with full authority, Ptolemy sent envoys to us asking that a truce be made with him also and that he be included in the same agreement. We saw that it was no small thing to give up part of an ambition for which we had taken no little trouble and incurred much expense, and that too when an agreement had been reached with Cassander and Lysimachus and when the remaining task was easier. Nevertheless, because we thought that after a settlement had been reached with him the matter of Polyperchon¹⁰ might be arranged more quickly as no one would then be in alliance with him, and because of our relationship to him (Ptolemy),¹¹ and still more because we saw that you and our allies were burdened by the campaign and the expenses, we thought it was well to yield and to make the truce with him also. We sent Aristodemos and Aischylos and Hegesias to draw up the agreement. They have now returned with the pledges, and the representative of Ptolemy, Aristoboulos, came to receive them from us. Know then that the truce has been established and that the peace is made. We have written in the treaty that all the Greeks are to swear to aid each other in preserving their freedom and autonomy, thinking that while we lived in all human expectation these would be protected, but that afterwards freedom would remain more certainly secure for all the Greeks if both they and the men in power are bound by oaths.¹² For them to swear also to help to guard the terms of the treaty which we have made with each other seems to us neither discreditable nor disadvantageous for the Greeks; therefore it seems to me best for you to take the oath which we have sent. In the future also we shall try to provide both for you and for the other Greeks whatever advantage we have in our power. It seemed best to me then to write you also about these matters and to send to you Akios to speak further (on the subject). He brings you copies of the treaty which we have made and of the oath. Farewell.

OGIS 6

[———he has sent] Akios, who [is in every respect] well-disposed [to our city] and continues [always] to maintain [his zeal] and (who) [requests (us)] to declare to him whatever the city might need; and he has sent also the agreements which have come about between himself and Cassander and Ptolemy and Lysimachus and copies of the oaths; and (he has sent a report of) what has been done concerning the freedom and autonomy of the Greeks. Be it resolved by the *demos*, since Antigonus has been responsible for great goods for the city and for the rest of the Greeks, to praise Antigonus and to rejoice with him over what has been done; and for the city to rejoice also with Greeks at the fact that, being free and autonomous, they will continue [for] the future to exist in peace. In order that Antigonus may be honored in a manner worthy of what has been done and that the *demos* may be seen to render thanks for the good things it has already received, (be it resolved) to set aside a precinct for him and to make an altar and to set up as fine an image as possible; and for the sacrifice and the festival to take place in his honor each year, just as it was even formerly carried out; and to crown him with a gold crown of 100 gold [staters]; and to crown also Demetrius and Philip,[13] each with (a crown of) fifty gold pieces; and to proclaim the crowns [at the] contest during the festival; and for the city to sacrifice (the offering of) glad-tidings at the news sent by Antigonus; and for all the citizens to wear garlands; and for the treasurer to provide the expenditure for these things. (Resolved) also to send him gifts of friendship; and to have the agreements and the letters from Antigonus and the oaths which he sent inscribed on a stele, just as Antigonus instructed, and to set it up in the sanctuary of Athena; (and) for the secretary to look after (this); and for the treasurer to provide the expenditure for this as well. (Resolved also) for all the citizens to swear the oath that has been sent just as Anti[gonus instructed]; (and) for those chosen———.

7. TWO LETTERS OF ANTIGONUS TO TEOS

RC 3 and 4 (*Syll.*[3] 344)   306-302

At some point in the last years of the fourth century Antigonus decided to unite the cities of Teos and Lebedos into a single, new city of Teos. This was to involve the removal of all the inhabitants of Lebedos to Teos (which was perhaps to be rebuilt on the peninsula slightly to the west of its existing location). These two letters from Antigonus to Teos contain various regulations for and instructions about the synoecism, which was in fact never finally accomplished. They (or at least the second of them) were written between 306 (when Antigonus adopted the royal title: Diod. 19.53.2) and 302 (when Cassander's general Prepelaos won over Teos: Diod. 20.107.5). The two letters can have been separated by no long time, as some of the instructions issued in the first had not been carried out when the second was written.

[———whoever] is sent to the Panionion, we thought it best that he should perform all the] common (ceremonies) for an equal period and should bivouac and attend the festival with [your envoys] and be called Tean.[14]

We thought it best that a building lot [be given] to each of the L[ebedians] among you equal to that which he leaves behind in Lebedos. Until the new houses are built, houses [are to be furnished to all] the Lebedians without charge: if the present city remains, one-[third of the] existing houses; if it is necessary to tear down the present city, half of the existing houses [are to be left], and of these one-third are to be given [to the Lebedians] and you are to have two-thirds; if a certain part of the city is torn down and the remaining houses [are enough] to receive both you and the Lebedians, [the] third part of these] are to be given to the Leb[edians]; if the remaining houses are not enough to receive both you [and the Lebedians], enough of the houses which are going to be torn down are to be left. [And when] enough houses [have been completed] in the city that is being built, then the houses which [were left] are to be demolished, [as many as] lie outside the walls of the city. [All the Lebedians] are to build houses on their lots within three years; otherwise the [lots] are to become public property. [We thought] it right that the roofs of the houses be given to the Lebedians,[15] a quarter of the total number each year for four years, [so that] the houses [may be finished as soon as possible].

[We thought] it right also that a place be assigned the Lebedians where they may bury their [dead].

(We thought it right) that [whatever] the city of Lebedos owes [as interest] be met from the common [revenues each year], and that these debts [be assumed] by your city on the conditions under which the Leb[edians owe] them.

As to the *proxenoi* of the city of Lebedos or those benefactors who possess [citizenship] or some other grant or honor from the Lebedians, (we thought it right) [that they have the same among] you, and that their names be inscribed within a year in the place where your *proxenoi* [and benefactors are] inscribed.

As to the suits based on injury or breach of contract [now standing] in either city, [we thought it right] that the litigants be reconciled or the cases adjudged separately [according to the] laws [of each city] and according to our *diagramma,* within two years from the time when [the *diagramma*] is promulgated. As to those suits which (you) have against Lebedians or the Lebedians have [against you, (we thought it right) that both cities make] an agreement, and put the agreement into writing; and if any objection is raised [against the] agreement, that the matter be decided in (before) the umpire (city)[16] within six months; that the umpire [city be] Mitylene, as both have agreed. [We think it best] that the drafters of the agreement should write the other terms as they may choose, but as we hear that the suits over contracts and over injuries are [so numerous] that if [they were judged according to] the [law], even without interruption, no one would be able to wait for the end — for up to now [it does not appear that any progress] has been made with these nor have the contracts been executed because the suits have [long] remained [unadjudicated] — and if the interest accumulates [from year to year, no one] would be able to pay it. We think it best for the drafters of the agreement to provide, if [the debtors pay] of their own accord, that they pay no more than double the value [of the debt], and if they go to court and are adjudged liable, (that they pay) three times its value.

Whenever the agreement [is ratified], (we think it right) that the suits be filed and judged within a year; and that anyone who does not file his suit [or have it judged] in the time prescribed, if the courts are sitting, should no longer be able to file it or [to have it judged; and if any] of your (citizens) or of the Lebedians is not in the city during the prescribed period, that it should be possible to serve a summons upon him [in his absence] before the town hall and before his house, notifying the [proper official...] in the presence of two responsible witnesses.

(We thought it right) that in the future [penalties] be paid [and received according to] whatever laws you may think are fair to both cities; [that each city appoint] as law-drafters three (men) not younger than forty years [who are incorruptible], and let the men chosen swear that they will draw up such laws as [they consider] to be best and to be of benefit to the city. After they have taken the oath, [let them draw up what] laws [they think] will be fair to both cities and let them submit them within [six months]. (We thought it right) that anyone else who wishes be permitted to draw up and submit a law. (We thought it right) that those of the laws [submitted] be put into practice which the law-drafters may agree upon and the *demos* ratify, [and that those which are opposed] be sent to us so that we may either decide about them [or designate a city] to do so; that (you) send (to us) also the [laws] which are agreed upon and that you indicate which were submitted by the law-drafters and [which were submitted by others, so that] if any have obviously drawn up a law not for the best but [inappropriately], we may charge him with it and punish him; that these things be done within a year. [Until all the] laws should have been drawn up, your envoys thought it best [to use the laws] of your city, [but those from] Lebedos asked permission to send for and [to use] those from some other city. [Since] we thought it fairer to send for [laws] from another city, [we directed] both parties to name the city whose laws they wished to use, and as both agreed to use the laws of the Koans we decided that this should be done, [and we have requested the Koans] to give you the laws to copy.[17] We think [it best] that three men [be appointed] as soon as this answer is read and that they be sent [to Kos in] three [days] to copy the laws; that those who are sent [shall bring back the] laws sealed with the seal of the Koans in [thirty] days; that when the laws [are brought back] you and the Lebedians shall elect the (new) magistrates [within] ten [days].

As to those men who have been *choregos* or trierarch or have performed another [liturgy] in either city, we think it best that they no longer [be liable for the same liturgy]. The envoys of the Lebedians [asked] that they be relieved of [the liturgies] for such time as the synoecism is in process. We think it best, if all of you remain [in the old city], that the Lebedians should be immune from the liturgies for three years. [If any of you] move into the peninsula, that they also should be immune for the [same period and that those whose] houses are not moved (*or* torn down?) should assume the liturgies.

The envoys of the L[ebedians] said [that it was necessary] to set aside from the revenues [one thousand] four hundred gold staters for the supply [of grain, so that] anyone who wished, taking this money against security, [might import grain into the] city and sell it throughout the year whenever he wished, and that [at the end of the year] he should return the money to the city, both the capital and the interest at the rate [at which he took it.[18] When they particularly requested us] to order that this be done even now so that there might be [a sufficient quantity] of grain [in the city] — for you could not produce enough — your envoys expressed [their approval but asked] that more money be appropriated as the synoecism [was being completed] and the population was becoming [larger] as you moved into the same place. Previously we were un[willing] to grant that [any] city should undertake the importation of grain or maintain a supply of grain, [for we were not willing to have the] cities spend for this purpose large sums of money unnecessarily; we did not [wish] even now to give this permission, for the tributary [land][19] is near [and thus if a need] of grain arose, we think there could easily be brought from [there as much as] one wished. Our anxiety on this point was due [to a desire] to benefit the [cities], since you and all the others [know that there is] no private profit [for us] in the business, but we maintain the regulation [in the hope that] the cities may become free of their debts. Seeing [that as far as lies in our power] we have made you free and autonomous[20] in other respects [we thought] to exercise some care over your debts also that they might be paid off as soon as possible. [As, however], this plan for the supply of grain seems [advantageous], we think it best, in order that we may [omit] nothing [which is both just] and also advantageous to the *demos* that the [supplies] of grain should be established as the Lebedian envoys said, believing that there should be provided against security a total of one thousand [four hundred] gold staters.

(We think it best) that the import and export of all [grains] be declared [in the portico of the] market, so that if it should not pay any persons to bring the grain into the [market and thence to] export it, they may have the right to export (directly), paying the duty on what is declared [in the market]. As to what villages or farms there may be outside [the city], we think it best that each man be ordered to register [as much produce] as he wishes to export (directly) from the farmland, so that he may export (it) having made declaration [to the market-commissioner and] paid [the] taxes.

Your envoys [and those from the Lebe]dians asked that three men be appointed from each city to frame any regulations furthering the synoecism [which may have been omitted. It seems to us desirable] that the men be appointed within thirty days [of the time when this answer] is read, and that the ones chosen draw up any measures which have been omitted [by us]; that of their provisions those [are to be valid] which are agreed upon by both (cities), and that the disputed points are to be referred to us within the two following months, (so that) after hearing [both sides] we may decide as we think [is best] for both.

RC 4

King Antigonus to the *boule* and the *demos* of the Teans, greeting. When we [before studied] how the synoecism might be completed most quickly, we did not see from what source the [necessary] money would come [for you] to be able [to give immediately] to the Lebedians the value of their houses, because the amount arising from the revenues comes in over a [rather long] period of time. [When we received] your envoys and those from the Lebedians and asked [them if they had any] expedient to suggest to us, and they said they had none except taxation, examining [their proposals] we find that only your wealthiest citizens have always advanced the property taxes. [It seems good to us, then,] that there should be six hundred (designated as) wealthy, [and that these] should advance money in proportion to their property, so that there may be [for the Lebedians] one-fourth of the compensation available at once, and that repayment be made to these men first, after an interval [of a year] from the revenues [of the city,] all of them being appropriated for this purpose.[21]

(It seems to us best) that the men who are going to bring the appraisers [of the houses] from Kos [and the] men who are going to copy the laws should be chosen as soon as the abrogation(?)[22] [takes place and] be sent out in five days from the time they are chosen, and that those who are [sent] for the laws should bring them from Kos and report them in the period which we specified in the answer (i.e., the previous letter). [Those] who are sent [for the] appraisers should bring the appraisers back as quickly as possible.

[We think best————] that the houses in your city which must be given to the Lebedians for [temporary residence] be counted [within] fifteen [days] from the reading of [this] answer, and that those who are to count [the houses and] assign them to the temporary occupants be elected by each [tribe] at the next assembly.

8. THE HELLENIC LEAGUE OF 302

Staatsverträge 446 (Moretti 44)   302

As early as 307/6 Antigonus had sought to establish a united coalition of the Greeks in Greece (Diod. 20.46). Nothing came of it then, but in 302 representatives from a number of Greek states met with Demetrius at the Isthmus and the charter of the new Hellenic League was drawn up (Diod. 20.102, Plut. *Demetrius* 25). The fragmentary state of the text (found at Epidauros) makes it impossible to determine who the original members were or exactly how many in number, but there would seem to have been at least a half dozen, including Elis and the Achaean League. The immediate aim of the venture was to unite the Greeks with Antigonus and Demetrius in the war against Cassander, but the provisions were drawn up with the view that the organization would continue to exist in peace time. Whether it could have done is perhaps doubtful, but there was certainly no chance of its surviving the defeat and death of Antigonus at Ipsus in 301.

Fragment I

————there is to be friendship and [alliance for all time] between [those...sharing in the] synhedrion[23]...and Antigonus and Demetrius ..., so that they have the [same] enemies and friends [———] by land and sea the Kings Antigonus and Demetrius [———]. [If any] of the allies or those sharing in the synhedrion [———] any of the cities sharing in the agreement [———] ravage the land or capture garrisons [———or] seek to destroy [the monarchy of Antigonus and] Demetrius and their descendants or [cities? constitutions?———].

Fragment II

[———it is not to be allowed for the cities] to do anything other [than what has been written; if any act contrary (to the agreements) either in] word or deed, let [anyone who wishes] bring a charge [about them to the prohedroi;[24] let the syn]hedroi pass judgment [and, if they are convicted, let them pay as a penalty whatever they seem to deserve to suffer] or to pay. [Let care be taken . . . to ensure that the] sea is clear [of pirates?———]; to use the ancestral constitutions———nor with the purpose of revolution———[if someone proposes or votes that———for the proposer and the] one who put the vote to be judged [by the synhedroi; if the synhedroi do not judge, let] anyone who wishes [bring a charge] about them [———].

Fragment III

————it shall not be permitted to [interfere with either the] ambassadors [from the Greeks (?) to] the synhedroi [or those] dispatched [by the] synhedroi, or with those sent out on common [campaign, either as they are going out] (to the places) to which the individual contingents have been ordered or as they are returning to their [cities?], or to kidnap them or to seize them [on any] charge. If anyone [does these things,] let [the] magistrates in each of the cities prevent him, and let the sy[nhedroi pronounce judgment.] Let the synhedroi assemble in time of peace [at the sacred games?], but in time of war as often as seems beneficial to the synhedroi and to [the strateg]os left behind by the kings for the common protection. The synhedrion shall sit for as many days as the prohedroi of the synhedrion announce. The meetings of the synhedrion shall take place, until such time as the common war[25] is concluded, wherever the prohedroi and the king or the strategos appointed by the kings announce; when peace comes, wherever the crowned games[26] are held. The resolutions of the synhedroi shall be [binding]. Let them conduct business when more than half their number is present, but if less than half is present they are not to conduct business. Concerning resolutions passed in the *synhedrion*, it shall not be possible for [the] cities to demand an account from the *synhedroi* who are sent.[27] When the war [ends] there shall be five [*prohe*]*droi* chosen by lot from among the *synhedroi*. No more than one may be selected by lot from any league or city. These shall bring together the *synhedroi* and [the] common secretaries [and the] assistants; and they shall put forward the matters about which [it is necessary] to deliberate; and they shall [pass on the resolutions to the secretaries, having themselves [clear?]copies, and they shall introduce [all?] the legal cases, and shall take care that all business is conducted [as is needful,] having the power to fine anyone acting in a disorderly way. [If anyone wishes] to introduce [any matter] of advantage to the kings [and the Greeks,] or to report [anyone as] acting contrary to the interests of the allies [or] disobeying the resolutions, or to bring any other business before the *synhedroi*, let him register [with the *prohedroi*] and let them bring the matter before the *synhedroi*. [The] *prohedroi* chosen by lot [are to be] required to render account for [everything] which they do.[28] Let [whoever wishes] (to bring charges against them) register it with the *prohedroi* next chosen by lot. Let [those who take over] bring the charge before the *synhedroi* at the first sitting [next ensuing]. Until the common war is ended, the *prohedroi* shall [always be those] (sent) from the kings. [If] any city does not send the *synhedroi* [to the] assemblies according to the agreements], let it pay a fine for each of those (so absent) of two [drachmas or minas][29] for each [sitting] until the *synhedroi* adjourn, unless any [of the *synhedroi* declares on oath] that he was ill. And if any city does not send the assigned military contingent according to the call sent out, let it pay a daily penalty for each cavalryman of 50 drachmas; for each hoplite of 20 drachmas; for each [light-armed soldier] of 10 drachmas; and for each sailor [10?] drachmas; until [the] time of the campaign [has expired for all] the other Greeks.

Fragment IV

It shall not be permitted instead of these ——— to dispatch cavalrymen instead of infantrymen (?) ——— [the] mercenaries have been enrolled and the [mercenary-leaders?] ——— [If any?] city or individual transgresses any [of what ——— has] been written, let [the *synhedroi*] fine [them] ——— the fines for private individuals ——— for the cities the *strategos* ——— the money collected———for whatever the *synhedroi* may decide———.

Fragment V

——— [Those who are going to share in the *synhedrion* (?) are to have the] agreements and the [oaths inscribed upon] stone stelae and [have them set up, the...in..., the...in...,] the Eleians in [Olympia,———], the Achaeans in [Aigion, ———; and the others who join the] *synhedrion* [are also to have] the agreements [and the oaths inscribed in the most famous sanctuaries] among them. [(The) oath: I swear by] Zeus, Ge, Helios, P[oseidon, Athena, Ares, and all the gods and goddesses: I will abide] in the alliance [with the Kings Antigonus and Demetrius (?)] and their [descendants (?) and . . . who share in (?)] the *synhedrion*; and I shall have the same enemies and friends. And [I shall] not [bear arms to bring suffering (?) . . . against any of those] abiding by the [treaty, neither by land nor by sea (?), nor] shall I ravage the territory [. . ., nor shall I subvert the] kingdom of An[tigonus and Demetrius and their descendants. If] anyone else [does any of these things (?), doing something contrary to] the things [written] in [the treaty (?), I shall not allow (him to do so) to the extent of my power], but [I shall] go to war [against him. . . who transgresses (?). . .the] alliance [———].

9. EPHESOS RECOVERS FROM WAR

*Syll.*³ 364   after 297

After the defeat of Antigonus and Demetrius at Ipsos in 301, Ephesos continued to support Demetrius. The present inscription shows that its territory suffered heavily in the ensuing war between Demetrius and Lysimachus. As a result, many were left holding ruined property which they had used as security in contracting loans. This property could not be sold for anything like its full value, if indeed buyers could be found at all, and the lenders would therefore be entitled to seize the whole of the pledged property in repayment of the loan. To prevent this happening a long (the surviving text is only part of what was originally inscribed) and complicated series of provisions was enacted. The dominating principle is that the land, after having a fair valuation placed on it, should be divided between the owner and his creditor(s), the latter receiving land in proportion to the amount of the debt. Thus, if the loan were for 1000 drachmas and the land valued at 4000 drachmas, the creditor could expect to receive one-quarter of the land.

The judges. — It is to be possible for the judges, if the matter does not seem to them to be ready for judgment, but the landowner has placed a greater value (on the property) and the creditor a lesser one, to value it for as much as may seem well to them. There is to be no counter-estimate of the (amount of the) debt. — If the valuation is agreed but the loan is disputed, or if the loan is agreed but the valuation is disputed, the judgment is to be about what is disputed. — The decisions of the judges the *eisagogeis* are to inscribe on a whitened tablet and, along with the settlements of the arbitrators, which (the disputants) have agreed to before the court, to hand over to those who have been chosen to supervise the common war.³⁰ When those who have been chosen to supervise the common war receive the judgments and the arbitration-settlements, they are to select by lot, from the thirty who have been chosen by the *demos*, five men for each five-day period as dividers of properties, and they are to select by lot also the areas and to record these; and the men selected by lot are to perform the divisions in the areas that have fallen to them, not sundering the holdings of the creditor or those of the landholder, but dividing the parts so that these are contiguous with one another; and of the land let them give over to the creditors [and to the landholders] amounts in proportion to the value inhering, taking into account both the (amount of the) loan and the valuation; let them except in the process of division of the land roads leading to religious sites and to water and to farm-buildings and around graves. — If any dispute the division that has occurred, let them declare this to those who have been chosen to supervise the common war and to the one in charge of the court. — Let the one designated to be in charge of the court lead the judges out to the place, and let the judges, if the division seems to them not to have been justly made, make it fair by adding to each (one's share, as may be required) in proportion to the (amount of the) loan and the valuation. The partitionings accomplished by the arbitrators or the judges are to be reported to those who have been chosen to supervise the common war, including a record of the men's names, the areas, and the boundaries of the divisions.— Those who have been chosen (to supervise the common war), having had all this inscribed on whitened tablets, are to turn them over to the *neopoiai* to be set up in the temple precinct. And let them give copies of these also to the copying-clerk, in order that it may be possible for any citizen who desires to look over the partitionings of the landed properties. And this process of division is to be the same for all. — If they reach agreement between themselves in some other way about the division and register with those who have been chosen to supervise the common war, it is to be for them just as they agree between themselves; and copies of the valuations and loans are to be received by the landholder from the creditor joining with him in the agreement, and, on behalf of an orphan, by the guardian, and the fellow-guardians which each may have received; no one is to receive copies from anyone else, and those assigned to be in charge of these things are not to give them (to anyone else). Otherwise, both the one who receives and the one who gives to another are to be accursed, and both the one who receives and the one who gives are to be liable to prosecution as being disobedient and as plotting against the best interests of the city. — As many as have lent money on security of residual value,[31] these are to have recovery from the portion remaining to the landholder — whether there be one or many of them, the first (being settled with) first, the others subsequently—and the law is to be for these just as for the initial lenders. — If any, after mortgaging property to some, have borrowed from others as if on unencumbered property, deceiving the subsequent lenders, it is to be possible for the subsequent lenders, being treated as the previous lenders according to the reckoning of the common war, to have the property. If anything remains owing to them, the lenders are to have recovery from the entire property of the debtor, in any way they can and free from all penalty. And if there is a guarantor, recovery from the guarantor is to be just as from those who guarantee [unsecured] loans. — Concerning guarantors who provide guarantees with respect to the property [itself]: if the value of the property is equal to the loan for which [he is] the guarantor, based on the valuation in effect before the war, then the guarantor is to be released from his guarantee. If the amount owing is greater than the value of the property, then let the guarantor pay, proportionately, the excess of the amount owing over the value of the property,[32] as do those who guarantee unsecured loans, except if extra interest is being charged for a longer period than that of the [guarantee] made in the (original) transaction. — If the creditor is charging additional interest contrary to the (original) transaction and the [length of time] agreed in the transaction, let the guarantor not pay the excess brought about by this additional charge, unless the creditor has postponed the recovery (of the loan) with the knowledge and consent of the guarantor. If they dispute about this, they are to receive judgment before the foreign court,[33] unless they have been brought to some agreement by the arbitrators, and the creditor is to initiate the court case. — If any guardian, having borrowed (money from the orphan) during his [guardianship], is in possession of the orphan's money in any way, he is not to share in the (provisions relating to the) common war. — As many as owe dowries for their own daughters or sisters, having assigned them from their paternal property, or being guardians, either appointed in the father's will or chosen by the *demos*, have not given to the orphan girls under their guardianship the dowries assigned by their fathers, or who, having married and then been divorced, have not paid back the dowries, which are to be paid back according to law, these are to pay the dowries and the interest according to the (original) transaction; and it is not to be open to them to take into account the (provisions relating to the) common war, but let the guardians make up the deficiency in the dowry of the orphan girls out of the rest of the estate under their guardianship. — As many as have borrowed on real security since the prytany of Demagoras and the month of Posideon, for these the (provisions relating to the) common war are to apply as for the others, but the valuations of the properties are to be those of the time when the loans and the (original) transactions took place, in order that, if any entered into arrangements with their property laid waste or after the farm-buildings had been destroyed, their valuations may reflect the state of the property on the basis of which they made the arrangements.[34] — As many as have made transactions, before (the prytany of) Apollas and the month Lenaion, contrary to the (provisions relating to the) common war, these transactions are not to be valid, but those in debt to them are to be covered by the (provisions relating to the) common war. — As many as have made transactions on real security since the month of Lenaion and (the prytany of) Apollas, their transactions are to be valid and the (provisions relating to the) common war are not to apply to them, since they prospered by maintaining faith during the war, but they are not to receive interest of more than one-twelfth.—Concerning lenders who have entered upon possession of property: As many as, having entered upon possession of properties, in accordance with arrangements made, prior to the month Posideon in the year of Demagoras, hold and possess the properties, for these the possessions are to be valid, unless they (i.e. debtor and creditor) have willingly come to some agreement with one another. If any dispute about full ownership, they are to receive judgment according to the laws. As many as entered upon possession subsequent to the month Posideon in the year of Demagoras, when the borrowers were in possession of the property according to the decree and had been brought back by the *demos*, (in such cases) the properties are to belong to the borrowers and possessors, the loans to the lenders, the division taking place as for the other lenders. — If the lenders disagree with the debtors, saying they entered upon possession prior to the prytany of Demagoras and the month Posideon, they are to receive judgment just as do the others who have suffered damage in the common war. — If any have themselves willingly and without coercion come to some agreement with the lenders, although the lenders have not entered upon possession, their agreements are to be valid. If the one says that he was coerced and the other denies it, they are to receive judgment about these matters in the foreign court, but they are first to submit to arbitration before the arbitrators in accordance with this law. — As many as have departed after abandoning their property, and the creditors have begun cultivation, (in these cases) the property is to belong to the creditors. If the debtors wish to recover their property by paying back what the creditors have spent, and the interest at one-fourteenth, and anything that may have been expended in the land or lost due to cultivation, taking into account the revenues produced, it is to be possible for them, if they pay (all this) back in the year of Danaos, to share in the (provisions relating to the) common war on the same terms as the others. — Concerning the expenditures made, and the losses in cultivation, and the revenues produced, if they come to agreement with one another or are brought to agreement by the arbitrators, these (agreements) are to be (valid), otherwise they are to receive judgment before the foreign court just as do the others, and the one who abandoned the property is to initiate the court case. If any, in the years of Demagoras or Mantikrates or Apollas, up to the month Posideon, ———.

10. THE IONIAN LEAGUE HONORS HIPPOSTRATOS OF MILETOS

*Syll.*³ 368   289/8

The victory of Seleucus and Lysimachus at Ipsos in 301 won for the latter control of Asia Minor. The present text reflects at least one aspect of his administration of the area as well as his attitude toward Ephesos, which had been so steadfast in its support of Demetrius after Ipsos. The decree of the federal council of the ancient Ionian League is preserved in two copies, one from Smyrna and one from Miletos. The latter is translated here (A), along with the two related Milesian decrees inscribed along with it (B and C).

A.

Resolved by the *koinon* of the Ionians. Whereas Hippostratos, son of Hippodemos, of Miletos, a friend of King Lysimachus and appointed *strategos* in charge of the cities of the Ionians, continues to treat in a friendly and beneficent way each city individually and the Ionians as a whole, with good fortune, be it resolved by the *koinon* of the Ionians: to praise Hippostratos son of Hippodemos for his virtue and the good-will which he continues to hold toward the *koinon* of the Ionians, and for him to be free from all taxes in (the) cities of the Ionians; the same provisions are to apply to Hippostratos himself and to his descendants. And (resolved) to erect a bronze equestrian statue of him in the Panionion; and for two cities to be chosen to see to it that the statue of Hippostratos is erected with dispatch, in order that all the rest may know that the Ionians honor with the appropriate honors men who are noble and provide service to the cities. And (resolved) for each of the council-members to take back to their own cities the decisions of the Ionians, in order that the decisions of the Ionians may be there written up in the public archives. And (resolved) to have this decree inscribed on the base of the statue of Hippostratos in the Panionion and for each of the cities (to have it inscribed) in their own city on a stone stele. The cities chosen were Miletos and Arsinoeia.[35]

B.

In the year of Telesias, in (the month) Panemos. Resolved by the *demos* to have inscribed in the public archive the decree ratified at the Panionion. Supervisors of the statue of Hippostratos son of Hippodemos, chosen according to the decree decreed by the Ionians were Archidemos son of Aristokrates and Ameinias son of Krateas.

C.

In the year of Telesias, in (the month) Lenaion. Resolved by the *boule*; Protomachos son of Pylios spoke: In order that the honors decreed by the *koinon* of the Ionians for Hippostratos son of Hippodemos may be carried out with dispatch, be it resolved by the *boule* for the *teichopoioi* to see to it and to let a contract for the preparation of the stele and the inscription of the decisions and for the treasurer in office for the month of Lenaion to provide the money from the wall-building funds.

11. LYSIMACHUS AND PRIENE

Priene 14 (*OGIS* 11) and *RC* 6 (*OGIS* 12;   ca. 285 (?)
Priene 15)

During Demetrius' invasion of Asia Minor in 287/6 (for this as the context of these inscriptions see Welles, *RC*, pp. 43-44) many cities either fell to his attacks or, as all of Lydia and Caria, went over to him. Priene was among those that remained loyal to Lysimachus. It endured the ravaging of its territory by Demetrius' soldiers and the hostile population of the Maeander plain until Lysimachus' forces were able to bring relief. In return for this the city voted to establish a cult in his honor, much as had been done at Samothrace in return for helpful military intervention (*Syll.*³ 372). The first text is part of a decree of Priene communicating the city's resolutions to Lysimachus, the second (also fragmentary) is the letter written by the king in return. Lysimachus' good will, thus secured, had its limits (cf. no. 12).

Priene 14

(For) King [Lysimachus]
Resolved by the *demos*; proposal [of the *strategoi* (?). Whereas] King Lysimachus both in [past times always] continued to exercise care [for the *demos* of the Prie]neans and now, having dispatched a force [against the Magnesians] and the other Pedieis,³⁶ led [it (the *demos*)] back [into the] city,³⁷ be it resolved by the *demos*, to choose as ambassadors ten men [from among] all the citizens who, going to him, shall both deliver the decree and rejoice with the king at the fact that he and his forces are well and that the other matters are in a satisfactory state, and who shall make clear [the] good-will which the *demos* continues to hold toward King [Lys]imachus and who shall crown him with a [gold] crown of 1,000 gold pieces. And [the] *demos* shall erect [in the *agora*] a golden image³⁸ [of the king] and shall set up beside it on the right ——— [to build] also an altar dedicated to him [in the *agora*; and for all] the [priests and priestesses of] the city [to sacrifice each] year, and for all the citizens to wear garlands, and for the priests and the magistrates and all the citizens to hold a procession [on the birthday of King] Lysimachus; [and] for [the magistrates] to gather together (for a banquet); and for the one in charge of [fiscal administration to give] to [the] *hieropoioi* of the tribes [for the sacrifices as much money as is given also for the Panathenaia ———].

RC 6

[King Lysimachus to the *boule* and] the *demos* [of the Prieneans], greeting. [Your] ambassadors, Antisthenes [and those with him, came and delivered] to us [your] decree and themselves rejoiced at [the fact that] we are in good health and (likewise) our friends [and] forces and affairs through [the entire] land, and they spoke along the lines of what is written in the decree, declaring about [the] good-will which the demos holds towards us and that, when we sent (instructions) to obey, (the *demos*) obeyed So[sthenes the (?)] *strategos* with enthusiasm and [in no way] stood apart from what was useful to us, although the land was being [ravaged] by the Magnesians [. . .] and the [soldiers] marching along with them.[39] [Wishing therefore to exercise care for] all [of you in common] and [each one] individually, and [considering it to be] to our advantage [that you should be our friends as] even previously, [we grant,] as [your ambassadors] requested[40] ———.

12. LETTER OF LYSIMACHUS TO SAMOS

RC 7 (*OGIS* 13)   283/2

Disputes between cities over territory, common enough throughout antiquity, tended during the Hellenistic period to lead to arbitration rather than to war. In the present case Priene has claimed a right to the area of Batinetis in the district of the Samian Anaia (on which cf. nos. 63, 64). Both sides presented their cases before Lysimachus, and the following letter, of which only the first part is preserved, contains his decision. Why the Prieneans made the claim in the first place is not clear, for it seems from the opening of Lysimachus' letter that there was not much question as to whose the territory was. It may be they thought the king would simply favor them over the Samians. The tone of the letter and the fact that it was inscribed at Samos indicate that he did not. For the date and circumstances of the judgment, see *RC*, pp. 48-50 and cf. Tod, *International Arbitration* 135-136.

King Lysimachus to the *boule* and the *demos* of the Samians, greeting. Your envoys and those sent by Priene appeared before us in the matter of the land which they have in fact disputed earlier in our presence. If we had known beforehand that you had had this land in your possession and use for so many years we should never have undertaken to hear the case at all; as it was, we thought that your occupation was a matter of only a very short time, for so [the] Prienean envoys declared to us in their former [statements]. At any rate, when your (envoys) and those from Priene were here, it was necessary to hear through the arguments [of both groups]. The Prieneans tried to prove from the histories and [the other] testimonials and documents, including the six years' truce, that the original [possession] of the land of Batinetis had been theirs. [Later] they agreed that when Lygdamis[41] attacked Ionia [with] his army the rest left the country and the Samians withdrew [to the island; that Lygdamis, after occupying the land three (*or* seven *or* ten) years, returned [to them] the same possessions and the Prieneans [took them over]; that no one of the Samians was there at all [unless one] happened to be among them as a resident alien, and he placed [the produce of his fields] at the disposal of the Prieneans; that later, the Samians, [returning], seized the land forcibly;[42] that consequently Bias [was sent from] the Prieneans [with full powers] about a settlement with the

Samians, and that [he] concluded the settlement and that the inhabitants [left the land of Ba]tinetis. [They claimed that affairs] had remained in this state in former times and that up to quite recently[43] [they had been in possession of the land]; now they asked us on the basis of this original [possession to give them back] the land. The [envoys] sent by you [claimed] that you had received your existing [possession] of the [land of] Batinetis [from your ancestors.] They admitted that, after the [invasion] of Lygdamis, the Samians like the rest [left the land and withdrew to] the island; that afterwards . . . a thousand S[amians] settled ———.

13. ATHENS HONORS PHILIPPIDES

*Syll.*³ 374   283/2

Passed in the year of the death of Demetrius Poliorcetes, this decree honors the comic poet Philippides for service to the *demos* extending over more than fifteen years. Plutarch (*Demetrius* 12.6 ff.) records his enmity toward Stratokles, the strenuous supporter of Demetrius, and adds: "Philippides was a friend of Lysimachus, and on his account the *demos* received much good treatment at the hands of the king." Such is the story told by this inscription, wherein Lysimachus is, not surprisingly, the only living ruler mentioned.

In the archonship of Euthios, in the third prytany, that of (the tribe) Akamantis, for which Nausimenes, son of Nausikydes, of (the deme) Cholargos was secretary, on the eighteenth day of Boedromion, the nineteenth day of the prytany; a regular assembly; of the *prohedroi* Hieromnemon, son of Teisimachos, of (the deme) Koile put the vote along with his fellow-*prohedroi*; resolved by the *boule* and *demos*; Nikeratos son of Phileas, of (the deme) Kephale spoke: Whereas Philippides has continued in every circumstance to show his good-will toward the *demos* and, having journeyed abroad to King Lysimachus and having first spoken with the king he obtained as a gift for the *demos* 10,000 Attic *medimnoi* of grain which were distributed to all the Athenians in the archonship of Euktemon,[44] and he spoke also about a mast and yard-arm in order that they might be given to the goddess at the Panathenaia with the *peplos* — things that were brought in the archonship of Euktemon; and when Lysimachus the king won the battle which took place at Ipsos[45] against Antigonus and Demetrius, those citizens who died in the [fighting] he had buried at his own expense; (as for those who) had been taken prisoner, after presenting himself to the king (and) obtaining their release, those who wished to continue as soldiers he arranged to be assigned in divisions, while those who wished to depart, after clothing them and providing money for travel from his own funds, he sent off whithersoever each wished (to go), and of these there were more than three hundred; and he also asked and obtained that as many citizens as had been captured and held in Asia by Demetrius and Antigonus be released; and he continues always to be helpful to any Athenians who encounter (him) in the way that each calls upon him; and after the *demos* obtained its freedom,[46] he has continued to speak and to do what is of benefit for the safety of the city, calling the king to aid with money and with food, in order that the *demos* might remain free and might regain the Piraeus and the garrisons as quickly as possible, and on all these matters the king often bore him witness before the Athenian ambassadors who approached him; and having been elected *agonothetes* in the archonship of Isaios, he willingly answered the call of the *demos* from his own funds and made the ancestral [sacrifices] to the gods on behalf of the *demos*, and the [———] he gave to all the Athenians (for) all the [contests, and] he was the first to establish an additional contest in honor of Demeter [and Kore], in remembrance of the [freedom] of the *demos*, and he [looked after] the other contests and [sacrifices on behalf of the city], and [after spending a great deal of his own] money on these things he submitted his accounts according to the laws, and never did he ever [do] anything contrary to democracy in either [word or] deed. In order that it may be clear [to all that the *demos*] knows how to return thanks to its [benefactors] in a manner worthy of the benefactions; with good [fortune; Resolved] by the *boule*: that the *prohedroi* chosen by lot [to preside] (over the assembly of the *demos*), when the number of days [required by law] for the request have passed, shall raise these matters at the first legal meeting of the assembly, and shall put to the *demos* the proposal of the *boule*, to wit, that the *boule* resolves: to praise Philippides son of Philokles of (the deme) Kephale for his valor and for the good-will which he continues to hold toward the *demos* of the Athenians, and to crown him with a gold crown according to the law, and to proclaim the crown during the Great Dionysia at the competition of tragedians, and to erect a bronze statue of him in the theater, and to grant to him and to whoever in future is his eldest descendant, public maintenance in the *prytaneion* and *prohedria* at all the contests that the city puts on. (Also resolved that) those in charge of administration are to look after the fabrication and proclamation of the crown; (that) the secretary for the prytany is to have this decree inscribed on a stone stele and set up by the temple of Dionysos, and those in charge of administration are to allocate 20 drachmas for the inscription of the stele [from] the funds expended by the *demos* on decree-related matters.

14. KNIDIAN LOANS TO MILETOS

Milet I 3 138   283/2

In 283/2 Miletos found itself without sufficient money on hand to pay the second instalment of its (annual?) tribute to Lysimachus. To cope with the situation the Milesians adopted the expedient of borrowing this money at Knidos. The Knidians were approached by envoys from Miletos, who sought the official support of Knidos for the venture, on the understanding that citizens of Miletos would guarantee the loans. This support was forthcoming, and the assembly at Knidos voted to invite contributory loans for Miletos and to underwrite these as well. The amount thus raised was 12 1/6 talents (of which three talents were lent for a year free of interest and the rest at the modest rate of six per cent.) If it may be assumed that this approximated to the amount needed and that the instalment in question was the second of two for the year, Miletos was paying Lysimachus a tribute of something like 25 talents a year. In this inscription the Milesians express their gratitude to the Knidians and publish the names of both the Milesian guarantors and the lenders from Knidos.

Resolved by the *demos*; proposal of the *epistatai*; Episthenes son of Alkis spoke: Whereas the *demos* of the Knidians is continually well-disposed and friendly toward the *demos* of the Milesians, showing itself eager to contribute to the welfare of the city on all other occasions and now, after we dispatched Kallikrates and Philippos as ambassadors about the provision of guarantees and the loan of the money which we must pay as the second instalment to King Lysimachus, (the *demos* of the Knidians) has sent to us a decree about these matters, and the ambassadors report that the *demos* of the Knidians has passed a decree about the provision of guarantees for the lenders and has called upon those who wish to provide a service to the *demos* of the Milesians, giving security to the lenders and praising them and exhibiting all zeal and good-will for the collection of money; with good fortune, be it decreed by the Milesians: to praise the *demos* of the Knidians for its virtue and for the good-will which it continues to hold toward the *demos* of the Milesians, and for it to be a subject of attention for the *boule* and the *demos*, and for the *prytaneis* and the *epistatai* to look after any matters about which the *demos* of the Knidians send to us, and for it to be (designated as) a benefactor of the *demos* of the Milesians; and to praise the private individuals who are lending the money and providing this service to the city; and, in order that the city of the Knidians shall be honored and the individual lenders as each is worthy, the *demos* is to choose 75 *synhedroi* from among all the Milesians who, having met together and drawn up the list of honors with which the *demos* of the Knidians and those who have lent the money to the city ought to be honored, will bring (these) before the assembly at which it is lawful for the *demos* to deliberate about its benefactors; and, in order that security be provided for the lenders, the *demos* is to choose 75 men who will give surety and provide guarantees to the lenders on behalf of the *demos*; and to have inscribed on a stone stele the names of the lenders, each with his father's name and the city from which he hails, and to have this set up in the temple of Apollo, adding besides the amount of money which each is lending, as the funds are advanced (?), and the term of the loan; and for the *teichopoioi* to look after and to let a contract for the preparation of the stele and the inscription of the names; and for the treasurer to provide the expenses from the wall-maintenance funds; and, in order that the city of the Knidians may know what has been decreed, for the previously chosen ambassadors, Kallikrates and Philippos, to deliver the decree to the *demos* of the Knidians and to call upon them to maintain the same good-will and friendship toward our city for all time and to join in see-ing to it that the money is brought safely to our city, and for these same ambassadors to have full authority to act on behalf of the city and the aforementioned guarantors in drawing up contracts and in arranging guarantees for the lenders. Resolved by the *demos* to have the decree inscribed on a whitened tablet.

The following announced that they would provide guarantees:
(There follows here the list of the 75 Milesians who
undertook to guarantee the loans on behalf of the city.)
The following Knidians made loans to the Milesians of Rhodian silver:
Stiphos son of Akroteles and Timodamas son of Lachartos:
6000 drachmas.
Philophron son of Philistas and Archippos son of
Timaithios: 3000 drachmas.
Diotimos and Mellinos, sons of Agathoboulos and Timas son of Timas:
6000 drachmas.
Kleisilochos son of Anaxippidas: 2000 drachmas.
Antigonos son of Epigonos: 6000 drachmas.
Thessalakon son of Kallippos: 3000 drachmas.
Stipholaidas son of Akrotatos: 2000 drachmas.
Antikrates and Philokrates, sons of Epikrates: 3000 drachmas.
Menippos son of Apollodoros: 3000 drachmas.
Euphragoras, Kleumenes and Kleumbrotos, sons of Philistas:
3000 drachmas.
Kallikles son of Athenokritos of Halikarnassos: 6000
drachmas.
Athenodoros son of Theodoros of Cyrene: 12,000 drachmas.
These made loans for three years; the loan begins in the month Artemision in (the stephanephorate) of Alexippos; interest is three obols per mina per month.
The following made loans without interest for a year:
Athenagoras son of Kleon: 6000 drachmas.
Boularchidas son of Archipolis: 6000 drachmas.
Epikydes son of Theanos: 4000 drachmas.
Nikandros son of Symmachos of Halikarnassos: 2000 drachmas.
The total (of the loans): 12 talents and 10 minas of Rhodian (silver).

15. LETTER OF SELEUCUS I AND HIS SON ANTIOCHUS TO AN OFFICIAL

RC 9   281

With the defeat and death of Lysimachus at Koroupedion in 281 mastery of Asia Minor fell to Seleucus. Realizing this, Athymbria, a small community centering on the temple of Hades and Kore near Nysa sent a deputation to him seeking confirmation of their traditional rights of receiving and protecting suppliants, of inviolability, and of exemption from taxation. In the present letter the king, along with his son and co-regent Antiochus, directs Sopatros, the governor of the district, to give the Athymbrians a favorable reply. Particularly noteworthy is his insistence upon the importance of the good-will of the Greek cities. Not long after this letter was written, Seleucus was murdered by Ptolemy Keraunos as he crossed to Europe (late 281).

[King] Seleucus and Antiochus to Sopat[ros, greeting]. The Athymbrians [having sent] to us [as envoys] Iatrokles, Artemidoros and Timotheos concerning their [right of receiving suppliants, their inviolability, and their tax-exemption], we have [. . .] the details and have written to you that you may reply [to them at greater length]. [For our policy is always] through benefactions [to please] the citizens [of the Greek cities and by no means least] with reverence to join in increasing [the honors] of the gods, [so that we may be the object of good-will] transmissible for all time [to those who come after] us. We are convinced that even in previous times we have given [many great] proofs of [our] personal [reverence, and] now also, [wishing] to be consistent with [our actions from the beginning], [we grant] to all the temples which [have received the right of inviolability ————].

16. ILION AND ANTIOCHUS I

Ilion 32 (*OGIS* 219)   279-274

After successfully dealing with a rebellion in the Seleukis that began at the death of Seleucus in 281, Antiochus I crossed the Taurus mountains into Asia Minor and within five years succeeded in concluding peace both with Antigonus Gonatas and with the Gauls. During the very early years of the new reign, the city of Ilion had already established a cult of Antiochus. In the present inscription, they confer upon him honors that reflect his successes in Asia Minor. Ilion had been loyal in support of Seleucus (cf. the end of this decree and *Ilion* 31 [*OGIS* 212]) and was always solicitous of his son (cf., probably, no. 18).

The *epimenios* being Nymphios son of Diotrephes, the *epistates* being Dionysios son of Hippomedon, Demetrios the son of Dies spoke: Whereas King Antiochus, son of King Seleucus, when he first took over the kingship and adopted a glorious and noble policy, sought to restore the cities of the Seleukis,[47] which were beset by difficult circumstances on account of those who were in rebellion, to peace and to their former prosperity, and, marching out against those who attacked his kingdom, as was just, (sought) to recover his ancestral empire; wherefore, embarking upon a noble and just enterprise and having not only his friends and forces eager to support him to the end in his struggle for the state but also the supernatural as a kind ally, he restored the cities to peace and his kingdom to its former condition; and now, coming to the area on this side of the Taurus (mountains) he has with all zealous concern at once established peace[48] for the cities and brought his affairs and his kingdom to a greater and more brilliant condition, mostly thanks to his own virtue, but also thanks to the good-will of his friends and his forces; so, in order that the *demos*, since even previously — at the time when he took over the kingship — it regularly made vows and sacrifices to all the gods on his behalf, may show the king clearly that it is now well-disposed and has the same policy, be it resolved by the *boule* and the *demos*, for the priestess and the *hieronomoi* and the *prytaneis* to pray to Athena Ilias, along with the ambassadors, that his presence has been (for the good) of the King and of his sister the Queen and of his friends and forces, and that all other good things accrue to the King and the Queen, and that their affairs and kingdom remain (steadfast), progressing just as they themselves intend; and for all the other priests and priestesses to pray, with the priest of King Antiochus,[49] to Apollo the founder of his line and to Victory and to Zeus and to all the other gods and goddesses. With the prayers to Athena let the *hieronomoi* and the *prytaneis*, with the priestess and the ambassadors, perform the customary and ancestral sacrifice; (with the prayers) to Apollo and the other gods let the *strategoi*, with the other priests and priestesses, (perform the sacrifice). When they make the sacrifices, let all the citizens and *paroikoi* wear garlands, and let them, meeting [in their houses] perform sacrifices to the gods on behalf of the King and the *demos*. And, [in order that] the rôle of the *demos* in promoting these things pertaining to honor and glory [may be clear to all], (be it resolved) to praise him for the virtue and courage he always has, [and to set up] a golden image [of him] on horseback in the sanctuary of Athena in the most conspicuous [place] by the altar of white stone, and to inscribe upon it: "The *demos* [of the Ilians (dedicates this statue of) King] Antiochus, son of King Seleucus, on account of his piety towards the sanctuary, he who has become [benefactor and] savior of the *demos*." And for the *agonothetes* and the s[*ynhedroi*] to make a proclamation [at the Panathenaia at the] athletic contest, [when the] city and the other cities crown [Athena] Ilias with the [crown of valor], making the announcement [———]; and to choose as ambassadors from among all [the Ilians three men, who], saluting him for the [*demos* and rejoicing at the fact that] he and [his sister the Queen and their children] and his friends and the [forces] are (all) in good health, [shall report to him the decreed honor], and, relating [the good-will of the *demos*, which it has always] continued [to hold toward both] his father King S[eleucus and the whole royal house], shall call upon [him ———.]

17. KOS GIVES THANKS FOR THE DEFEAT OF THE GAULS

*Syll.*³ 398   278

At the time of his death in battle against Seleucus at Koroupedion in 281 Lysimachus had for four decades been (among other things, to be sure) filling the rôle played in the fourth century and before by the kings of Macedon and in the third and second (from ca. 277/6 to 167) by the Antigonids in Macedon, namely, withstanding the almost constant pressure of the various tribes to the north. Whether anyone could have withstood the Gallic forces in the winter of 280/79 is unknown; Seleucus was murdered later in the year of Koroupedion on his way to Greece, and his murderer, Ptolemy Keraunos, ended his brief reign of Macedon fighting against the invaders. The Gauls reached Delphi but soon began to fall prey to the guerrilla conducted from the mountains by the peoples of central Greece, above all the Aetolians, and to the weather. At Delphi itself the Greeks were aided by a severe hail/snow storm (the "white maidens" of the oracle in Diod. 22.9.5; cf. Justin 24.8 and the "epiphany" in the present text). The northward retreat of the Gauls was, for them, disastrous. This decree of the Koans is the earliest surviving reference to the events of 280-278 and must have been passed as soon as it became clear that the Gauls were indeed leaving Greece.

Diokles son of Philinos spoke. Whereas, the barbarians having made a campaign against the Greeks and against the sanctuary in Delphi, it is announced that those who came against the sanctuary have met with vengeance at the hands of the god and at the hands of the men who went to the aid of the sanctuary at the time of the barbarians' attack, and that the sanctuary has been preserved and, moreover, adorned with the arms of the attackers, and that most of the rest of the attackers perished in their battles with the Greeks; — in order that the *demos* may be manifest in sharing with the Greeks pleasure at the victory that has occurred and in rendering thankofferings to the god on account of the epiphany that took place amidst the dangers surrounding the sanctuary and the safety of the Greeks; — with good fortune, be it resolved by the *demos*: that the *architheoros* and the *theoroi* who have been chosen, when they arrive in Delphi, are to sacrifice a gilt-horned ox to Pythian Apollo on behalf of the safety of the Greeks, and to pray that good things befall the *demos* of the Koans and that they conduct their political affairs with concord in democracy, and that it go well for all time with those of the Greeks who went to the aid of the sanctuary and that the *prostatai* also are to make a sacrifice to Pythian Apollo and to Zeus the Savior and to Victory; let them sacrifice to each of the gods an unblemished victim; the day on which they make the sacrifice is to be held sacred and garlands are to be worn by the citizens and the *paroikoi* and all the others resident in Kos; let the sacred herald proclaim that the *demos* holds the day sacred in honor of the safety and victory of the Greeks, and that it will be well and propitious for those wearing garlands; let them make the sacrifice in the month Panamos; let the treasurer provide for the sacrifice in Delphi 400 drachmas, for that in Kos 160 drachmas; let the *prostatai* see to it that the money is dispatched to the *theoroi* and that the sacrifices in Kos take place; let the *poletai* let a contract for inscribing of this decree on a stone stele and for setting it up in the sanctuary of Asklepios.

C. The Period of Stability (276-221)

18. A GIFT OF LAND BY ANTIOCHUS I

Ilion 33 (*RC* 10-13)   ca. 274

This dossier, inscribed all together at Ilion, relates to a substantial gift of royal land to one Aristodikides of Assos by Antiochus I (on the dating and the ascription to this Antiochus, which is not certain, cf. *RC*, p. 64). Of Aristodikides nothing further is known, but the fact that he is designated "friend" of the king is significant. It shows that "he belonged. . .to the half-military, half-political nobility of merit which grew up rapidly under the Hellenistic dynasties, and if we may draw any conclusions from the extensive land grants made to him, his place in it must have been high" (*ibid.*). The dossier is introduced by a covering letter to Ilion from Meleager (13), Antiochus' deputy in Asia Minor (cf. no. 66), and there follow three letters of Antiochus to Meleager (10-12): the first announces the initial gift to Aristodikides, the second increases it (this after an intervention by Aristodikides), and the third amends it in the light of problems encountered along the way.

13

Meleager to the *boule* and the *demos* of the Ilians, greeting. Aristodikides of Assos has given us letters from King Antiochus, the copies of which we have written for you below. He has also himself come to us, saying that although many others address themselves to him and confer on him crowns — a fact which we ourselves know because certain embassies have come to us from the cities — he wishes, both because of the sanctuary and because of the good-will he entertains toward you, to join to your city the land given him by King Antiochus.[50] What he thinks should be granted him by the city, then, he himself will make clear. You would do well to vote all his privileges and to inscribe the terms of the grant which he will make on a stele and to place it in the sanctuary, so that the grant may remain securely yours for all time. Farewell.

10

King Antiochus to Meleager, greeting. We have given to Aristodikides of Assos two thousand *plethra* of cultivable land to join to the city of the Ilians or the Skepsians. Do you therefore give orders to convey to Aristodikides from the land adjacent to that of Gergis or Skepsis, wherever you think best, the two thousand *plethra* of land, and to add them to the boundaries of the (land) of the Ilians or the Skepsians. Farewell.

11

King Antiochus to Meleager, greeting. Aristodikides of Assos has come to us, asking us to give him in the Hellespontine satrapy Petra, which formerly Meleager held, and of the land of Petra fifteen hundred *plethra* suitable for cultivation, and two thousand other *plethra* of cultivable land from that adjacent to the lot previously given to him. And we have given him both Petra, unless it has been given previously to someone else,[51] and two thousand *plethra* of cultivable land besides, because he as our friend has furnished us his services with all good-will and enthusiasm. Do you therefore having made an investigation, if this Petra has not already been given to someone else, convey it with its land to Aristodikides, and from the crown land adjacent to the land formerly given to Aristodikides give orders for the surveying and conveyance to him of two thousand *plethra*, and that he be permitted to join (his holding) to any of the cities he wishes in our country and alliance. If the crown peasants of the region in which Petra lies wish to live in Petra for protection, we have ordered Aristodikides to allow them to live (there). Farewell.

12

King Antiochus to Meleager, greeting. Aristodikides has come to us, saying that, because it had been assigned to Athenaios the commander of the naval base, he has not even yet received the place Petra and the land belonging to it which we previously wrote giving it to him, and he has asked that there be conveyed to him instead of the land of Petra the same number of *plethra* elsewhere, and that there be granted to him two thousand *plethra* besides, which he may join to any of the cities in our alliance he wishes, just as we wrote before. Seeing therefore that he is well-disposed and enthusiastic in our interest we are anxious to favor the man highly, and we have given our consent in this matter also. He says that his grant of the land of Petra was fifteen hundred *plethra*. Do you therefore give orders to survey and to convey to Aristodikides of cultivable land both the twenty-five hundred *plethra*[52] and, instead of the land belonging to Petra, fifteen hundred other *plethra* suitable for cultivation from the crown land adjacent to that originally given him by us. (Give orders) also to permit Aristodikides to join the land to any of the cities in our alliance he wishes, just as we wrote in our earlier letter. Farewell.

19. CHREMONIDES' DECREE

Staatsverträge 476 (*Syll.*³ 434/5)   265/4

Although it is not a war vote, this decree effectively marks the beginning of the war named after its proposer. The target was Antigonus Gonatas of Macedon, here cast in the rôle of enemy of the cities of Greece, who had been extending his influence and control in Greece since securing the throne of Macedon in 277/6. The instigator of this bellicose co-operation between Athens and Sparta was clearly Ptolemy II of Egypt, whose influence in Greece had been waning directly as Antigonus' increased. The attempt proved disastrous for the Spartans, who were defeated in a battle near Corinth that cost them their king, Areus, for the Athenians, who capitulated to Antigonus in 261/0 after a siege that Ptolemy's admiral Patroklos had failed to break, and for Ptolemy himself, who eventually lost his naval domination of the Aegean after a defeat at the hands of the Macedonian navy.

Gods. In the archonship of Peithedemos, in the second prytany, that of (the tribe) Erechtheis, on the ninth (day) of Metageitnion, the ninth (day) of the prytany, (in) a statutory assembly. Of the *prohedroi* Sostratos, son of Kallistratos, of (the deme) Erchia, and his fellow *prohedroi* put the motion to the vote. Resolved by the *demos*: Chremonides, son of Eteokles, of (the deme) Aithalidai, spoke: Whereas in former times the Athenians and the Lacedaemonians and the allies of each, after making friendship and common alliance with one another, together fought many noble struggles alongside one another against those who were trying to enslave the cities, from which deeds they both won for themselves fair reputation and brought about freedom for the rest of the Greeks, and (whereas) now, when similar circumstances have overtaken all Greece on account of those who are trying to overthrow the laws and the ancestral institutions of each (of the cities), King Ptolemy, in accordance with the policy of his ancestors and his sister,[53] shows clearly his concern for the common freedom of the Greeks, and the *demos* of the Athenians, having made an alliance with him, has voted to urge the rest of the Greeks toward the same policy; and, likewise, the Lacedaemonians, being friends and allies of King Ptolemy, have voted an alliance with the *demos* of the Athenians, along with the Eleians and Achaeans and Tegeans and Mantineians and Orchomenians and Phialians and Kaphyans and as many of the Cretans as are in the alliance of the Lacedaemonians and Areus[54] and the other allies, and have sent ambassadors from the *synhedroi*[55] to the *demos* (of the Athenians), and their ambassadors having arrived, make clear the zealous concern which the Lacedaemonians and Areus and the rest of the allies have toward the *demos* of the Athenians, and bring with them the agreement about the alliance; (and) in order that, a state of common concord having come to exist among the Greeks, the Greeks may be, along with King Ptolemy and with each other, eager contenders against those who have wronged the cities and violated their treaties with them, and may for the future with mutual good-will save the cities; with good fortune, be it resolved by the *demos*: that the friendship and alliance of the Athenians with the Lacedaemonians and the Kings of the Lacedaemonians, and the Eleians and Achaeans and Tegeans and Mantineians and Orchomenians and Phialians and Kaphyans and as many of the Cretans as are in the alliance of the Lacedaemonians and Areus and the rest of the allies, be valid for all [time, the one which] the ambassadors bring with them; and that [the] secretary of the prytany have (it) inscribed on a bronze stele and [set up] on the Acropolis, by the temple of Athena Polias; and that [the] magistrates [swear] to the ambassadors who have come [from them the oath] about the alliance, according to [ancestral custom]; and to send [the] ambassadors [who have been] elected by the *demos* to receive the oaths [from] the [rest of the Greeks]; and further, that [the *demos* immediately] elect [two] *synhedroi* [from among] all [the Athenians] who shall deliberate [about the common] good with Areus and the *synhedroi* [sent by the allies]; and that [those in charge] of public administration distribute to those chosen (as *synhedroi*) provisions for as long as they shall be away [whatever] the *demos* shall decide [when electing them]; and to praise [the ephors] of the Lacedaemonians and Areus and the allies, [and to crown them] with a gold crown in accordance with the law; [and further, to praise the] ambassadors who have come from them, Theom [. . . of Lacedae]mon and Argeios son of Kleinias of Elis, [and to crown] each of them with a gold crown, in accordance with [the law, on account of their zealous concern] and the good-will which they bear toward [the rest of the allies] and the *demos* of the Athenians; and that [each of them] be entitled to receive [other] benefits from the *boule* [and the *demos*, if they seem] to deserve [any]; and to invite them [also to receive hospitality] tomorrow [in the *prytaneion*], and that the secretary of the prytany have inscribed [this decree also and the agreement] upon a [stone] stele and have it set up on the Acropolis, and that those in charge of [public administration] allocate [the expense for the inscription and erection] of the stele, [whatever it] may be. The following were elected *synhedroi*: Kallippos of (the deme) Eleusis, [and ———].

The treaty and alliance [of the Lacedaemonians and the allies] of the Lacedaemonians with [the Athenians and the allies] of the Athenians, [to be valid] for all [time]: [Each (of the parties)], being [free] and autonomous, [is to have its own territory, using its own political institutions in accordance with] ancestral tradition. If anyone [comes with war as their object against the land] of the Athenians or [is overthrowing] the laws, [or comes with war as their object against] the allies of the Athenians, [the Lacedaemonians and the allies] of the Lacedaemonians [shall come to the rescue in full strength to the best of their ability. If] anyone comes with war as their object [against the land of the Lacedaemonians], or is overthrowing [the] laws, [or comes with war as their object against the allies] of the Lacedaemonians, [the Athenians and the allies of the Athenians shall come to the rescue in full strength to the best of their ability.] ——— The (following) Athenians

swear the oath to the Lacedaemonians [and to those from each] city: the
strategoi and the [*boule* of 600 and the] archons and the phylarchs and the
taxiarchs [and the hipparchs]. "I swear by Zeus, Ge, Helios, Ares, Athena
Areia, [Poseidon, Demeter] that I shall remain in the alliance that has been
made; [to those abiding by this oath] may many good things befall, to those
not, the opposite." [Of the Lacedaemonians] (the following) swear the
same oath to the Athenians: the [kings and the ephors (and)] the *gerontes*.
And the magistrates [are to swear the same oath also in the other] cities. If
[it seems preferable to the Lacedaemonians and] the allies and the
Athenians (to add something) or to remove something in respect to (the
terms of) the alliance, [then whatever is decided upon by both] will be in accord with the oath. (The cities are) to have [the agreement] inscribed [upon]
stelai and have (them) set up in a sanctuary wherever they wish.

20. ANTIOCHUS I AND THE IONIAN LEAGUE

Erythrai 504 (*OGIS* 222)   268-262

This inscription (from Klazomenai) contains resolutions of the Ionian League
about the cult of Antiochus I. His birthday is to be celebrated, as was Alexander's,
and a sacred precinct is to be established as the seat of his and his son's worship by
the League. Besides the obvious fact that the Ionian cities are seeking to please
Antiochus in this increasingly standard way, one may note that they count upon him
to support established democracies. In this respect the Seleucids were the heirs of
the policy of Antigonus toward the Greek cities. (For the origins of the various
restorations, see the notes to *Erythrai* 504.)

——— (on) the fourth (of the month. . .) in order that we may celebrate the
[day on which King Antiochus] was born with [all] reverence [and]
thankfulness: (be it resolved also) to give to [each] of those who [take part
in the festivities] as much as is given for the [procession and sacrifice (in
honor) of] Alexander. And in order that [King Antiochus and] Queen
Stratonike[56] may know [what has been decreed by the *koinon* of the]
Ionians in respect to the honors, (be it resolved) [to choose immediately
from among . . .[57]] two (men) from each city who have [before this time]
served as ambassadors to King [Antiochus, and for these] to deliver [to the
king] this decree [from the *koinon*] of the Ionian cities [. . . and for them to
accomplish whatever good] they may be able to for the *koinon* [of the
cities]. And let the ambassadors [call upon] King [Antiochus to take [every]
care for the [Ionian] cities [in order that (the cities),] being free and [being]
democracies, may [with concord] continue to conduct their own internal
political affairs according to (their) ancestral [laws]. And [let] the ambassadors [make clear] to him that [by doing this] he will be responsible for
[many] good things for the cities [and at the same time he will be following

the] policy of his ancestors.[58] [And let the ambassadors] call upon King Antiochus to indicate [the place which may to him] seem to be [the finest], in which the sacred precinct [of the kings shall be consecrated] and the festival [shall be] celebrated. (And be it further resolved), [when] the embassies [have returned], for the city [in which they perform (?) the] sacrifice of the Alexandreia[59] [to summon all the *demoi*] who share in the [sacrifice, in order that, according to the decision] of the *synhedrion*, they may deliberate [about...and the sacrifices] and about the rest of the matters, how [they will come to pass and at what] times they should be carried out. [And when the] decree [has been ratified] for the *synhedroi* (there) present from the cities to perform a sacrifice to all the gods and goddesses and to Kings Antiochus [and Antiochus][60] and Queen Stratonike, and to sacrifice victims free from blemish, and for the *synhedroi* and everyone else in the city to wear garlands; and for the priests and priestesses to open the temples and burn incense, praying that the resolutions may be of benefit to Kings Antiochus and Antiochus and to Queen Stratonike and to [all] those sharing in the honors. And (be it further resolved) to have this decree inscribed on a stele, and (with it) the names and patronymics of the *synhedroi* who have come from the cities, and placed in the sacred precinct by the altar of the kings; and that the *demoi* in the individual cities have this decree inscribed, and (with it) the names and patronymics of the *synhedroi*, [and set up in whatever place] may seem most conspicuous.

21. PTOLEMY II AND MILETOS

Milet I 3 139 (incl. *RC* 14)   ca. 262

This inscription from Miletos contains three elements: (A) a letter from Ptolemy II to the city thanking it for its support; (B) a decree of Miletos instructing the council to have Ptolemy's communication and envoy brought before a meeting of the assembly; (C) a proposal of one Peithenous (who was *stephanephoros* at Miletos in 261/0) adopted at that meeting of the assembly. The troubles which Miletos endured in support of Ptolemy are probably the same as are reflected in the list of Milesian *stephanephoroi* (*Milet* I 3 123). From 266/5 through 263/2 this eponymous magistracy was held by Apollo himself: the situation was such that no one else could be found to take on the position. This is the period of the Chremonidean War, to which the military activity referred to in Peithenous' decree (including an attack by sea — presumably by the Macedonian navy) would thus belong. These events at Miletos may accordingly be seen as having taken place not long before the decisive defeat inflicted upon Ptolemy's fleet by Antigonus Gonatas in the battle of Kos (258?).

A. (*RC* 14)

King Ptolemy to the *boule* and the *demos* of the Milesians, greeting. I have in former times shown all zeal on behalf of your city, both giving land[61] and exercising care in all other matters, as was proper because I saw that our father was kindly disposed toward the city and was responsible for many benefits for you and relieved you of harsh and oppressive taxes and tolls which certain of the kings had imposed.[62] Now also, as you have guarded fittingly your city and your friendship and alliance with us — for my son[63] and Kallikrates[64] and the other friends who are with you have written me what a demonstration you have made of your good-will toward us—we consequently praise you highly and shall try to requite your people through benefactions, and we call upon you for the future to maintain the same policy toward us so that, this being the case, we may exercise even more care for your city. We have ordered Hegestratos to address you at greater length on these subjects and to give you our greeting. Farewell.

B.

Resolved by the *boule* and *demos*; proposal of the *epistatai*; Epameinon, son of Hestiaios, spoke: that the secretary of the *boule* is to bring before the assembly on the fourth day from the end of this month the letter which Hegestratos brought from King Ptolemy and to have it read to the *demos*, and also the *epistatai* are to bring Hegestratos before the assembly, and that the *demos*, having heard (Hegestratos and the letters) is to take counsel for what seems to be best.

C.

Resolved by the *demos*; proposal of the *epistatai*; Peithenous son of Tharsagoras spoke: (concerning) the other matters (let it be) as the *boule* has decreed; whereas, when the *demos* had even previously chosen friendship and alliance with the god and savior Ptolemy,[65] it happened that the city became prosperous and renowned and that the *demos* was judged worthy of many great goods, for which reasons the *demos* honored him with the greatest and most noble honors, and (whereas) his son, King Ptolemy, having succeeded to the throne, and having renewed the friendship and alliance with the city, has shown all zeal in promoting the interests of all the Milesians, giving land and arranging the peace for the *demos* and being responsible for other good things as well for the city, and now, when many great wars overtook us by land and sea and the enemy attacked our city by sea, the king, having learned that the city had stood honorably by its friendship and alliance with him, dispatched letters and the ambassador Hegestratos and praises the *demos* for its policy and promises to take all care for the city and to requite it even more with benefactions and calls upon the *demos* to maintain its friendship toward him for the future as well, and (whereas) the ambassador Hegestratos made similar declarations about the good-will which the king holds toward the city; be it resolved by the *demos* to praise King Ptolemy, because in all circumstances he has the same policy about

44

what is of benefit to the city; and, in order that for the future as well the *demos* may make manifest its zeal in the interest of his [son] and himself, to call upon the citizens to take the oath to maintain for all time the friendship and alliance which exist between the city and King Ptolemy and his descendants; and for the ephebes, when, after [finishing their training] and completing the prescribed requirements, they leave the gymnasium, to swear to abide by the ratified decisions of the *demos* and to maintain the friendship and alliance with King Ptolemy and his descendants; and, in order that both the policy of the king toward the city and the good-will of the *demos* toward the king may be remembered for all time, to have this decree and the letter (of the king) inscribed on a stone stele and to have it set up in the sanctuary of Apollo beside the statue of Ptolemy the god and savior; and for the *teichopoioi* to let a contract for the preparation of the stele and the inscription of the decree and the letter, and for those chosen to be in charge of the defense of the city to provide the expense from the wall-maintenance fund; and for the ambassadors previously chosen by the *demos* to deliver the decree to the king. Resolved by the *demos* to have the decree inscribed on a whitened tablet.

22. LETTER OF ANTIOCHUS II TO ERYTHRAI

Erythrai 31 (*RC* 15; *OGIS* 223)   after 261 (?)

It is not altogether certain whether the author of this letter is Antiochus I or II. On balance, the flattering tone of the letter (and the similar character of the gestures made by Erythrai) accord better with the beginning of a reign. It is, moreover, less likely to have been Antiochus I, always at war, who remitted the Gallic war tax than his son, who will have been particularly anxious at the outset of his reign to secure the loyalty of important Greek cities (*RC*, p. 81; see, however, Habicht, *Gottmenschentum*[2] 96-99, where the letter is assigned to Antiochus I and seen in connection with no. 20). (The aim of the Gallic fund itself may have been either to meet actual war costs or to pay the Gauls to leave Antiochus and those places subject to him in peace.) After the king's letter was inscribed a decree of the Erythraians; of this little survives, as of the Erythraian decree (*Erythrai* 30) referred to by Antiochus at the beginning.

King Antiochus to the *boule* and the *demos* of the Erythraians, greeting. Tharsynon and Pythes and Bottas, your envoys, delivered to us the decree by which you voted the honors and the crown with which you crowned us, and gave us likewise the gold intended as a gift of friendship. Having discoursed on the good-will which you have always held toward our house and on the gratitude which the people entertain toward all their benefactors, and likewise on the esteem in which the city has been held under the former kings, they asked with all earnestness and zeal that we should be friendly to you and should aid in advancing the city's interests in all that pertains to glory and honor. We have then accepted in a friendly spirit the honors and the crown and likewise the gift, and we praise you for being grateful in all things — for you seem generally to pursue this policy. We have therefore from the beginning continued to entertain good-will toward you, seeing that you act sincerely and honestly in all matters, and we are now even more attracted to you, recognizing your nobility from many other things and to no small extent from the decree which has been delivered to us and from what was said by the embassy. And since Tharsynon and Pythes and Bottas have shown that under Alexander and Antigonus your city was autonomous and free from tribute, while our ancestors were always zealous on its behalf; since we see that their judgment was just, and since we ourselves wish not to lag behind in conferring benefits, we shall help you to maintain your autonomy and we grant you exemption not only from other tribute but even from [the] contributions [to] the Gallic fund. You shall have also [. . . and] any other benefit which we may think of or [you ask for]. We call upon you also, remembering that [we have always] tried earnestly———good-will as is just and———consistent with your previous actions———that you will remember suitably [those by whom] you have been benefitted. [More about these matters and] and the other questions which we discussed your envoys [will report to you], whom [we praise] both for their [other conduct and] especially for the concern they have shown [for the interests of the *demos*]. Farewell.

23. EUMENES I AND HIS MERCENARIES

Staatsverträge 481 (*OGIS* 266)   263-241

At some point in his reign (perhaps more likely near the beginning than the end) Eumenes was faced with a mercenaries' revolt that evidently lasted for four months. The following inscription, found at Pergamon, contains the concessions made by Eumenes to bring an end to the trouble and the oaths sworn by Eumenes and the soldiers.

Requests which Eumenes son of Philetairos granted to [the] soldiers [in] Philetairea and to those in Attaleia. To pay as the cash value of the grain (allowance) four drachmas the *medimnos*, and of the wine (allowance) four drachmas the *metretes*. Concerning the year: that it be reckoned as having ten months, and he will not observe an intercalary (month).[66] Concerning those who have rendered the full number (of campaigns) and who are not in service: That they receive the pay for the time they have served. Concerning the affairs of orphans: that the next of kin take them over, or the one to whom (the decedent) has left (them). Concerning taxes: that the freedom from taxes in the 44th year[67] shall obtain. If anyone goes out of the service or asks to be dismissed, let him be released, removing his own belongings free of impost. Concerning the pay which was agreed for the four months: that the agreed amount be given, and let it not be reckoned as part of the (regular) pay. Concerning the "poplar-corps":[68] that they receive the grain for the period for which (they were granted) also the garland.

Let him inscribe the oath and the agreement on four stone stelae, and let him set them up, one in Pergamon in the sanctuary of Athena, one in Gryneion, one in Delos, one in Mitylene in the (sanctuary) of Asklepios.

The oath sworn by Paramonos and the commanders and the soldiers under them in Philetairea-under-Ida and Polylaos and the commanders and soldiers under him in Attaleia and Attinas (the) hipparch and the cavalrymen under him and Holoichos and the Trallians under him: "I swear by Zeus, Ge, Helios, Poseidon, Demeter, Ares, Athena Areia, and the Tauropolos, and all the other gods and goddesses. I settle with Eumenes, son of Philetairos, from the best motives, and I shall bear good-will toward him and his offspring, and I shall not plot against Eumenes, son of Philetairos, nor shall I take up arms against him nor shall I desert Eumenes, but I shall fight on his behalf and on behalf of his state as long as I am alive and until I die. And I shall provide other service with good-will and without hesitation, with all zeal to the best of my ability; and if I perceive anyone plotting against Eumenes, son of Philetairos, or otherwise acting against him or his state, I shall not allow (him) to the best of my ability, and I shall, immediately or as quickly as I am able, announce the one doing any of these things to Eumenes, son of Philetairos, or to whoever I consider will most quickly reveal it to him. And I shall preserve, if I take anything over from him, either city or garrison or ships or money or anything else that may be handed over to me, and I shall return (it) correctly and justly to Eumenes son of Philetairos or to whomever he may command, provided he does what has been agreed. I shall not accept letters from the enemy, and I shall not receive an ambassador nor myself send (such) to them; and if anyone brings (letters) to me, I shall take them, sealed, and I shall lead the one who brought them as quickly as I am able to Eumenes son of Philetairos, or I shall take (them) and lead (him) to whoever I consider will most quickly reveal (the matter) to him. And I shall not deal fraudulently regarding this oath by any means or pretext whatsoever. And I release Eumenes the son of Attalus[69] from the oath, and also those who swore with him, when the matters agreed upon have been carried out. And may it be well for me and mine if I keep my oath and remain in good-will towards Eumenes son of Philetairos, but if I should break the oath or transgress any of the agreements, may I and my line be accursed.

Oath of Eumenes: I swear by Zeus, Ge, Helios, Poseidon, Apollo, Demeter, Ares, Athena Areia, and the Tauropolos, and all the other gods and goddesses. I shall maintain good-will towards Paramonos and the commanders and the others under pay in the command in Philetaireia-under-Ida, those under the orders of Paramonos, and towards Arkes, and towards the garrisons under him, and towards Philonides and towards those serving without pay who have joined in swearing the oath and towards all that is theirs and towards Polylaos and the commanders and all other soldiers placed under his command in Attaleia, infantry and cavalry and Trallians, as long as they campaign with us; and I shall not plot, nor shall anyone else on my account, nor shall I betray them or [anything of] what is theirs to any enemy, [neither those in charge (?)] of them nor those chosen by the rank and file, in any way or under any pretext whatsoever, nor shall I carry [arms] against (them), nor ———.

24. BERENIKE'S JOURNEY TO SYRIA

P. Cair. Zen. II 59251[70]   252

Part of the agreement between Ptolemy II and Antiochus II that ended the Second Syrian War (259-253) was the marriage of the latter to Ptolemy's daughter Berenike, thus displacing Antiochus' first queen, Laodike, and preparing the dynastic rivalry in the Seleucid house that erupted into the Third Syrian War on the death of Antiochus. Ptolemy accompanied his daughter as far as Pelusium, the eastern edge of Egypt, and the dioiketes Apollonios escorted her, with an undoubtedly large retinue and her enormous dowry, as far as the Syrian border between Ptolemaic and Seleucid possessions. During the journey, Artemidoros, the private physician of the finance minister, writes as follows to Zenon with various requests. On Apollonios' agent Zenon, who appears in many papyri in this volume, see M. Rostovtzeff, *A Large Estate in Egypt* (Madison 1922) and Cl. Préaux, *Les Grecs en Egypte d'après les archives de Zénon* (Bruxelles 1947).

Artemidoros to Zenon, greeting. If you are well, it would be excellent. I too am well, and Apollonios is in good health, and other things are satisfactory. As I write to you, we have just arrived in Sidon[71] after accompanying the queen as far as the border, and I expect to be with you soon. You will please me by taking care of yourself so that you may be well and by writing to me if you want anything that I can do for you. And please buy me, so that I may get them when I arrive, three *metretai* of the best honey and 600 artabas of barley for the animal, paying the price of these things from the sesame and kroton; and please take care of the house in Philadelphia so that I may find it roofed when I arrive. Try also as best you can to keep watch on the oxen and the pigs and the geese and the rest of the livestock there, for in this way I shall have a better supply of provisions. And take care that the crops are harvested in some manner, and if any outlay is necesssary, do not hesitate to pay what is necessary. Farewell. Year 33, intercalary Peritios 6. (Address) to Zenon. To Philadelphia. (Docket) Year 33, Phamenoth 6. Artemidoros.

25. CORRESPONDENCE ABOUT A SALE OF LAND BY ANTIOCHUS II TO THE DIVORCED QUEEN LAODIKE

RC 18-20 (*OGIS* 225 +)   254/3

This dossier, from the sanctuary of Apollo at Didyma, containing a letter of Antiochus II and two letters of subordinate Seleucid officials, deals with the sale of a tract of land in Asia Minor to his recently divorced wife Laodike. At the time preparations were being made for the dynastic marriage of Antiochus to Berenike, daughter of Ptolemy II of Egypt (see no. 24). The price paid, 30 talents, is minimal for land estimated at 15,000 ha (cf. *RC,* p. 96), but the effect of the sale was to remove the property from the royal domain and turn it into privately owned land in the territory of a city (cf. no. 18). A gift would have been potentially revocable by the king. The extensive publicity to be given the transaction seems also to have been aimed at guaranteeing Laodike's ownership of the property. The dossier as inscribed begins with what remains of the covering letter (19) of Metrophanes, who was governor of the Hellespontine satrapy, in which the land was located, or *diocetes* of the kingdom (Bengtson, *Strategie* II, 103). This was addressed to the hyparch of the district. Then came the royal letter (18) and the required survey report (20) of the hyparch. Lost is the letter of the *oikonomos* referred to in the hyparch's report, which originally stood before the others.

19

[——— the copy of the edict written] by him [———] and to the other [——— to place] the stelae in [the designated cities. Do you] then in accordance with the letter of the [king] place the contract and give orders to have the deed of sale and the survey inscribed on two stone stelae, and of these to set up the one in Ephesos in the sanctuary of Artemis and the other in Didyma in the sanctuary of Apollo, and to supply from the royal treasury the money required for this. Let it be your care that the stelae be erected as soon as possible, and when it is done write to us also. We have written to Timoxenos the archivist to file the deed of sale and the survey in the royal records at Sardes, as the king has directed. [Year 59,] Daisios.[72]

18

King Antiochus to Metrophanes, greeting. We have sold to Laodike (the village) Pannoukome and the manor-house and the land belonging to the village, bounded by the land of Zelia and by that of Kyzikos and by the old road which used to run above Pannoukome, but which has been plowed up [by the] neighboring farmers so that they might take the place for themselves — the present Pan[noukome] was formed afterward — and any hamlets there may be in this land, and the folk who live there with their households and all their property,[73] and with the income of [the] fifty-ninth year, at (a price of) thirty talents of silver — so also any of the folk of this village who have moved away into other places — on the terms that she will pay no taxes to the royal treasury and that she will have the right to join the land to any city she wishes; in the same way also any who buy or receive it from her will have the same right and will join it to whatever city they wish unless Laodike has already joined it to a city, in which case they will own the land as part of the territory (of the city) to which it has been joined by Laodike. We have given orders to make payment in the treasury at...in three installments, the first in the month Audnaios in the sixtieth year,[74] the second in Xandikos,[75] the third in the following three months. Give orders to convey to Arrhidaios, the manager of Laodike's property, the village and the manor-house and the land belonging to it and the folk with their households and all their property, and to have the sale entered in the royal records in Sardes, and inscribed on five stelae; (give orders) to erect the first in Ilion in the sanctuary of Athena, another in the sanctuary at Samothrace, another in Ephesos in the sanctuary of Artemis, the fourth in Didyma in the sanctuary of Apollo, and the fifth in Sardes in the sanctuary of Artemis; and (give orders) to survey the land immediately and to mark it with boundary stones, and [to inscribe] the boundaries of the land also on the stelae [just mentioned. Farewell. Year 59], the fifth of Dios.[76]

20

[The copy of] the [survey. ———] Pannou[kome and the manor-house and the land belonging to it and the] peasants [who live there, and there has been conveyed] to Arrhidaios the manager of Laodike's property by [...] krates the hyparch, the village and the manor-house and the [land] belonging to it, according to the written order of Nikomachos the *oikonomos* to which were subjoined that from Metrophanes and that from the king which had been written to him, according to which it was necessary to make the survey: from the east, from the land of Zelia by land of Kyzikos, the ancient royal road which runs to Pannoukome above the village and the manor-house — this was pointed out by Menekrates the son of Bacchios of Pythokome, it having been plowed up by the (peasants) living next to the place; from this to the altar of Zeus which lies above the manor-house and which is, like the tomb, on the right of the road; from the tomb the royal road itself which leads through the Eupannese to the river Aisepos. [The] land has been marked with stelae according to the boundaries as pointed out.

26. PTOLEMY III EUERGETES: THE ADOULIS INSCRIPTION

OGIS 54   ca. 246

This inscription, the text of which survives thanks to the copy made of it at Adoulis on the Arabian Gulf by the sixth-century monk Cosmas Indicopleustes, commemorates the campaign made by Ptolemy III at the opening of his reign. His opponent was Seleucus II, who had himself just come to the throne. The conflict, the Third Syrian War, is known also as the Laodikean war, after Laodike, whom Antiochus II had set aside in order to marry Berenike, daughter of Ptolemy II (cf. nos. 24-25). After the death of Antiochus II, Laodike's son succeeded him as Seleucus II, and she forthwith saw to the murder of Berenike and her infant son at Antioch. Ptolemy, too late to save his sister (cf. no. 27), immediately undertook a march into the Asian heartland of the Seleucid realm. This campaign is referred to also by Jerome in his commentary on the Book of Daniel (11.8): "and he (Ptolemy) came with a great army, and entered into the province of the king of the north, i.e., Seleucus called Callinicus, who was reigning in Syria with his mother Laodice, and dealt masterfully with them and obtained so much as to take Syria and Cilicia and the upper parts across the Euphrates, and almost all Asia. And when he heard that a rebellion was afoot in Egypt, plundering the kingdom of Seleucus he took 40,000 talents of silver and costly vases, and 2,500 images of the gods, among which were those Cambyses had carried away to Persia when Egypt was taken." (Cf. also Bevan, *House of Ptolemy* 192 ff.).

Great King Ptolemy, son of King Ptolemy and Queen Arsinoe the Brother- and Sister Gods,[77] the children of King Ptolemy and Queen Berenike the Savior Gods,[78] descendant on the paternal side of Herakles the son of Zeus, on the maternal of Dionysos the son of Zeus,[79] having inherited from his father the kingdom of Egypt and Libya[80] and Syria[81] and Phoenicia and Cyprus and Lycia[82] and Caria and the Cyclades isalnds,[83] led a campaign into Asia with infantry and cavalry and fleet and Troglodytic and Ethiopian elephants, which he and his father were the first to hunt from these lands and, bringing them back into Egypt, to fit out for military service. Having become master of all the land this side of the Euphrates[84] and of Cilicia[84] and Pamphylia[85] and Ionia[86] and the Hellespont[87] and Thrace[87] and of all the forces and Indian elephants[88] in these lands, and having made subject all the princes in the (various) regions, he crossed the Euphrates river and after subjecting to himself Mesopotamia and Babylonia and Sousiane and Persis and Media and all the rest of the land up to Bactriane[89] and having sought out all the temple belongings that had been carried out of Egypt by the Persians and having brought them back[90] with the rest of the treasure from the (various) regions he sent (his) forces to Egypt through the canals that had been dug ———.

27. REPORT ON THE THIRD SYRIAN WAR

W. Chr. 1   ca. 246

This much-discussed papyrus contains a report, damaged in many places, of military operations by the Ptolemaic armed forces against those of the Seleucid Queen Laodike in the early part of the Third Syrian War (cf. no. 25), as Ptolemy

III, who is himself the writer here, advanced to support the claims of his sister Berenike. Ptolemy reports that Berenike had, while one of Ptolemy's officers was conquering some Seleucid city, given orders for some 1500 talents of silver in Soloi to be captured and brought to Seleukia, which they succeeded in doing, with the help of the people of Soloi. The Seleucid *strategos*, trying to escape across the Tauros to Ephesos, was beheaded by the natives. Ptolemy then arrived in Seleukia to a tumultuous welcome, but left soon for Antioch, where a similar greeting met him, and where he found Berenike. This passage has aroused much controversy, because ancient authors assert that Berenike was dead when Ptolemy arrived in Antioch; the present passage is rather enigmatic: Berenike may well have been dead, which would explain why she was not active in this welcoming scene; or perhaps the king was trying to conceal her death from his readers, in order to use her as a living weapon for political propaganda in Asia, which he in fact did.[91]

—— and asking him [to do] nothing in violation of the treaty or hostile, he said that the [benevolence] on our part and [that of our sister (?)] would be evident [to them for the future], and after this, [giving] his right hand [to them and] putting Epigenes in charge of the [citadel and handing] the city [over to him], together with the day——

At the same time Pythagoras [and Aristokles, with five (?)] ships, when our sister sent orders to them, eagerly [set out], and [furnishing] the remaining service and sailing along the coast to Cilician Soloi, they gathered the money collected there and transported it to Seleukia, it being 1500 talents [of silver, which] Aribazos, the *strategos*[92] in Cilicia was planning to send to Ephesos to Laodike, but when the Soleians and the soldiers there agreed with one another and the men of Pythagoras and Aristokles helped them [energetically] and . . . , and since they were all brave men, it happened that the money was captured and the city and citadel came into our hands. But when Aribazos escaped and reached the pass of the Tauros, some of the natives in the area cut off his head and brought it to Antioch.

[But we], when we. . . affairs on the [ships], at the beginning of the first watch, embarked onto as many ships as the harbor in Seleukia would hold and sailed along the coast to the fort called Posideon[93] and anchored about the eighth hour of the day. From there, early the next morning we weighed anchor and arrived at Seleukia. When the priests and the magistrates and the other citizens and the commanders and the soldiers crowned themselves (with garlands) and met us on the [road] to the harbor, [no extravagance of] good-will and [friendship toward us was lacking.]

[And when we arrived] in the city, [the private individuals asked us to sacrifice the] victims offered [on the altars] built by them [by their houses][94] and [the sacred heralds] announced the honors in the Emporion. This day [we spent in the city], but on the next. . . [and embarking on the ships ——] all those who had [sailed with us and the] soldiers from there and the generals [and the other] commanders, as many as were not in charge of the city and the [citadel with the] garrison. . . [we arrived] at Antioch. [And there] we saw such a preparation (for our arrival) and so [great a mass of the populace] that we were astonished. For the satraps and other commanders and the soldiers and the priests and the colleges of magistrates and all the young men from the gymnasium and a further crowd, crowned (with garlands), [came to meet] us outside the gate, and they led all the sacrificial victims to the road in front [of the gate], and some greeted us with their hands while others [greeted us] with applause and noise ——— (15 lines lost or damaged).

——— [at no] time were we so glad as [in their zeal]. And when we. . . all the offered victims. . . and since the sun was already setting, we went at once to our sister and afterward engaged in business, giving audience to the commanders and soldiers and other persons in the country and taking counsel about the entire matter ———.

28. DELPHI, SMYRNA, AND SELEUCUS II

OGIS 228   242 (?)

> This and no. 29 emanate from the time of the Third Syrian War (246-241) and provide an insight into the situation of Seleucus II in Asia Minor, and especially into the attitude of the city of Smyrna and its actions on his behalf. In gratitude for its strenuous support Seleucus wrote to "the kings and the dynasts and the cities and the leagues" (no. 29), asking them to confirm as sacred and inviolable Smyrna and its sanctuary of Aphrodite Stratonikis. The present inscription (found at Delphi) contains the favorable response accorded the request by the Delphians.

Gods. [Resolved by the] city of the Delphians: Whereas King Seleucus, son of King [Antioch]us, having sent a letter to the city, requests that the temple of Aphrodite Stratonikis and the city of the Smyrnaeans be sacred and inviolable (and whereas) he himself, having obeyed the oracle of the god[95] and having done what he requests of the city, has granted to the Smyrnaeans that their city and land should be free and not subject to tribute, and guarantees to them their existing land and promises to return their fatherland;[96] and (whereas) the Smyrnaeans, having sent as ambassadors Hermodoros and Demetrios, ask that the things granted to them be inscribed in the temple, as the king requests, be it resolved by the city of the Delphians, that the temple of Aphrodite Stratonikis and the city of the Smyrnaeans is to be sacred and inviolable, just as the king has sent (to ask) [and] the city of the Smyrnaeans requests. And it has been enjoined upon the *theoroi* announcing the Pythia[97] to praise King Seleucus for these things and for his piety and for his having acted in accordance with the oracle of the god, and to sacrifice to Aphrodite. (Resolved also) for the city to have this decree inscribed in the sanctuary of the god, and the letter on the wall of the magistrates' building.

29. MAGNESIA, SMYRNA, AND SELEUCUS II

Staatsverträge 492 (*OGIS* 229)　　　　　　　　　　　　　soon after 242 (?)

The opening phases of the Third Syrian War were marked by successes on the part of Ptolemy III (see no. 26). When Seleucus II crossed the Tauros mountains in 246 to meet the invader in Seleukis, trouble arose at Magnesia-by-Sipylos, where the soldiers (at least) revolted from Seleucus. This led immediately to war between Magnesia and Smyrna, which remained steadfast in its loyalty to the Seleucid cause and which for a time got much the worst of the fighting. A cessation of hostilities was arranged by the time Seleucus again crossed over into Seleukis (242?), and this was followed by a more permanent (and quite favorable for Smyrna and Seleucus) reconciliation by which Magnesia was effectively absorbed into Smyrna. The inscription contains three separate, but closely related in time and substance, elements. (A) is a decree of Smyrna dealing with the negotiations between the city and the soldiers at Magnesia. (B) is the text of the agreement negotiated between them, according to which those at Magnesia became citizens of Smyrna. (C) is the decree of Smyrna by which the city absorbed also the fortress at Old Magnesia and the forces there. As remarkable as the vigorous efforts of Smyrna on Seleucus' behalf is the authority he evidently gave the city to act independently in his interest.

A.

Resolved by the *demos*, proposal of the *strategoi*. Whereas previously, at the time when King Seleucus crossed over into Seleukis, when many and great perils beset our city and territory, the *demos* maintained its good-will and friendship toward him, not terrified at the attack of the enemy nor caring about the destruction of its property, but reckoning everything to be secondary to standing by its policy and to supporting his state to the best of its ability, as has been its way from the beginning; wherefore King Seleucus too, being disposed piously toward the gods and lovingly toward his parents, being magnanimous and knowing how to return gratitude to those who benefit him, honored our city, both on account of the good-will of the *demos* and the zeal which it evinced for his state and on account of the fact that his father the god Antiochus[98] and the mother of his father the goddess Stratonike[99] are established among us[100] and honored with substantial honors by the people in common and by each of the citizens individually, and he confirmed for the *demos* its autonomy and democracy, and he wrote to the kings and the dynasts and the cities and the leagues, asking that the temple of Aphrodite Stratonikis be (recognized as) inviolable and our city (as) sacred and inviolable.[101] And now, when the king had crossed over into Seleukis, the *strategoi*, anxious for affairs to remain in a state beneficial to the king, sent to the *katoikoi*[102] in Magnesia and to the cavalry and infantry in open camp and dispatched from among themselves Dionysios to call upon them to maintain forever the friendship and the alliance with King Seleucus, promising that, if they preserved his state and had the same enemy and friend, they would have from the *demos* and from King Seleucus all kindness and noble things and that gratitude worthy of their policy would be returned to them. Those in Magnesia, being called upon and being themselves eager to maintain the friendship and the alliance with the king and to preserve his state for him, zealously accepted what was asked by the *strategoi* and promised to hold the same policy toward our *demos* in all matters of benefit to King Seleucus, and they have dispatched to us envoys, from the *katoikoi* Potamon and [Hi]erokles, from those in open camp Damon and Apolloniketes, to speak with us and to convery the agreement by which they ask that the (treaty of) friendship be concluded with them; and the envoys, brought before the *demos*, have discoursed on all matters, in accordance with what was written in the agreement; with good fortune, be it resolved to conclude the (treaty) of friendship with those in Magnesia on all terms of benefit to King Seleucus, and to appoint three envoys (to go) with them, who shall convey the agreement that the *demos* may decide, and who shall speak about what is written in it and call upon them to accept and to carry out what is written in the agreement; and if those in Magnesia accept (it), let the envoys who shall have been appointed administer to them the oath written in the agreement; and when those in Magnesia have accepted these things and have sealed the agreement and sworn the oath and the envoys have returned, let all the rest of the things written in the agreement be carried out, and let this decree be inscribed according to the law; and let it be inscribed [on] stelae on which also the agreement shall be inscribed. And let the *epimenioi* of the *boule* invite the envoys who have come from Magnesia to be received as guests in the *prytaneion*. And let Kallinos the treasurer give to the envoys appointed (the) travel-allowance (specified) by [law] for as many days as the *demos* assigns. Five days were assigned; appointed as ambassadors were Phanodemos son of Mik[ion], Dionysios son of Dionytas, Parmeniskos son of Pytheas.

B.

In the priesthood of Hegesias, the stephanephorate of Pythodoros, the month Lenaion; with good fortune: On the following terms the Smyrnaeans (on the one side) and (on the other) the *katoikoi* in Magnesia, both the cavalry and the infantry in the city, and [those] in open camp and the other inhabitants concluded the (treaty of) friendship, and the Smyrnaeans gave citizenship to the *katoikoi* in Magnesia, the cavalry and infantry in the city, and to those in open camp and to the [others who] live in the city, on the condition that those in Magnesia preserve with all zeal for all time for King Seleucus the alliance and good-will toward the affairs of King Seleucus, and that they return to King Seleucus as much as they have received from King Seleucus, after guarding (it) to the extent of their ability. They shall be citizens with the Smyrnaeans according to the laws of the city, without faction and reckoning the same as enemy and friend as the Smyrnaeans. Those in Magnesia shall swear to the Smyrnaeans and the Smyrnaeans to those in Magnesia, each of them the oath written below in the agreement. When the oaths have been carried out, let all the accusations that arose in the course of the war be done away with, and let it not be possible for either side to bring accusations about what happened during the war either through a court case or in any other way at all; otherwise, let every accusation brought be invalid. Citizenship in Smyrna, on equal terms and the same as for the other citizens, is to be given to the *katoikoi* in Magnesia, the cavalry and infantry in the city, and to those in open camp. Citizenship is likewise to be given to the others [who] live in Magnesia, as many as may be free and Greeks. Let those who are secretaries of the (military) divisions deliver to the *demos* the registers of the cavalry and infantry in Magnesia, both those in the city and those in open camp, and (let) the men appointed by the *katoikoi* in Magnesia (deliver to the *demos*) the list of the other inhabitants. When the secretaries provide the registers and the appointed men the list of the other inhabitants, let the *exetastai* have them swear on oath at the *metroon* over freshly sacrificed victims, [the] secretaries that they have from the best motive brought the list of the *katoikoi* really with them, cavalry and infantry, [both those] drawn up [in the city and those in] open camp; the men who bring the list of the [other inhabitants, that they have from the best motive brought the list of those who] live in Magnesia and who are really free and Greeks. Let [the] *exetastai* hand over the [lists] that have been brought to the record-keeper of the *boule* and the *demos*, and let him deposit (them) in the public archive. Let the *exetastai* assign all the names that have been brought to tribes by lot and enter them in the allotment-lists,[103] and let those entered in the allotment-lists share in everything in which the other citizens share. Let the enrolled citizens use the laws of the Smyrnaeans in contract and injury cases involving Smyrnaeans, even in Magnesia. And let them accept also in Magnesia the coin of the city as legal. And let those in Magnesia receive the magistrate whom the *demos* may send to have control of the keys and to be in charge of the protection of the city and to preserve the city for King Seleucus. And let the Smyrnaeans provide for lodging to those of the ones from Magnesia who are building houses as many beds as the *demos* may decide, for six months from the time the agreement is sealed; let the treasurer of the sacred revenues, with the *strategoi,* lease the houses and provide the expense from the revenues of the city. The *katoikoi* of Magnesia, both the cavalry and the infantry in the city, and those in open camp, and the others who are being enrolled in the state are to swear the following oath: "I swear by Zeus, Ge, Helios, Ares, Athena Areia and the Tauropolos, and the Sipylene Mother, and Apollo in Pandoi, and all the other gods and goddesses, and the fortune of King Seleucus: I shall abide by the agreements which I conclude with the Smyrnaeans for all time; and I shall preserve the alliance and good-will toward King Seleucus and the city of the Smyrnaeans; and I shall preserve what I have received from King Seleucus to the extent of my ability and shall return (it) to King Seleucus; and I shall transgress nothing of what is in the agreement, nor shall I change for the worse the things written in it, in any way or on any pretext whatsoever; and I shall be a citizen, with concord and without faction, according to the laws of the Smyrnaeans and the decrees of the *demos*, and I shall join in preserving the autonomy and the democracy, and the other things which have been granted to the Smyrnaeans by King Seleucus, with all zeal and at all times, and I shall not wrong any one of them, nor shall I allow another (to do so), to the extent of my ability; and if I perceive anyone plotting against the city, or the territories of the city, or seeking to subvert the democracy or the *isonomia*, [104] I shall reveal (this) to the *demos* of the Smyrnaeans and shall go to its aid, contending with all zeal, and shall not desert it, to the extent of my ability. May it be well for me if I abide by this oath, but if I break it may there be ruin for myself and for the family sprung from me.'' The Smyrnaeans are to swear to those from Magnesia the following oath: ''I swear by Zeus, Ge, Helios, Ares, Athena Areia, and the Tauropolos, and the Sipylene Mother, and Aphrodite Stratonikis, and all the other gods and goddesses: I shall abide for all time by the treaty which we have concluded with the *katoikoi* [in] Magnesia, the cavalry and infantry in the city, and those in open camp and the others who are being enrolled in the state, transgressing nothing of what is in the agreement nor changing for the worse the things written in it, by no device and on no pretext whatsoever. And I shall bear good-will both toward King Seleucus and toward the *katoikoi* in Magnesia, those in the city and those in open camp, and (toward) the others who live [in] Magnesia, as many as are free and Greeks, and I shall make them all citizens, (them) and their descendants, on equal terms and the same as for the other citizens, and assigning them by lot to tribes I shall enter them in the one each may draw by lot, and I shall not wrong any one of them nor shall I allow another (to do so), to the extent of my ability. And if I perceive anyone plotting against them or their descendants or their property, I shall reveal this as quickly as I can, and shall lend support with zeal. And I shall give them the right to share in the magistracies and the other public affairs of the city in which also the other citizens share. May it be well for me if I abide by this oath, but if I do not may there be ruin for myself and the family sprung from me.'' Let the Smyrnaeans and those from Magnesia apoint men, [each of them as many as] each may reckon to be sufficient, to administer the oath to the peoples of those in Smyrna and of those in Magnesia. [Let them administer the oath after announcing] on the previous day that those in the city are to be present for the completion of the oath specified in the agreement. Let those appointed from Magnesia administer [the oath written above] to the Smyrnaeans, and those from Smyrna to those in Magnesia. In Smyrna let [the treasurer Kal]linos provide the victims for the oath-swearing from what the *demos* may decree, in Magnesia the treasurers to whom the people may assign the task. And let the Smyrnaeans have the agreement inscribed on [white stone] stelae and set up in the sanctuary of Aphrodite Stratonikis and in Magnesia-on-the-Maeander in the sanctuary of Artemis [Leukophrye]ne, and (let) the *katoikoi* in Magnesia (have it inscribed and set up) in the *agora* by the altar of Dionysos and the statues of the kings, and in Pandoi in [the sanctuary of] Apollo, and in Gryneion in the sanctuary of Apollo. And let the record keeper of the *boule* and the *demos* have the copies of the agreement entered [in] the public archive. And let those whom the *koinon* of those in Magnesia may appoint seal the (copy of the) agreement which is to be given to the Smyrnaeans with their own seals and with the existing public seal, and let the *strategoi* and the *exetastai* of the Smyrnaeans seal the one to be given to Magnesia with the seal of the city and with their own. Let these matters be carried out by both peoples with good fortune.

C.

Resolved by the *demos*, proposal of the *strategoi*: whereas the *demos*, taking forethought for all the things of benefit to King Seleucus, formerly continued to join in strengthening his kingdom and to preserve his state insofar as it could, and endured the loss and destruction of much of its property and withstood many dangers for the sake of preserving its friendship toward King Seleucus, and now, being eager to join in preserving for him and holding together his state as far as is possible, (the *demos*) has concluded a (treaty of) friendship with the *katoikoi* in Magnesia and the cavalry and infantry soldiers in open camp and the others who live in Magnesia, in order that they might maintain the alliance and good-will of King Seleucus; reckoning it to be necessary for the city to take over also the place Old Magnesia[105] and to make a guardpost with it, in order that, with this taken over as well, all the important affairs might remain (solid) for King Seleucus, they (the *demos*) sent to those living in the place and called upon them to choose friendship toward King Seleucus and to hand over the keys to the magistrate sent by the *demos* and to accept the guard-force which will join with them in maintaining the place for King Seleucus, promising that, if they do these things, they will have from the city all the kindnesses and noble things; those living in the place chose with all zeal friendship for King Seleucus and accepted the requests made by the *demos* and handed over the keys to the magistrate sent by the *demos* and received into the place the guard-force from the city: with good fortune, be it resolved that they are to be citizens and to have all the same things the other citizens have, and that they are to have, free from the tithe, their allotments, the two which the god and savior Antiochus[106] granted them and about which Alexander[107] has written; and if the territory, which the *katoikoi* who were previously in Magnesia hold, is joined to our city, they are to have the three allotments[108] as a gift and are to keep their present freedom from taxes; and as many of them as are without allotments, (resolved) for a cavalryman's allotment[109] to be given them from the (lands) located by the place; and Timon and the infantry under Timon, who have been assigned from the phalanx to the guard-force of the place, are to have citizenship and the same freedom from taxes [which] also the others have, and they are to be in the place; and Omanes, and the Persians under Omanes, and those sent from Smyrna to guard the place — Menekles and those under him — are to have citizenship and the other kindnesses which have been decreed also for the others from Magnesia, and the *demos* is to take thought as to how the drink and food allowances, and as many other things as used to be given to them from the royal treasury, may be given to them from the royal treasury. (Resolved) to have this decree inscribed on the stelae which will be set up in the sanctuaries by the *demos* and [by those] from Magnesia; and for it to be recorded in the public archives as well.

30. DECREE OF THE ACHAEAN LEAGUE

Staatsverträge 499 (*Syll.*³ 490)   ca. 234

During the 230's a number of Peloponnesian cities joined the Achaean League upon the abdication of their pro-Macedonian tyrants (cf. Polybius 2.44.4 f. for Megalopolis, Argos, Hermione, and Phlious). That the same thing happened at Orchomenos is made most likely by the present inscription (found near Orchomenos), which contains measures taken by the Achaeans to deal with certain difficulties existing at Orchomenos when it joined the league. Orchomenos subsequently joined the Aetolian League, fell under the control of Kleomenes of Sparta in 228 (Pol. 2.46) and then of Antigonus Doson (Pol. 2.54). In 199 it re-entered the Achaean League (Livy 32.5).

[———] transgresses [———] sends [———] if a magistrate [———] or a private citizen casts his vote that ——— [let him owe as a fine] thirty talents sacred to Zeus [Amarios, and let it be open to anyone who so wishes] to bring a capital [charge] before the *koinon* [of the Achaeans. Let] the Orchomenians and the Achaeans [swear] the same [oath] as follows, in [Aigion the *synhedroi* (? or *damiourgoi*) of the Achaeans and the *strat*]*egos* and the hipparch and the nauarch, in [Orchomenos the magistrates of the Orchomenians]: "I swear by Zeus Amarios, Athena Amaria, Aphrodite, and [all the] gods (that) I shall in all respects abide by the stele[110] and the agreement and the decree [passed by the *koinon*] of the Achaeans; and if anyone does not so abide, I shall prevent him to the best of my ability. To me if I keep this oath may good things befall, (to me) if I break it, the opposite."

It shall not be permitted for anyone of those who obtain a lot or a house in Or[chomenos] after they (the Orchomenians) have become Achaeans to alienate it within a period of twenty years. If there existed from the time before the Orchomenians became Achaeans any charge against Nearchos[111] or his sons, let all such charges be null and void; and no one shall [seek a judgment against (?)] Nearchos or his sons nor shall Nearchos or any of his sons (seek a judgment) on any charges existing before the Orchomenians became Achaeans; anyone who seeks such a judgment shall pay a fine of 1000 drachmas, and the judgment shall be invalid.

Concerning [the] golden (statue of) Victory from (the sanctuary of) Zeus Hoplismios, which the Methydrians deposited as security for the money which the Methydrians [who] moved to Orchomenos then divided up among themselves, and which some of them (subsequently) [brought back to Methydrion]: if they do not return the money to the Megalopolitans, even as [the] city of the Orchomenians has [granted], those who do not act justly are to be liable to prosecution.[112]

D. The Period of Roman Intervention (221-189)

31. PHILIP V AND LARISA

*Syll.*³ 543   215

This inscription contains two letters of Philip V of Macedon and two decrees of the Thessalian city of Larisa. Philip is here trying to help resuscitate the city after the damage it suffered during the last months of the Social War (220-217). At the same time he has the Romans very much on his mind, as the noteworthy reference to them in the second letter indicates. In the year before the second letter belongs the battle of Cannae and the start of negotiations between Philip and Hannibal.

The *tagoi* being Anankippos son of Thessalos, Aristonous son of Eunomos, Epigenes son of Iason, Eudikos son of Adamas, Alexias son of Klearchos; the gymnasiarch being Aleuas son of Damosthenes; Philip the king has sent the following letter to the *tagoi* and the city:

King Philip to the *tagoi* and the city of the Larisaeans greeting. When Petraios and Anankippos and Aristonous returned from their embassy,[113] they revealed to me that your city too is in need of more inhabitants on account of the wars.[114] Until we shall consider that others too are worthy of your state, for the present it is my decision that you pass a decree in order that citizenship may be given to those of the Thessalians or the other Greeks who dwell among you. For when this has been accomplished and all have remained together on account of the kindnesses, I am convinced both that many other useful things will accrue both to me and to the city and also that the land will be worked to a greater extent. Year 5, the 21st day of Hyperberetaios.[115]

The city has voted the following decree: On the 26th day of Panamos, a special assembly having taken place with all the *tagoi* presiding; since Philip the king has sent a letter to the *tagoi* and the city, (saying) that Petraios and Anankippos and Aristonous, when they returned from their embassy, revealed to him that our city is in need of more people to inhabit it on account of the wars; (he says that) until he shall consider that others are worthy of our state, for the present it is his decision that we pass a decree in order that citizenship may be given to those of the Thessalians and the other Greeks who dwell among us; (and he says that) when this has been accomplished and all have remained together on account of the kindnesses, he is convinced both that many other useful things will accrue to him and to the city and that the land will be worked to a greater extent; it is decreed by the state to act in regard to these matters according to what the king wrote, and to give citizenship to those of the Thessalians and the other Greeks who dwell among us, both to them and to their descendants, and that all other rights should belong to them, as many as belong to the Larisaeans, each choosing the tribe of which he wishes to be a member; and that this decree is to be valid for all time, and that the treasurers shall pay for it and the names of those enrolled as citizens to be inscribed upon two stone stelae, and shall set up one in the temple of Apollo Kerdoios, and the other on the acropolis, and shall pay whatever expense arises from this.

And later Philip the king sent another letter, the following, to the *tagoi* and the city; the *tagoi* being Aristonous son of Eunomos, Eudikos son of Adamas, Alexippos son of Hippolochos, Epigenes son of Iason, Nymeinios son of Mnasias; the gymnasiarch being Timounidas son of Timounidas:

King Philip to the *tagoi* and the city of the Larisaeans greeting. I learn that those who were enrolled as citizens in accordance with my letter and your decree and who were inscribed on the stelae have been struck out. If indeed this has happened, those who advised you have missed the mark regarding what is of benefit for (your) fatherland and regarding my decision. For that it is the fairest thing of all for the city to grow strong, with as many as possible having a part in the state, and for the land to be worked not badly, as is now the case, I believe that not one of you would disagree, and it is also possible to look at the others who make use of similar enrolments of citizens, among whom are the Romans, who receive into the state even slaves, when they have freed them, giving them a share in the magistracies, and in such a way not only have they augmented their own fatherland, but they have also sent out colonies to almost seventy places.[116] So even now I still call upon you to get on with the business without rivalry, and to restore to citizenship those selected by the citizens; but if any (of them) have done anything irremediable against the throne or the city or for any other reason are not worthy to have a part in this stele, (I call upon you) to postpone consideration of them until I shall hear their cases after returning from my campaign;[117] announce, however, to those intending to bring accusations against these (that they take care) not to show themselves as doing this out of rivalry. Year 7, the 31st day of Gorpiaios.[118]

The city has voted the following decree: On the last day of Themistios, Alexippos presiding (over the meeting) concerning sacred affairs, Alexippos having spoken, it is decreed by the state: the *tagoi* are to set up in the town center a whitened tablet on which they have inscribed the names of as many of the rest of those enrolled as citizens in accordance with the letter of the king, and the letters of the king, and the decrees — both the previous one and today's — (the *tagoi*) are to have inscribed on two stone stelae and to set these up, the one in the temple of Apollo Kerdoios and the other on the acropolis in the temple of Athena; and the treasurers are to provide the expenditure arising for this out of the public revenues; and this decree is to be valid for all time.

The following have been enrolled as citizens in accordance with the letters of the king and the decrees of the city: (There followed here a list of names; those that survive include one from Samothrace, 142 from Krannon, and more than sixty from Gyrton.)

32. ALLIANCE BETWEEN ROME AND AETOLIA

Staatsverträge 536   211

During the first Macedonian war the Romans concluded an alliance, almost certainly in 211, with the Aetolian League, the effect of which was to keep Philip of Macedon occupied while securing for the Romans a good deal of saleable booty (notably, the inhabitants of the captured cities). The agreement, and its execution, also gained for the Romans the ill-will and suspicion of a large part of Greece (cf. esp. Polybius 9.37-39; 10.25; 11.4-6). The fragmentary inscription containing part of the treaty was found at Thyrrheion in Akarnania; Livy 26.24 gives what purports to be a fuller version, along with an account of the preceding negotiations (cf. also Livy 25.33). The nature of the terms lost at the end of the inscription cannot be gathered from Livy but may be at issue in a hostile exchange between Flamininus and the Aetolian Phaineas at the end of the second Macedonian war (Polybius 18.38).

————[against] all these———let the magistrates of the Aetolians do, as may be wont to be done. If the Romans take by force any of these peoples, let it be permitted, as far as concerns the *demos* of the Romans, for the *demos* of the Aetolians to have these cities and lands; whatever (the) Romans take besides the city and land, let (the) Romans have. If Romans and Aetolians together take any of these cities, let it be permitted, as far as concerns the *demos* (of the Romans) for the Aetolians to have these cities and lands; whatever they take besides the city, let it belong to both together. If any of these cities go over to, or surrender to, the Romans or the Aetolians, [let it be permitted, as far as concerns the] *demos* of the Romans, for the Aetolians to take these people and the cities and the lands [into their] state———autonomous———from Rome———the peace———.

33. LAMPSAKOS, MASSILIA AND ROME

*Syll.*³ 591   197/6

This is the surviving part of a decree of Lampsakos in honor of Hegesias. The embassy, which is described here and for the conduct of which Hegesias is being honored by his city, belongs to the winter of 197/6, probably to the first part of 196. The ten commissioners were with Flamininus at Corinth for the spring and early summer of 196 (see Polybius 18.44-47 and Livy 33.30-34), and they had left Rome by the time Hegesias arrived there. Very early in 196 Antiochus had tried and failed to gain control of Lampsakos and Smyrna by siege or diplomacy (Livy 33.38), and it was likely this activity (or the expectation of it) that prompted this Lampsakene embassy. Lampsakos and Smyrna (along with Alexandria Troas, also in northwestern Asia Minor) played an important role in Rome's dealings with Antiochus from 196 on: see especially Polybius 18.52 (196); Livy 35.15-17 (193); Polybius 21.13 and Diodorus 29.7 (190, with reference back).

[——— in the decrees] inscribed above. [When the *demos* was looking for] and with all [zeal] calling upon those who would offer themselves, and when the *demos* passed a decree [to the effect that] there would be some honor from the [*demos*] for those who undertook the embassy on behalf of the city to the [Massilio]tes and the Romans, and that when the ambassadors returned the *boule* would formulate a proposal as to how they would be honored, and when [some] had withdrawn after being put forward, and others, even after being elected, had declared on oath (that they could not go) — all on account of the extent of the journey [and the expense], then Hegesias, after being put forward and after being elected and requested by the *demos*, instead of abjuring (the embassy), [thinking] nothing of the dangers associated with the journey, but reckoning his own affairs [of less importance] than what was of benefit to the city, [accepted] the position of ambassador; and, after leaving home and arriving [in] Greece and, along with his fellow-ambassadors, having met with the general of the Romans in command of the fleet, [Lucius],¹¹⁹ he explained to him at length that the *demos*, being the [kinsman]¹²⁰ and friend of the *demos* of the Romans, had sent [them] to him, and that he [and his] fellow-ambassadors requested and called upon him [to take thought] for our city, inasmuch as we are kinsmen of the [Romans], in order that he might bring about [what might seem to be] beneficial for the *demos*; for it was incumbent upon them [always] to support (?) what is of benefit to the city, both on account of [the] kinship [obtaining] between us and them — which (kinship) even [they themselves accepted], and because of the fact that the Massiliotes, [who are friends] and allies of the *demos* of the Romans, are our brothers;¹²¹ and [whenever] they received [from him] fitting answers they sent [all these to the city], and on account of these the *demos* was of better heart; [for in] them he explicitly accepted the relationship [and] kinship obtaining between us and the Romans, [and he undertook that], if he made friendship or sworn agreement with anyone, he would include our city [in the agreement], and (that) he would maintain [the democracy] and the autonomy and the peace, [and (that) he would do whatever] could be of use, and (that), if anyone [attempted to cause us trouble], he would not permit (them) but would prevent (them). And (Hegesias), [along with his fellow]-ambassadors, meeting with the treasurer[122] in charge of the fleet...[and having persuaded] him always to be responsible for some good, [received] from him [too] a letter to [our] *demos* [which (the *demos*), recognizing] it to be of benefit, entered in [the public archives]; and travelling then [to...and wishing to accomplish everything] concerning which he had decrees, after making [the] long and dangerous voyage to [Massil]ia and (there) [going before the Six Hundred], he (so) disposed them and acted [so as to obtain] ambassadors to join with him in the embassy [from Massilia] to Rome; and judging it to be useful, they asked for [and obtained from the] Six Hundred a beneficial letter on [our] behalf [to the] *demos* of the Tolostoagian Gauls.[123] Travelling then [to Rome along with his] fellow-ambassadors and those sent along with them [from Massi]lia, and dealing with the Senate along with [them, he heard them (the Massiliotes) speak of] the good-will and the disposition which [they maintained toward] them (the Romans) and renew the existing [alliance with] them and explain to them [about us, that they (the Massiliotes)] were in fact brothers of our *demos* [and] held [the good-will] pursuant upon the kinship; and he (Hegesias) spoke [both about the other matters],[124] and about what the *demos* sought to bring about [for itself that it had sent] the embassy and, along with [his fellow-ambassadors] he called upon them [to have forethought for the safety] of their other friends and relations and to take thought on behalf of our city, on account of [the kinship and] the kindnesses obtaining between us and them [and the] commendation we had received from the Massiliotes, [asking that he] receive [an answer] beneficial to the *demos*; and (when) the ambassadors [besought] that we might be included [in the agreements] the Romans made with the [king,[125] the senate] included us in the agreements with [the king], just as they themselves write, and concerning [all] the other [matters] the Senate [referred] them to the consul [of the Romans], Titus,[126] and the ten [commissioners[127] appointed to deal with the affairs of Greece]; and going to Corinth, with [...and] Apollodoros, he (Hegesias) met with the general [and the ten commissioners, and] having spoken to them on behalf of the *demos* and having [called upon (them) with all] zeal to take thought [on our behalf and to contribute] to the preservation of [our] city as [autonomous] and democratic; concerning which things he received both [a benevolent decree] and letters to the kings[128] ———; [recognizing these] to be of benefit to it (the *demos*) he dispatched [them ———]. The *demos*, in accordance with what had previously been decreed ———.

34. LETTER OF FLAMININUS TO CHYRETIAI

RDGE 33 (*Syll.*³ 593)   197-194

The Thessalian city of Chyretiai was taken by storm and plundered by the Aetolians in 199 (Livy 31.41.5). After the battle of Cynoscephalae and Philip's surrender in 197 it presumably passed to the Romans along with other places once subject to Philip. The date of the present letter, by which confiscated property was given over to the city, cannot be fixed with certainty. It certainly precedes Flamininus' departure from Greece in 194 and is likely subsequent to the promulgation of the terms of the Roman settlement in 196. It may belong to the summer of 196, when Flamininus dealt with Thessalian legations at Corinth (Polybius 18.47), or to the spring/summer of 194, when Flamininus visited Thessaly and put things in order (Livy 34.51), or to almost any time between the summer of 197 and 194. What is clear is that Flamininus is anxious to blunt criticism of Roman behavior in Greece (this was forthcoming above all from the Aetolians), to demonstrate Rome's concern for the preservation of private property (cf. the rôle of the wealthy in his Thessalian arrangements: Livy 34.51.6), and in general to secure the good-will of as much of Greece as possible with a view to what was seen as the threat posed by Antiochus III.

Titus Quinctius, *strategos hypatos*[129] of the Romans, to the *tagoi* and the city of (the) Chyretians, greeting. Since even in other matters we have made altogether clear to everyone both our own policy toward you and that of the *demos* of the Romans, we wish also in what follows to demonstrate in every respect that we have taken a stand for what is honorable, in order that those who are not in the habit of acting from the best motives may not be able to rail against us in these matters either.[130] As many of your possessions, in land and houses, as remain of those belonging to the public property of the Romans, we grant them all to your city, so that in these matters also you may know our nobility and that in no matter whatsoever have we wished to be greedy, setting the highest premium upon kindness and love of glory. As many as have not recovered what belongs to them, if they prove their case to you and are evidently speaking reasonably, as long as you base your action upon my written decisions, I judge it to be just that (their property) be restored to them. Farewell.

35. STATUE OF FLAMININUS AT GYTHEION

*Syll.*³ 592   195 (or later)

The operations of 195, when Flamininus (consul in 198, proconsul 197-194) was instrumental in liberating Gytheion from Nabis of Sparta (Livy 34.29), lie behind the inscription on a statue base found there.

The *demos* of the Gytheians (dedicated this statue of) Titus, (son) of Titus, consul of the Romans, its savior.

36. EUMENES II AND THE WAR AGAINST NABIS

*Syll.*³ 595   195 (or later)

These two dedications at Pergamon stem from the same operations as the foregoing (see Livy 34.29 for Eumenes' presence at Gytheion). The first is from an offering made by Eumenes, the second from the base of a statue set up in Eumenes' honor.

[King Eumenes] (made this) offering to Athena Nikephoros [from] the booty [arising out of] the campaign [which he conducted with the Romans] and [the] other allies against Nabis the Laconian, [him who had subjected the Argives] and [Messenians].

[The] soldiers [and sailors who] sailed [with] him [to] Greece in the war against Nabis [the Laconian] (dedicated this statue of) [King Eu]menes, for his valor.

37. M. VALERIUS MESSALLA WRITES TO THE TEANS

RDGE 34 (*Syll.*³ 601)   193

About 205 the Teans had established a festival in honor of Dionysos and had in this connection successfully sought that numerous Greek cities recognize Teos as sacred and inviolable. The same request was communicated to the Romans in 194/3 through Antiochus' envoy Menippos. This letter is the Roman response. Note the end.

(From the) Romans. Marcus Valerius, son of Marcus, praetor,[131] and the tribunes of the *plebs* and the Senate, to the *boule* and the *demos* of the Teans, greeting. Menippos, the ambassador sent to us by King Antiochus,[132] chosen also by you as ambassador concerning your city, presented the decree and himself spoke with all zeal in accordance with it. We received the man kindly both on account of his previous reputation and on account of his innate good character, and we listened favorably to his requests. And that we continue always to value most highly piety towards the gods one might best reckon from the favor with which we have for these reasons met from the supernatural. We are convinced, moreover, that the special honor we show to the divine has become thoroughly clear to all from many other things as well. Wherefore, for these reasons and on account of our good-will towards you and on account of the esteemed ambassador, it is our decision that your city and land are to be sacred, as is even now the case, and inviolable and free from tribute at the hands of the *demos* of the Romans, and we shall try to increase both the honors to the god and our kindnesses to you, so long as you maintain your good-will towards us even after this. Farewell.

38. THE SCIPIOS WRITE TO HERAKLEIA-BY-LATMOS

RDGE 35 (*Syll.*³ 618)   190

   In the latter part of 190 L. Cornelius Scipio, consul for that year, led the Roman forces across the Hellespont into Asia Minor. His brother, P. Cornelius Scipio Africanus (consul 205 and 194) was serving as his legate (on the restoration of the names, see *RDGE*, p. 219). Around this time they were met by a large delegation from Herakleia-by-Latmos, which announced the decision of the city to entrust itself to the Romans (see note 133). This likely happened after the Romans entered Asia and before the Battle of Magnesia (Dec./Jan. 190/89), although the embassy could have been dispatched at any time after the Roman naval victory at Myonnesos (late summer 190). This letter contains the response of the Scipios.

[Lucius Cornelius Scipio], consul of the Romans, [and Publius Scipio, his brother], to the *boule* and *demos* of the Herakleotai, [greeting]. Your ambassadors, Dias, Dies, Diony[sios, . . .]am[an]dros, [Eu]demos, Moschos, Aristides, Menes, met with us, [noble] men who both presented the decree and themselves spoke, with no lack of love of honor, in accordance with what was set out in the decree. As it is, we are kindly disposed towards all the Greeks, and we shall try, now that you have come over into our [trust],[133] to show all possible concern, being always responsible for some good. We grant to you freedom, as we have also to [the] other cities that have surrendered absolutely to us, and (we grant to you), keeping all your possessions, to govern yourselves according to your own laws, and [in] other matters we shall try, treating you well, always to be responsible for some good. We accept your kindnesses and the [pledges] and shall ourselves try to be second to none in the requital of favors. We have dispatched to you Lucius Orbius to look after the [city and] the land, so that no one may cause you any trouble. Farewell.

39. LETTER OF C. LIVIUS SALINATOR TO DELPHI

RDGE 38 (*Syll.*³ 611)   189/8

In 189? the Delphians who had been freed from Aetolian control by M'. Acilius Glabrio (consul 191) after his victorious campaign in Greece in 191, sent three envoys to Rome in order to obtain senatorial confirmation of Delphi's autonomy (cf. *RDGE* 37 and p. 226). As we learn from the present inscription, these envoys never returned home. A second embassy was sent, probably late in 189, and it was their visit to Rome that elicited this letter from the consul of 188, C. Livius Salinator.

[Gaius Livius, son of Marcus],¹³⁴ consul [of the Romans, and] (the) tribunes of the plebs and [the] Senate, to the magistrates and city of the Delphians, [greeting]. The ambassadors dispatched by you, Herys son of Eudoros and Damosthenes son of Archelas, presented the letter and themselves spoke in accordance with what was set down in the letter with all zeal and with no lack of love of honor, and they reported also that you celebrated the gymnastic contest and the sacrifice on our behalf. And the Senate gave consideration, and they resolved, concerning the previous ambassadors, Boulon, Thrasykles, and Orestas, who came to us but perished on the return journey home, to write to our general, Marcus Fulvius,¹³⁵ in order that he might see to it that, when we have the business at Same under control, he search out the wrongdoers, and might see to it that they meet with fitting punishment and that all the belongings of the ambassadors are restored with their relatives. It was resolved also to write to the Aetolians about the wrongs that have occurred among you, in order that they might now seek out and restore to you everything that has been taken away, and that nothing (of the kind) may occur in the future. And concerning those dwelling in Delphi, the Senate has allowed you to have power to banish those whom you wish and to allow to dwell among you those who are acceptable to the *koinon* of the Delphians.¹³⁶ We have given to these (ambassadors), as they requested of us, the responses that were given to the ambassadors who came from you before, and for the future we shall try always to be responsible for some good to the Delphians, on account of the god and on account of you and on account of the fact that it is our ancestral custom to be pious towards the gods and to honor those who are responsible for all good things.

E. The Struggle for the Survival of Hellenism (189-30)

40. SENATUSCONSULTUM ON THE AFFAIRS OF THISBE

RDGE 2 (*Syll.*³ 646)   170

In the winter of 172/1 a Roman embassy, led by Q. Marcius Philippus, had attempted, among other things, to dissolve the Boeotian League and to secure the adherence of the various cities individually to Rome (see Livy 42.43-4 and cf. 42.46-7 and Polybius 27.5). Except in the cases of Thisbe, Koronea, and Haliartos they were immediately successful. Early in 171 the war of the Romans against Perseus actually began, the Roman forces in Greece being led by the consul P. Licinius Crassus and the praetor C. Lucretius Gallus. Of the Boeotian cities Haliartos alone remained steadfast in its alliance to Perseus. It was taken by Lucretius after a siege, plundered, and then destroyed. Lucretius next approached Thisbe. It surrendered. The city was turned over to the exiles (pro-Romans driven out by the supporters of Macedon) and to the supporters of Rome who had remained in the city. All the property of the pro-Macedonians, most of whom had by this time fled, was sold (see Livy 42.63, where Thisbe must be at issue and not Thebes). In 170 the pro-Romans at Thisbe sent a delegation to Rome with the aim of dealing with certain problems and securing their position. The Senate responded in the *senatus-consultum* preserved in the present inscription from Thisbe. It was issued by Q. Maenius, praetor in 170. On the Koroneans mentioned at the end of the letter, see *RDGE* 3 and L. Robert, *Etudes épigraphiques et philologiques* (Paris 1938) 287-92; their situation was analogous to that of the Thisbeans.

Quintus Maenius son of Titus, praetor, consulted the Senate in the Senate-house seven days before the Ides of October;[137] present for the writing (of the decree) were Manius Acilius son of Manius, (of the tribe) Voltinia, (and) Titus Numisius son of Titus.[138] Concerning the matters about which the Thisbeans who remained in our friendship spoke regarding their affairs: that there be given them those to whom they might relate their affairs. Concerning this matter it was so resolved: that Quintus Maenius, praetor, should appoint five from those in the Senate, who seem to him to be in accordance with the public interest and his own good faith. Resolved. On the day before the Ides of October;[139] present for the writing (of the decree) were Publius Mucius son of Quintus, Marcus Claudius son of Marcus, Manius Sergius son of Manius.[140] So concerning the matters about which the same ones spoke regarding land and regarding revenues and regarding mountain pastures: it was resolved that, as far as concerns us, it be permitted for them to have what had been theirs. About magistracies and about sanctuaries and revenues, that they might have control of them; concerning this matter it was resolved thus: that those who entered our friendship before Gaius Lucretius brought up his army to the city Thisbe should have control for the next ten years. Resolved. About land, houses, and their possessions: to whomever of them something belonged, it was resolved that they should be allowed to have their own property. So concerning the matters about which the same ones spoke, that those who deserted (to us) and are exiles there, should be allowed to fortify the citadel and to live there, as they requested, it was resolved thus: that they should live there and fortify it.[141] Resolved. Resolved not to fortify the city. So concerning the matters about which the same ones spoke, that the gold, which they collected for a crown in order that they might dedicate the crown on the Capitoline, might be returned to them, as they requested, in order for them to dedicate this crown on the Capitoline: resolved thus to return it. Likewise concerning the matters about which the same ones spoke, that they might hold (the) men who are at odds with our public interest and with their own: concerning this matter it was resolved to do as may seem to Quintus Maenius, praetor, (to be) in accordance with the public interest and his own good faith. Those who went away to other cities and did not appear before our praetor, that they might not return to their (former) position: concerning this matter it was resolved to send a letter to Aulus Hostilius, consul,[142] that he might give his attention to this, as may seem to him in accordance with the public interest and with his own good faith. Resolved. So concerning the matters about which the same ones spoke, regarding the trials of Xenopithis and Mnasis, that they might be sent from Chalkis and Damokrita, daughter of Dionysios, from Thebes: it was resolved that these (women) should be sent from these cities, and that they should not return to Thisbe. Resolved. So about their report that these women brought jugs with silver to the praetor: concerning this matter it was resolved to deliberate later in the presence of Gaius Lucretius.[143] So concerning the matters about which the same Thisbeans reported regarding grain and oil, that they had a partnership with Gaius Pandosinus: about his matter it was resolved to give them judges, if they wish to receive judges.[144] So concerning this matter it was resolved to give to (the) Thisbeans and Koroneans friendly letters to Aetolia and Phokis and to any other cities they may wish.

41. EUMENES II AND THE IONIAN LEAGUE

RC 52 (*OGIS* 763)   167/6

From the time of the first Macedonian War through the beginning of the third, the royal house of Pergamon was on the best of terms with Rome and profited more than a little from that friendship. As the war with Perseus drew toward a close, however, the Senate began to view Eumenes with growing disfavor, whether because he was really thought to have been trying to help Perseus (who had allegedly tried to have him murdered) or because he had simply ceased to be useful. He had in 168/7 sought help from Rome in dealing with a Gallic invasion, but the Roman ambassador more than anything encouraged further disaffection from Eumenes. In the winter of 167/6 he went to Italy himself, but the Senate, unwilling openly to admit its change of heart, hurriedly voted that it would receive no more kings. Informed of this at Brundisium Eumenes left Italy directly. It was on his way back to Pergamon that the envoys from the Ionian League (*koinon* of the Ionians) met him at Delos and informed him of the honors they had voted him; the present inscription (from Miletos) contains his response. The contrast with his treatment by Rome is complete. Nor was the situation unique, for Polybius (31.6) was led to remark that the more the Romans behaved harshly toward Eumenes, the more the Greeks were attracted to him.

King Eu[menes to the League of the Ionians, greeting]. Of your envoys, Menekles did not appear before me, but Eirenias and Archelaos meeting me in Delos delivered a fine and generous decree in which you began by saying that I, having chosen from the start the finest actions and having shown myself a common benefactor of the Greeks, had undertaken many and great struggles against the barbarians, exercising all zeal and forethought that the inhabitants of the Greek cities might always dwell in peace and in the best condition; and that, being indifferent [to] the coming danger and determining [to be zealous and ambitious in] what concerned the League, consistent with my father's policy, I had made clear on many occasions my attitude on these points, being well-disposed both in general and toward each of the cities individually and joining in bringing about for each many of the things pertaining to glory and repute, which actions [. . .] both my love of glory and the gratitude of the League. Wherefore, in order that you might show that you always return fitting honors to your benefactors, you have resolved to crown us with a gold crown of valor, to set up a gold statue in whatever spot of Ionia I may wish, and to proclaim the honors in the games celebrated by you and throughout the cities in the (games) held in each. (You resolved) [also to greet me] in the name of the League [and to join in rejoicing at] the fact that I and my relatives are in good health [and] my affairs [are] in good order, and to call upon me, seeing the gratitude of the people, to take [proper] thought for those things by which the League of the I[onians would be furthered] and would be always in the best [condition]. Thus in the future as well would I receive all that pertains to honor and glory. In accordance with the contents of the decree your envoys also spoke with great enthusiasm declaring that the good-will of the whole people toward us was most vigorous [and] sincere. The honors I accept kindly and having never failed, as far as it lay in [my] power, to confer always something of what pertains to [honor and glory] both upon all in common and individually by city, I shall now try not to diverge from such a precedent. May things turn out in accordance with my wish, for so will you have a demonstration of my policy clear through the facts themselves. In order that for the future, by keeping a day in my honor in the festival of the Panionia, you may celebrate the whole feast more illustriously, I shall present you with sufficient revenues from which you will be able to [establish] our memory suitably. The gold statue I shall make myself, because I desire that [the] favor should be altogether without expense for the League. [I wish] to have it set up [in the] precinct voted us by the Milesians. Since it was when you were celebrating the festival in this city that you voted us the honor, and since this city alone of the Ionians up to now has designated a precinct for us, and since it counts itself our relation through the Kyzikenes[145] and since it has done many glorious and memorable deeds for the Ionians, I thought that the erection of the statue in this (city) would be most suitable. In detail about my good-will toward all of you in common and to each individual city your envoys have heard and will report to you. Farewell.

42. EUMENES II, ATTALUS II, AND THE GAULS

RC 61 (*OGIS* 315 VI)   ca. 156

In spite of the clear attitude of Rome (cf. on no. 41) Eumenes continued in his attempt to deal with the Gauls. In this he was aided, and eventually succeeded (in 159), by his brother Attalus (II). The collection of letters of which the following is a part indicates that the matter was approached at least partly by way of intrigue, and in this they had the support of the priest of Cybele at Pessinus, himself a Gaul. The first three letters were written by Eumenes II (the date of *RC* 55 is 5 September 163), the next two by Attalus acting on his brother's behalf. The last but one is again from Attalus, but whether as king or minister is not clear; in *RC* 61 he is king. Much of the time had evidently been spent in planning a course of vigorous action, but when this was finally discussed by Attalus with his advisors (*RC* 61), hesitation won the day. The view of Rome that produced this result is, to judge from Polybius (see above all 23.17), one that had been valid for some three decades at least. The letters themselves were not actually inscribed until the late first century B.C., probably as part of an attempt to record the past of the temple of Cybele at Pessinus on its stones.

[King Attalus to priest Attis, greeting. If you were well, it would be] as I wish; I also was in good health. When we came to Pergamon and I assembled not only Athenaios and Sosandros and Menogenes but many others also of my kinsmen, and when I laid before them what we discussed in Apamea and told them our decision, there was a very long discussion, and at first all inclined to the same opinion with us, but Chloros vehemently held forth the Roman fact and counseled us in no way to do anything without them. In this at first few concurred, but afterwards, as day after day we kept considering, it appealed more and more, and to start something without them began to seem to hold great danger; if we were unsuccessful (there would be) envy and detraction and baneful suspicion — that which they felt also toward my brother — if we failed, certain destruction. For they would not, it seemed to us, regard our disaster with sympathy but would rather be delighted to see it, because we had undertaken such projects without them. As it is, however, (it seems that) if — may it not happen — we were worsted in any matters, having done everything with their approval, we would receive help and fight our way back, with the good-will of the gods. I decided, therefore, always to send to Rome men to report constantly on cases where we are in doubt, while [we] ourselves make [careful] preparation [to protect] ourselves, [if necessary ———].

43. WILL OF PTOLEMY THE YOUNGER

SEG IX 7   155

On the morrow of the Sixth Syrian War (170-168), Egypt was ruled by two sons of Ptolemy V: Ptolemy VI Philometor and his younger brother Ptolemy VIII (called Physcon for his corpulence), who later became Euergetes II. The co-regency was not a stable one, and in 164 Ptolemy VI was forced to flee. He found little sympathy at Rome, where first he went, but did succeed in establishing himself on Cyprus. In 163 he was asked by the Alexandrians to return to Egypt, whereupon the two brothers decided to partition the kingdom. Ptolemy VI took Egypt and Cyprus, Ptolemy VIII Cyrene. Hostilities continued nonetheless, while the younger Ptolemy sought to secure Cyprus. In 155, so Ptolemy VIII maintained, his brother tried to have him assassinated. In this context belongs this text from Cyrene, containing the younger Ptolemy's will. In 155/4, it may be added, he went to Rome and showed the scars from the alleged murder attempt to the Senate (Polybius 33.11, where there is no mention of the will). The senators decided at that point to help him secure control of Cyprus. Enough of Polybius' account of these events survives (cf. 31.2, 10, 17; 33.11) to give a clear picture of the Senate's shrewd pragmatism (see especially 31.10).

(In the) fifteenth year, (the) month Loios, with good-fortune. King Ptolemy, son of King Ptolemy and Queen Cleopatra, Gods Manifest, the younger, made the following testament, of which also a copy has been sent to Rome. May it be allowed me, with the favor of the gods, to take vengeance fittingly upon those who contrived the unholy plot against me and sought to deprive me not only of my kingship but also of my life. If anything human should befall me before I leave successors to my kingship, I leave the kingship which belongs to me to the Romans, with whom I have from the beginning truly maintained friendship and alliance; and to the same I entrust my affairs for them to preserve, beseeching them by all the gods and by their own good reputation, if any attack the cities or the country, to give aid, in accordance with the friendship and alliance which has existed between us and in accordance with justice, with all their might. As witnesses of these things I appoint Capitoline Zeus and the Great Gods and Helios and Apollo Archegetes,[146] with whom also the document concerning these matters has been deposited.

44. LETTER FROM ESTHLADAS TO HIS PARENTS

W. Chr. 10 (*Sel. Pap.* 101)   130

This papyrus provides further evidence of the civil war between Ptolemy VIII and his sister Cleopatra II, in which Hermonthis persistently took the side of the latter. The author, a Pathyrite, tells his parents that the Egyptian general of the king, Paos, is shortly to arrive with an army capable of conquering Hermonthis. Paos was probably successful, since Hermonthis was in Euergetes' hands in 127.

Esthladas to his father and mother, greeting and good health. As I have often written to you to keep up your courage and take care of yourselves until things settle down, once again please exhort yourselves and our dependants (to take courage). For news has come that Paos is sailing up in the month of Tybi with abundant forces to subdue the mobs in Hermonthis, and to deal with them as rebels. Look after my sisters also and Pelops and Stachys and Senathyris. Farewell. Year 40, Choiach 23. (Address) Deliver to Pathyris to my father.

45. DECREE OF AMNESTY AND REGULATION

P. Teb. I 5[147]   118

These royal decrees, issued by Ptolemy VIII Euergetes II and his two queens, Cleopatra II and III, marked the end of a prolonged period of civil and dynastic warfare that had occupied much of Euergetes' reign in Egypt (145-116). The variety and thoroughness of the measures taken show the disarray of the country in the wake of the conflicts. In particular, the great attempt to reestablish tranquil and productive relations between the crown and its tax base shows the disastrous effects of internal strife on the tightly regulated economic life of the country. Relations between Greeks and Egyptians are also treated with considerable innovative care. Throughout, the revitalization of royal revenues is at stake; the king must persuade the royal cultivators to return to their land, the workers in monopolized industries to return to their jobs, and the officials to stop oppressing the subjects. The last of these was perhaps the most difficult of all, as the king's control of his administration was not very secure. For this period in general, see Cl. Préaux, *Actes du Ve*

Congrès International de Papyrologie (Bruxelles 1938) 345-54.

King Ptolemy and Queen Cleopatra the Sister and Queen Cleopatra the Wife proclaim an amnesty to all their subjects for errors, crimes, accusations, condemnations and charges of all kinds up to the 9th of Pharmouthi of the 52nd year, except to persons guilty of willful murder or sacrilege.

They have also decreed that persons who have fled because they were guilty of theft or subject to other charges shall return to their own homes and resume their former occupations, and recover those of their belongings seized on account of these charges that have not yet been sold.

And they release everyone from debts for the period up to the 50th year in respect to the farming of the grain tax and the money taxes except for hereditary lessees who have given a surety.

Likewise, in respect to those who owe for the half-artaba tax and...and the two-artaba tax and the police tax and embankment work and similar obligations and the dike-tax, up to the same date. And they release also those in arrears for the *apomoira* and the *eparourion* and the rents and the other...up to the same time ———.

(And they have decreed that the officials of the custom-house shall not)...nor seize goods unless they find upon the wharf at the harbors of Alexandria something on which duty has not been paid or of which the importation is forbidden; these they are to bring to the *dioiketes*.

Likewise persons who travel on foot up the country from Alexandria by the land-route which leads..., and persons crossing from one tongue of land to another shall have no payment of any kind demanded or exacted from them except the legal duties.

[Likewise in the case of] persons importing goods through the foreign mart...the seizure [is to be made (?)] at the custom-house itself.

And they have decreed that all recipients of grants of land and all holders of temple or other conceded land, both those who have encroached on the Crown land and all others who hold more land than that to which they are entitled, shall, on giving up the excess and declaring themselves and paying a year's rent, be released from payments due from them up to the 51st year, and shall remain in valid possession (of their holdings).

And that the picked forces, and the native soldiers who hold ten or seven arouras, and their leaders, and all others placed [in that class], and the native marines, and those who..., shall have the legal ownership of the lands which they have possessed up to the [52nd year, and shall be free from accusation] and interference. And they release everyone from the *liturgikon* due.

And they have decreed that the sacred land and other sacred [revenues] which belong to the temples shall remain assured to them and that the temples shall receive the shares which they used to receive from vineyards and gardens and other land.[148]

And in like manner the appointed sums or what they received from the Treasury for the pay of the temples and the other sums granted to them up to the 51st year shall be paid to them regularly, as in the other cases, and no one shall be allowed to take anything from these sources of revenue.

No one shall take away by force anything of what has been dedicated to the gods, nor apply forcible persuasion to the superintendents of the sacred revenues, whether derived from villages or land or other temple revenues, nor shall the tax on associations or the crown-tax or the artaba-tax be paid upon what has been dedicated to the gods, nor shall anyone exercise control over the sacred land on any pretext, but they shall be left to be administered by the priests.

And they remit to the overseers of the temples and the chief priests and priests the arrears on account of both the tax for overseers and the values of woven cloths up to the 50th year.

Likewise they remit to holders of honorable offices, or of posts as prophet or scribe, or of other sacred offices in the temples, the arrears owed in the temples for the emoluments demanded on certain occasions up to the 50th year. Likewise they remit the penalties incurred by those who have extorted more (than their due) emoluments up to the same period.

Likewise to holders of such offices in the lesser temples, both shrines of Isis and feeding places of ibises and hawk-shrines and Anubis-shrines and the like they remit the corresponding arrears and penalties up to the same period ———.

And they have decreed that the expenses for the burial of Apis[149] and Mnevis should be demanded from the Crown revenues, as in the case of the deified personages. Likewise in the case of the other sacred animals the sums required (shall be paid by the Crown). (Likewise) those honorable offices and posts as prophet or scribe which have been bought for the temples out of the temple revenues, and of which the prices have been paid, shall remain assured to the temples, but the priests are not permitted to make over these offices to other persons.

And they have decreed that no one is to be [taken away] or forcibly ejected from the existing places of asylum on any pretext.

And since it sometimes happens that the *sitologoi* and *antigrapheis* use larger measures than the correct bronze measures appointed in each nome...in estimating dues to the Crown, and in consequence the cultivators are not charged the (correct number of) choinikes, they have decreed that the *strategoi* and the overseers of the revenues and the royal scribes shall test the measures in the most thorough manner possible in the presence of those concerned with the revenues, of the farmers, and the priests and the cleruchs and other holders of conceded land..., and the measures must not exceed (the government measure) by more than the two...allowed for errors. Those who disobey this decree are punishable with death.[150]

And they have decreed that the cultivators of vineland or gardens throughout the country, if they plant them between the 53rd and 57th years in the land which has become flooded or dry, shall be left untaxed for five years dating from the time at which they plant them, and from the sixth year for three years more they shall be required to pay less than the proper amount, (payment being made) in the fourth year, but from the ninth year onwards they shall all pay the same as the owners of taxable land, and that cultivators in the country belonging to Alexandria shall be allowed an extra three years' grace.

And they have decreed that those who have bought from the Crown houses or vineyards or gardens or other (holdings?) or boats or anything else whatever shall remain in undisturbed possession,[151] and they shall not have persons quartered in their houses.

And they have decreed that owners of houses which have been pulled down or burned shall be permitted to rebuild them according to the prescribed measurements; and that persons who own private [houses] in the villages shall likewise be allowed to rebuild their homes in the same manner to the height of..., and rebuild the temples to the height of 10 cubits, except the inhabitants of Panopolis.[152]

No one is to collect anything whatever from the cultivators and the taxpayers[153] and the persons connected with the revenues and the honey-workers and the rest for the benefit of the *strategoi* or superintendents of police or the chiefs of police or *oikonomoi* or their agents or the other officials in any way. Neither *strategoi* nor holders of official positions nor their subordinates nor any other persons whatever shall take the richest crown land from the cultivators by fraud or cultivate it at choice.

The following classes[154] — the Greeks serving in the army, the priests, the cultivators of Crown lands, the..., all the wool-weavers and cloth-makers, the swineherds, the gooseherds, [the...], oil-workers castor-oil-workers, honey-workers, and beer-makers, who pay the proper sums to the Crown — shall not have persons quartered in the one house in which each of them lives, and in the case of their other buildings which may be used for quarters, not more than half shall be occupied for that purpose.

And they have decreed that the *strategoi* and the other officials may not compel any of the inhabitants of the country to work for their private service, nor use their cattle for any purpose of their own, nor force them to feed calves and other animals for sacrifice, nor force them to provide geese or birds or wine or grain at a price or on the occasion of renewals, nor oblige them to work without payment on any pretext whatever.

And they remit to the police throughout the country the (penalties incurred by making) false returns in connection with the government inspections and the produce which they have lost; and they remit the sums which have been paid them for arrears or for other reasons but which have disappeared, up to the 50th year.

And (they have decreed) that those who have failed to deliver to the Crown at a price the oil-yielding produce from cleruchic or temple or other land up to the same period and those who have failed to supply transport for the assembly are released from the penalties which they have incurred.

Likewise that persons who have failed to provide reeds and light material for the embankments (are released from the penalties which they have incurred).

Likewise the cultivators of Crown lands, the . . ., and other holders of conceded land who have failed to plant the proper number [of arouras] up to the 51st year, (are released from) the penalties which they have incurred, but the planting (of the proper number) shall be made from the 52nd year onwards.

And (they remit the penalties incurred by) those who have cut down wood on their own property in contravention of the published decree.

And they have decreed, in cases in which Egyptians and Greeks are opposed, namely in cases of Greeks who bring actions against Egyptians, or of Egyptians against Greeks, with regard to all classes except the cultivators of Crown land and the tax-payers and all others connected with the revenues, that where Egyptians make an agreement with Greeks by contracts written in Greek, they shall give and receive satisfaction before the *chrematistai*; but where Greeks make agreements by contracts written in Egyptian they shall give satisfaction before the native judges in accordance with the national laws;[155] and that suits of Egyptians against Egyptians shall not be dragged by the *chrematistai* into their own courts, but they shall allow them to be decided before the native judges in accordance with the national laws.

And they have decreed that collectors of foreign debts must not on any pretext whatever get control over the persons of the cultivators of crown land or the taxpayers or the others whom the previously issued decrees forbid to be brought up for accusation; but the exactions in cases which come before the collectors shall be levied upon the rest of the debtor's property which is not exempted by the following decree.

And they have decreed that in the case of cultivators of crown land the collectors shall not sell up one house containing their working implements, or their cattle or other equipment necessary for cultivation, neither for a debt to the Crown nor for one to the temples nor for any other debt, on any pretext whatever. And in the same way they shall not sell the cloth-weaving tools of the cloth-weavers and the byssus-makers[156] and the wool-weavers and other persons engaged in similar trades on any pretext whatever; nor shall any other persons take possession of or use the tools required for cloth-weaving or byssus-manufacture than the taxpayers themselves and the byssus-workers, who alone shall use them in the temple themselves for the service of the sovereigns and the vestments of the other gods.

And (they have decreed) that no one holding an official position or anyone else shall impose labor upon the cloth-weavers and byssus-workers and robe-weavers gratis or at reduced wages. And they have decreed that no one may appropriate boats for his own use on any pretext whatever.

And that neither the *strategoi* nor any others who are in charge of the Crown, city or sacred interests may arrest anyone for a private debt or offense or owing to a private quarrel and keep him imprisoned in their houses or anywhere else on any pretext whatever; but if they accuse anyone, they shall bring him before the magistrates appointed in each nome, and shall give or receive satisfaction in accordance with the decrees and regulations.

46. LETTER OF Q. FABIUS MAXIMUS TO DYME

RDGE 43 (*Syll.*³ 684)   115 (?)

After the end of the Achaean war in 146 the Achaean League was drastically reorganized by the Romans. Its territory was reduced and a property qualification for League and city magistrates was established. Paucity of evidence for the years after 146 makes it impossible to establish the popularity or otherwise of the new arrangements, but the present text indicates that there was serious discontent at least in Dyme about 115 (on the date see note 157). New laws were drafted, public buildings were burned, and even some local magistrates (the *synhedroi* not with Kyllanios and the *damiourgos* condemned to death) were involved. The matter was reported to the Roman governor of the province of Macedonia (whose area of control included the Peloponnesos) who here outlines the actions he has taken.

In the term of Leon as *theokolos*, (and that) of Stratokles as secretary of the *synhedrion*. Quintus Fabius, son of Quintus, Maximus, proconsul of the Romans, to the magistrates and *synhedroi* and the city of the Dymaeans, greeting. Kyllanios and the *synhedroi* with him informed me about the wrongs that have been perpetrated among you — I speak of the burning and destruction of the town-hall and the public records, in which the leader of the whole disturbance was Sosos, son of Tauromenes, who also drafted the laws contrary to the constitution given by the Romans to the Achaeans — concerning which I held a detailed discussion in Patrai with my advisory council present. Since, therefore, those who carried out these things were to my mind manifestly laying the [foundation] of the worst state of affairs and of disorder for all the Greeks — for not only are these doings [in keeping with] a state of mutual disaffection and cancellation of debts, but they are also at odds with the freedom returned in common to all the Greeks and with our policy. As the accusers provided genuine proofs, I have judged to be guilty and condemned to death Sosos, who was the instigator of the deeds and who drafted laws aiming at the overthrow of the constitution given, and likewise [Phor]miskos, son of Echesthenes, one of the *damiourgoi*, who acted together with those who set fire to the town-hall and the public records — since even he [himself] confessed. Timotheos son of Nikias, who was with Sosos a law-drafter, since he seemed to have done less wrong, I ordered to proceed to Rome, having exacted an oath that he will be there on the first day of the ninth [month] and having informed the praetor in charge of foreigners[158] [of the decision] that he is not to return home before (then), unless ———.

47. LETTER OF KING ANTIOCHUS TO KING PTOLEMY

RC 71-72 (*OGIS* 257)   109

The last years of the Seleucid dynasty were dominated by internecine rivalry and a labyrinthine series of marriage alliances with the Ptolemies. At the end of the second century Antiochus VIII Grypus and Antiochus IX Cyzicenus were ruling in different parts of Syria. They were at once cousins, being sons of the brothers Demetrius II and Antiochus VII, and uterine brothers, as both were born of Cleopatra Thea. Each of them, moreover, during his life married two daughters of Ptolemy VIII Euergetes II (father of Ptolemy IX Soter II and Ptolemy X Alexander): Grypus married Cleopatra Tryphaena, and Cyzicenus married Cleopatra IV, and both married (in succession) Cleopatra Selene, who went on to wed Antiochus X. Of the sisters, Cleopatra IV and Cleopatra Selene both had Ptolemy IX (their brother) as a first husband. The letters here were probably written by Antiochus VIII to his ally Ptolemy X at a time when Antiochus was in control of Seleukia. Antiochus VIII and IX, both weak, "were forced to purchase support in any quarter and at any price at which it might be obtained. Here the cost was the recognition of the freedom of one of the capital cities, Seleucia in Pieria" (*RC*, p. 290). The text of the second letter (including the mention of the Romans) is full of uncertainties.

71

King Antiochus to King Ptolemy, also (called) Alexander, his brother, greeting. If you were well it would be as we wish; we ourselves were well and were remembering you with affection. The people of Seleukia in Pieria, the city holy and inviolable, [from of old] supported our father and to the end maintained steadfast their good-will [toward him. They have been constant in] their love toward us and have shown it [through many] fine deeds especially in the most desperate times we have experienced. We have therefore hitherto furthered their interests both generously and as they deserve and have brought them into [more conspicuous] regard. And now, being anxious to reward them fittingly with the first [and greatest] benefaction, [we decided that they be for] all time free, [and we included them in the treaties] which we have made with each other, [thinking] that thus both [our piety and our generosity] toward our ancestral city will be more apparent. [So that you also may] know [these concessions, it seemed] best [to write you]. Farewell. Year 203, Gorpiaios 29.

72

[King Antiochus to the magistrates and the] *boule* and the *demos* [of the people of Seleukia] in Pieria, the holy [and inviolable, greeting. If you and the city were well, it would be] as we wish. [We have sent you a copy of the letter] which we have written [to King Ptolemy and of the one to the Senate of the] Romans (?), [so that you may know ————].

48. DECREE FOR DIOPHANTOS, STRATEGOS OF KING MITHRIDATES VI

IPE I² 352 (*Syll.*³ 709)   ca. 107

In the years preceding the accession to the throne of Pontus by King Mithridates VI Eupator (about 112), the Greeks of the north coast of the Black Sea were under constant pressure from the Scythians of the steppe. The independence of Chersonnesos (on the Crimean peninsula), in particular, was threatened by the control over Olbia by the Scythian king Palakos. Under attack by the barbarians, the Greeks of Chersonnesos appealed for help to the new king of Pontus (about 110; Strabo 7.308-9). The *démarche* bore fruit for the Chersonnetai, for whom independence was secured, and for Mithridates, who made a solid beginning of establishing his control over the entire area. The successful campaign was conducted by Mithridates' general Diophantos of Sinope, in whose honor the Greeks of Chersonnesos passed the decree contained in the present inscription.

[———and...son of...]ithos spoke: Whereas [Diophantos, son of Asklapi]odoros, of Sinope, being [our] friend [and benefactor] and being trusted and [honored] second to none by King Mithridates[159] Eupa[tor], has always been responsible for good [for each] of us, urging the king on to the most noble and glorious deeds, having been summoned by him [and] taking on the war against the Scythians, [and] arriving in our city, he courageously accomplished the crossing of the whole army to the opposite shore; and when Palakos, king of the Scythians, suddenly attacked with a great throng, (Diophantos), drawing his army up in the moment of need and routing the Scythians, who were thought to be irresistible, brought it about that King Mithradates Eupator set up his first trophy from Scythian spoils, and rendering the neighboring Tauroi subject to him and establishing a city in the place, he moved off into the regions about the Bosporus[160] and, having in a short time carried out many great actions, he turned back into our area again and, taking with him those citizens in their prime, he advanced into the middle of Scythia, and when the Scythians surrendered to him the palaces at Chabaei and Neapolis it came to pass that almost all (of them) became subject to King Mithradates Eupator, for which the *demos* in its gratitude honored him with the appropriate honors, as having been released from the domination of the barbarians. When the Scythians made manifest their innate faithlessness and revolted from the king and sought to bring about a change in the state of affairs, and when, for these reasons, King Mithridates Eupator again sent Diophantos out with an army, although the season was closing on winter, Diophantos, taking his own troops and the most able of the citizens, set out against the very palaces of the Scythians, but hindered by storms and turning back to the coastal area he took Kerkinitis and The Walls and set about besieging those living round the Fair Harbor. When Pala[kos] thought the occasion was to his advantage and was collecting all his own forces, dragging along also the tribe of the Reuxinalians, the Parthenos, who ever stands over the Chersonnetai and who on that occasion was with Diophantos, foretold the action that was about to happen by the signs that occurred in the sanctuary and inspired the whole army with courage and daring. After Diophantos drew up his forces wisely it came to pass that the victory went to King Mithradates Eupator, a splendid one and worthy of being remembered forever; for of the (enemy's) infantry scarcely a one [was saved], and of the cavalry not many escaped. Leaving no time for inactivity, and advancing with [his army] at the height of spring[161] against Chabaei and Neapolis, all the heavy-armed soldiers ——— [with the result that some...] (managed to?) escape, and the rest of the Scythians about their own [affairs?]...took counsel. And after moving off into the regions about the Bosporus and arranging things there well and to the advantage of King Mithradates Eupator, when the Scythians with Saumakos began to cause trouble and killed the king of the Bosporus, Pairisadas, who had raised him (Saumakos), and laid a plot against Diophantos, he escaped [the] danger and boarded the boat that had been sent to him by our citizens, and coming here and encouraging the citizens, having as a zealous helper King Mithradates Eupator who dispatched him, he arrived at the height of spring[161] with his army and navy, and taking with him a specially picked group of citizens in three ships' crews, he set out from our city and took Theodosia and Pantikapaion; and punishing those who were responsible for the revolt and capturing Saumakos, who was the murderer of King Pairisadas, he sent him under arrest into the kingdom (Pontus), and he regained control of the area for King Mithradates Eupator, and, aiding the embassies dispatched by the *demos* he shows himself kind and zealous for everything of benefit to the Chersonnetai. So in order that the *demos* may be seen to return fitting thanks to its benefactors, be it resolved by the *boule* and the *demos* to crown Diophantos son of Asklapiodoros with a golden crown at the (festival of the) Parthenia at the procession, the *symmnamones* making the (following) proclamation: "The *demos* crowns Diophantos son of Asklapiodoros, of Sinope, on account of his virtue and his goodwill toward itself;" and to set up a bronze statue of him in armor on the acropolis by the altar of Parthenos and that of Chersonnesos; and for the magistrates listed to look after these matters, that they may be done as quickly and as splendidly as possible; and to have this decree inscribed upon the base of the statue, and for the treasurers of the sacred (funds) to provide the expense arising in these connections. These things were resolved by the *boule* and the *demos*, on the 19th of the month Dionysios, when Agelas the son of Lagorinos was *basileus*, and Menis the son of Heraklios was *proaisymnetes*, and Da[masikl]eios son of Athanaios was secretary.

49. CHAEREMON OF NYSA, MITHRIDATES AND ROME

*Syll.*³ 741, I + *RDGE* 48 (*Syll.*³ 741, II)   88 and following
+ *RC* 73-74 (*Syll.*³ 741, III-IV)

After the end of the Roman war against Mithridates of Pontus many of the Greek cities of Asia Minor were anxious to appear as pro-Roman as possible. At Ephesos, for example, an inscription of about 85 (*Syll.*³ 742) referred thus to Mithridates: "[having transgressed his] treaty with the Romans and collecting together [forces, he undertook] to make himself master [of territory that in no way belonged] to him"; and it goes on to speak of the Ephesians as having from the start maintained their good-will toward the Romans. In 88, however, the Ephesians had slaughtered the Romans and Italians who had taken refuge in the (theretofore) inviolate sanctuary of Artemis at Ephesus (Appian, *Mith.* 23.88). At the end of the war the city of Nysa honored its eminent pro-Roman Chaeremon with a statue. Inscribed on the base of it were three letters written in 88: (A) one to the city of Nysa from the Roman proconsul of Asia, C. Cassius, and (B and C) two of different tenor from Mithridates to his satrap of Caria, Leonippos. It is not clear whether the honor was conferred posthumously, for it would seem that Chaeremon was in the Artemision at Ephesos when the massacre just referred to occurred. Rhodes proved in the event a more secure place of refuge, and Chaeremon's descendants are known to have maintained connections with Rome (cf. *RDGE*, p. 262).

[The *de*]*mos* [of the Nysaeans and the *bou*]*le* [honored] Ch[aer]em[on], son of Pythodoros.

A

Gaius Cassius to the magistrates of the Nysaeans, greeting. Chaeremon, son of Pythodoros, your citizen, came to me in Apamea, and asked [that] I allow him (to come before) my advisory council. This I did allow him, since he promised to my advisory council, out of regard for the Senate and *demos* of the Romans, that he would give as a gift for the army 60,000 *modii* of wheat meal. I replied about this matter that he had done nobly, and that I myself in turn would see to it that he recognized that these things were pleasing to us. And [we shall report these things] to the Senate and the *demos* of the Romans.

B

King [Mithrid]ates to (the) satrap Leonippos, greeting. Whereas Chaeremon the son of Pythodoros, a man most hatefully and most inimically disposed to our state, has always consorted with our most hated enemies, and now learning of my proximity has removed to a place of safety his sons Pythodoros and Pythion and has himself fled, proclaim that if anyone apprehends Chaeremon or Pythodoros or Pythion living, he will receive forty talents, and if anyone brings in the head of any [of them], he will receive twenty talents.

C

King Mithridates to Leonippos, greeting. Chaeremon the son of Pythodoros has previously effected the escape of the fugitive Romans with his sons to the city of the Rhodians, and now, learning of my proximity, he has taken refuge in the temple of the Ephesian Artemis and from there he is sending letters to the Romans, the common enemy (of everyone). [His] confidence in face of the offenses he has committed is the starting point of the things being done against us. Consider how you may by all means bring him to [us] or how he may be kept in arrest and imprisonment until I am free of [the] enemy.

50. CORRESPONDENCE OF PLATON

P. Bour. 10, 12   88

These two letters form part of a dossier of letters written by Platon, *epistrategos* of the Thebaid, in the time of a revolt by the Egyptians of that region in 88. The revolt began under Ptolemy X Alexander, but that king is not mentioned as taking any measures, and by the end of the dossier, Ptolemy IX Soter II his brother has returned to power and Alexander has fled. It is interesting to note that in these letters Platon uses the priests and an Egyptian subordinate as the bases of support for the government, in keeping with the usual policy of the later Ptolemies of using Egyptians to control Egyptians. For another document of this group and a very full discussion of the entire archive, see *P. Ross. Georg.* II 10.

10

Platon to Nechthyres, greeting. We set out from Latopolis to take charge of things in the most advantageous manner under the circumstances, after having written to the inhabitants to assist you.[162] Please keep watch on the area and be on the defensive; and if any persons try to disobey you and engage in a (more severe?)[163] uprising, secure them until I reach you as soon as possible. Farewell. Year 26, Phamenoth 16. (Address) Give to Nechthyres.

12

Platon to the priests and other inhabitants of Pathyris, greeting. Philoxenos my brother has written to me in a letter brought to me by Orses about the arrival of King Soter, the very great god, at Memphis, and that Hierax has been put in charge, with very great forces, of the subduing of the Thebaid. I judged it good to inform you so that knowing this you may maintain your confidence. Farewell. Year 30, Phaophi 19. (Address) To the priests and others in Pathyris.

51. CN. POMPEIUS MAGNUS

*Syll.*³ 749, 751   ca. 67

These two inscriptions are from the bases of the statues of Pompey erected probably after his war against the pirates, a campaign especially gratifying to the islands
of the Aegean. (A) is from Delos, (B) from Samos. (In both, the Roman title *imperator*
renders the Greek *autokrator*.)

A

The *demos* of the Athe[nians and the *koinon*] of the Pompeis[tai in Delos
(dedicated) to Apollo (this statue of) Gnaeus] Pompeius [son of] Gna[eus,
(the Great], *imperator*.

B

The *demos* of the Samians (dedicated this statue of) Gnaeus Pompeius, son
of Gnaeus, (the) Great, *imperator*, the benefactor and savior ———.

52. REPORT ON DISTURBANCE IN THE COUNTRY

BGU VIII 1762   probably 58

The author and addressee of this report are both unknown, but the source is the
Herakleopolite Nome and time evidently the rule of Berenike IV and Cleopatra
Tryphaina in 58. The details are obscure, but it appears that an angry group was
pacified by promises that their complaints against an official would be heeded.

——— On the following day rather more (men) came to the gate of. . . and
shouted for the queens and the armed forces. When the *strategos* arrived
with Charias the clerk and the visitors from Alexandria, they learned of
many other injustices committed by Hermaiskos and his staff toward
everybody. They (the complainants) refuse to do any more work, either
private or royal, if Hermaiskos and his staff are not removed from the
nome when the *strategos* has made his report to the queens and *dioiketes*.
And when the *strategos* and the others encouraged them more and promised
to report the submissions to them, they dispersed. Therefore we report.

II

THE FOREIGN POSSESSIONS OF THE PTOLEMIES

53. ORDINANCES ABOUT REGISTRATION OF LIVESTOCK AND SLAVES IN SYRIA AND PHOENICIA

C. Ord. Ptol. 21-22   260

These royal *prostagmata* exemplify the workings of the Ptolemaic administration in Syria and Phoenicia, one of the Ptolemies' possessions outside Egypt which they controlled throughout the third century. The main lines are similar to those in Egypt: a *dioiketes* (chief finance minister), *oikonomoi* (district financial officers), komarchs, tax-farmers, hyparchies in place of nomes. Similar, too, is the emphasis on registration: livestock are to be registered by a set date and taxes up to that date are remitted, provided that registration is made. If it is not, severe penalties await the violators. The pasture tax on livestock was a major source of tax revenue, and was based on the number of animals. The second part of the papyrus deals with registering slaves; the acquisition of Syrian natives as slaves (through debt, for example) is strictly limited to certain cases connected with government exactions. The Ptolemies in general tried to minimize the Greek tendency to enslave non-Greek peoples, since in Syria and in Egypt the latter formed a class of peasants producing rent and taxes on royal land and private estates, and the loss of their manpower was a serious threat. The papyrus was first published by H. Liebesny in *Aegyptus* 16 (1936) 257-91, with a full commentary; the text was reprinted as *SB* V 8008.

———— to the *oikonomos* assigned in each hyparchy, within 60 days from the day on which the [ordinance] was proclaimed, the taxable and tax-free [livestock]...and take a receipt. And if any [do not do as] has been written above, [they shall be deprived of] the livestock and shall be [subject to the penalties] in the schedule. [Whatever] of the livestock was unregistered up to the proclamation of [the ordinance shall be free of taxes] for former years,[164] of the pasture tax and crown tax and the other penalties, but from the 2[5]th year they shall pay the sum owing by villages...As for those... who make a registration in the name of another, the king will judge concerning them and their belongings shall be confiscated. Likewise, ————

Those holding the tax contracts for the villages and the komarchs shall register at the same time the taxable and tax-free livestock in the villages, and their owners with fathers' names and place of origin, and by whom the livestock are managed. Likewise they shall declare whatever unregistered livestock they see up to Dystros of the 25th year in statements on royal oath.

And they shall make each year at the same time declarations and shall pay the sums due as it is set out in the letter from the king, in the proper months according to the schedule. If any do not carry out something of the aforesaid, they shall be liable to the same penalties as those registering their own cattle under other names.

Anyone who wishes may inform (on violations), in which case he shall receive a portion of the penalties exacted acccording to the schedule, as is announced in the schedule, and of the goods confiscated to the crown he shall take a third part.

By order of the king: If anyone in Syria and Phoenicia has bought a free native person or has seized and held one or acquired one in any other manner ——— to the *oikonomos* in charge in each hyparchy within 20 days from the day of the proclamation of the ordinance. If anyone does not register or present him he shall be deprived of the slave and there shall in addition be exacted for the crown 6000 drachmas per head, and the king shall judge about him. To the informer shall be given. . . drachmas per head. If they show that any of the registered and presented persons were already slaves[165] when bought, they shall be returned to them. As for those persons purchased in royal auctions, even if one of them claims to be free, the sales shall be valid for the purchasers.

Whoever of the soldiers on active duty and the other military settlers in Syria and Phoenicia are living with native wives whom they have captured need not declare them.

And for the future no one shall be allowed to buy or accept as security native free persons on any pretext, except for those handed over by the superintendent of the revenues in Syria and Phoenicia for execution, for whom the execution is properly on the person, as it is written in the law governing farming contracts.[166] If this is not done, (the guilty party) shall be liable to the same penalties, both those giving (security) and those receiving it. Informers shall be given 300 drachmas per head from the sums exacted.

54. LETTERS OF TOUBIAS

P. Cair. Zen. I 59076, 59075[167]

These two letters record gifts made by Toubias, the wealthy head of the powerful Toubiad family in the Transjordan, which was under Ptolemaic rule at the time, to the *dioiketes* Apollonios and to the king. Toubias, like many rulers who operated as vassals of the Ptolemaic kings, retained very considerable local autonomy within the framework of royal rule, and if he is not the king's equal, neither is he quite an ordinary subject; his gifts are, even if suggested by Apollonios, those of one ruler to another. Both letters were written by a well-trained Greek scribe in Toubias' employ.

59076

Toubias to Apollonios [greeting]. If you and all your affairs are flourishing, and everything else is [as you wish it], many thanks to the gods. I too have been well, and have thought of you at all times, as was right.

I have sent to you Aineias bringing a [eunuch] and four boys, house-slaves and of good stock, two of whom are uncircumcised. I append descriptions of the boys for your information. Farewell. Year 29, Xandikos 10.

Haimos. About 10. Dark skin. Curly hair. Black eyes. Rather big jaws with moles on the right jaw. Uncircumcised.	Atikos. about 8. Light skin. Curly hair. Nose somewhat flat. Black eyes, scar below the right. Uncircumcised.	Audomos. About 10. Black eyes. Curly hair. Nose flat. Protruding lips. Scar near the right eyebrow. Circumcised.

Okaimos. About 7. Round face. Nose flat. Gray eyes. Fiery complexion. Long straight hair. Scar on forehead above the right eyebrow. Circumcised.

(Address) To Apollonios. (Docket) Toubias, about a eunuch and four boys he has sent to him (Apollonios). Year 29, Artemision 16, at Alexandria.

59075

Toubias to Apollonios, greeting. As you wrote to me to send [gifts for the king in the] month of [Xandikos], I have sent on the tenth of Xandikos [Aineias] our agent [bringing] two horses, six dogs, one wild mule bred from an ass, two white Arab donkeys, two wild mules' foals, one wild ass's foal. They are all tame. I have also sent you the letter which I have written to the king about the gifts, together with a copy for your information. Farewell. Year 29, Xandikos 10.

To King Ptolemy from Toubias, greeting. I have sent you two horses, six dogs, one wild mule bred from an ass, two white Arab donkeys, two wild mules' foals and one wild ass's foal. Farewell.

(Address) To Apollonios. (Docket) Toubias, about the items sent to the king, and the copy of his letter to the king. Year 29, Artemision 16, at Alexandria.

55. LETTER OF APOLLONIOS ABOUT GRAIN EXPORTING

PSI IV 324[168]   261

The marketing of wheat surpluses was one of the Ptolemies' largest sources of foreign revenue, and very tight controls were put on it to safeguard the royal interest. It is clear here that Syria was regulated much as was Egypt, with the crown maintaining if not a monopoly at least a large-scale export business handled through private merchants.

Apollonios to Apollodotos,[169] greeting. If anyone exporting grain from Syria pays you either the price or a deposit, receive it from them through the bank and give us double sealed receipts, writing the name of the payer and the amount of silver and whether he is paying on behalf of another. Farewell. Year 25, Artemision 12.

56. MEMORANDUM TO ZENON

P. Cair. Zen. I 59037[170]   258/7

The author of this memorandum to Zenon was evidently one of his Carian friends (he came from Kaunos), who gives him news about the latest problems in a large financial scandal in Halikarnassos. The late Danaos had been involved in some transaction (a tax-farming contract, perhaps) with the crown, but had defaulted; his son has reached an agreement with the chief Ptolemaic financial official in the area for the settlement of the problem, but Halikarnassian and Alexandrian politics are delaying the settlement. Zenon is asked to cut the red tape.

——— that. . . was sent from the son of Danaos and (letters) were written to him (Apollonios) in Xandikos of the 28th year from Apollodotos[171] and Kratinos the son of Danaos to the effect that (the affair) should be settled with payment of twenty talents to the king; but the emissary had not delivered the letters to him, but is living in Alexandria in the house of Aristoboulos,[172] following evil ways. His name is Hedylos.

(Know) also that Pankris, the associate of Danaos, is trying to get the office of *nomophylax* through Epikydes,[173] but that the latter is referring it to him (Apollonios). Therefore (take care) that he obtains no favors, for he is hostile and spreading the word that the trouble about Danaos happened because of him (Apollonios).

Get for me letters from him (Apollonios) to Apollodotos and Laagos and Hikesios, and let them be favorable about me, and you write yourself. And get (a letter) also to Iason the banker saying that he (Apollonios) is reconciled to him by my intercession, for he has already written to Apollodotos.

57. AFFAIRS IN KALYNDA

P. Cair. Zen. III 341a-b[174]   248

The involvement of the central government in all manner of local financial affairs in the cities overseas (Caria, here) is nowhere better displayed than in this text, where help from the *dioiketes* is sought by a Kalyndian whose own city government has not paid what it owed him in connection with supplying wine for a festival. The second part concerns an attempt by another citizen of Kalynda to secure to himself the reconcession of his father's exemption from having troops quartered on him or furnishing supplies for these troops. In an appended note (not translated here), Zenon asked Apollonios to write to the *oikonomos*, council, and assembly to ask that the privilege be confirmed. It is noted that the man's mother was an aunt of Zenon.

To Apollonios the *dioiketes*, greeting from Theopropos, *theoros*[175] from Kalynda. In year 38 my farmer Theron purchased from the city a concession to supply wine for the festival which is held yearly in Kypranda, and I supplied the wine on his behalf, amounting to 84 *metretai*, at 10 drachmas the *metretes*, which makes 850 drachmas[176] (borrowing at the legal rate of interest, as Theron had no private means and had made the purchase through me).[177] And as the treasurers Diophantos and Akrisios had only given me 600 drachmas in payment of this sum and were withholding the balance of 250 drachmas because all the subscriptions had not been paid up, I brought them before the *strategos* Motes and the *oikonomos* Diodotos,[178] claiming my 250 drachmas. The treasurers Diophantos and Akrisios demanded that a decree should be issued for them to act on, saying that without a decree it was beyond their authority to repay the money. But the *prytaneis* and the clerk procrastinated and had not written the decree up to the time when, having been appointed a *theoros* by the city, along with Diophantos one of the treasurers, I came to see the king. If therefore it seems good to you, kindly write to our city and to the *strategos* and the *oikonomos* to let the 250 drachmas be paid to me (together with the interest whatever it may amount to from the time when I paid out money to buy the wine for the city, as I had myself to borrow from other people and am still incurring interest), (seeing that in former cases also other contractors have been paid by decree (?) owing to the subscriptions being insufficient to provide for the payment), in order that I may not suffer wrong but be one of the many that have experienced your benevolence. Farewell.

Neon to Damonikos, greeting. If you are well and other matters are going according to your desires, it would be well. I myself am well and all the others.

Would you please speak to Zenon[179] about the billeting and the hay and the green fodder for the sixty-days' obligation, asking that an order be given for my personal exemption; for at present we have people quartered on us and have also to provide hay and green fodder for the cavalryman, as they are paying no attention to the first letter. But let him write also to the same effect to the *boule* and *demos*. I am trying to come and join you myself at all costs. Until I come, then, speak to him yourself, taking along Ariston, Epharmostos,[180] and Apollonios.[181] I have written to Apollonios as well as Epharmostos, asking them to speak to Zenon on your behalf also.

58. VISIT OF A ROMAN SENATOR

P. Teb. I 33[182]   112

By the time of this letter Egypt was no longer a power of the first rank, and Roman favor counted for a great deal. Roman visitors of senatorial rank, as here, were therefore naturally treated with the utmost deference.

Hermias to Horos, greeting. A copy of the letter to Asklepiades is below. Take care that its instructions are followed. Farewell. Year 5, Xandikos 17, Mecheir 17.

To Asklepiades. Lucius Memmius, a Roman senator, who occupies a position of great dignity and honor, is making the voyage from Alexandria to the Arsinoite Nome to see the sights. Let him be received with special magnificence, and take care that at the proper spots the guest-chambers be prepared and the landing-places to them be got ready with great care, and that the gifts of hospitality mentioned below be presented to him at the landing-place, and that the furniture of the chamber, the customary bites of food for Petesouchos[183] and the crocodiles, the necessaries for the view of the labyrinth,[184] and the victims to be offered and the supply for the sacrifices be properly managed; in general take the utmost pains in everything that the visitor may be satisfied, and display the utmost zeal
———.

III

LIFE IN GREEK CITIES

59. ISOPOLITY BETWEEN PERGAMON AND TEMNOS

Staatsverträge 555 (OGIS 265)   early 3rd century (?)

A state of isopolity existed when the citizenship of one city was made equivalent to that of another and vice-versa. In the present text such an agreement is struck between Pergamon and the Aeolian city of Temnos, the citizens of each becoming full citizens of the other. The arrangement was apparently initiated by Pergamon (where also the inscription was found). The Pergamene decree is followed on the stone by a joint resolution of the two cities, which is written in the Aeolic dialect used at Temnos.

Boule and *demos* [decided]; proposal of the *strategoi*: [whereas the] *demos* of the Temnitans is in fact affectionately disposed towards the *demos* of the Pergamenes, with good fortune, be it resolved by the *boule* and the *demos*, to dispatch two envoys who, arriving (in Temnos), shall declare the goodwill towards them, and who shall address them to the effect that both cities decree isopolity; and, if this seems suitable to the Temnitans, for those dispatched to conclude (an agreement) about this as fully-empowered (representatives). Chosen were Apollonides, son of Apelles, and H[. . .] son of Hermippos. With good fortune, resolved by the Temnitans and Pergamenes, (at Temnos) the *prytanis* being the one after [Herak]leides, son of Ditas, in the month Heraion, in [Pergamon] the *prytanis* being Aristokrates, son of Hiera[. . .], in the month Heraion: for Temnitans to have citizenship in Pergamon and for Pergamenes (to have citizenship) [in Temnos], sharing in what the other [citizens share in], and for [the Temnitan] in Pergamon and the Pergamene in Temnos to have the right of owning land and house; and for the Temnitan to pay [taxes in Pergamon, as much as the] Pergamene pays, and for the Pergamene (to pay taxes) [in Temnos, as much as the] Temnitan pays ———.

60. PRAXIKLES' LOAN TO ARKESINE

*Syll.*³ 955   late 4th-early third century

Sometime around 300 the city of Arkesine on Amorgos borrowed three talents from a certain Praxikles of Naxos. The present inscription contains the terms of the loan. The interest (10%) is not in the least unusual, but the provisions about security are striking. The document is eloquently discussed by Tarn (in J.B. Bury et al., *The Hellenistic Age* [Cambridge 1923] 108 ff.; cf. below, note 186) and provides a fair indication of the uncertainty of the times.

[Good Fortune.] At Naxos in the month Hekatombaion, the *aisymnetai* being...enes and Sostratos; at Arkesine in the month Miltophorion, the [*arch*]*on* being Ktesiphon. Praxikles son of Polymnestos lent to the city of the Arkesineans three talents of Attic silver, guaranteed for Praxikles against all risks, at interest of five obols per mina per month, the *daneistai*,[185] Protomachos and Dio...es, having gone on public mission (to Naxos) according to the decree which Stesagoras proposed.

Mortgaged to Praxikles is all the public property of the city and the private property belonging to the Arkesineans and those dwelling in Arkesine, that within the land and that overseas.

The treasurers who collect the revenues of the Arkesineans will pay the interest each year. If they do not pay, let those who do not pay be liable to Praxikles for 150 per cent of the money owed from their own private resources, (this money to be recoverable) by all manner of execution, just as if consequent upon final court decision in accordance with the *symbolon*[187] of the Naxians and the Arkesineans; and let this money not be to the credit of the city against the loan, but let the city pay the interest. If (the city) does not pay, let the interest which it does not pay be subject to interest, payable to Praxikles, along with the principal sum at the same annual rate of interest.

They will pay back the principal sum within six months from the time Praxikles or whomever Praxikles sends demands it.

Whenever they pay the interest or the principal sum, they will pay (it) in Naxos to Praxikles, or to whomever Praxikles orders, in Attic or Alexandrian coin, which the city uses, [guaranteed against all risk], whole, genuine, uncut (?), undamaged, free of all imposts wherever Praxikles orders.

If they do not pay back the money according to the written terms, the Arkesineans agree and covenant to owe to Praxikles six talents; and it shall be permitted to Praxikles, free from all penalty, to exact this money by all manner of execution from the public property of the Arkesineans, and from the private property of the Arkesineans and those dwelling in Arkesine, both the whole amount from one individual and from all alike, in whatever way he can, just as from the losers of a final court decision in (before) the umpire city in accordance with the *symbolon* of the Naxians and Arkesineans. And whatever Praxikles seizes or exacts is not to be to the credit of the Arkesineans toward the repayment of the money they owe. And the Arkesineans also release from penalty and from liability to court action any who exact the money at Praxikles' behest. If any of the Arkesineans or of those dwelling in Arkesine obstructs the exactors or interferes with the exaction in any way or under any pretext whatever, let him pay as penalty to Praxikles a talent of silver, and [let him be liable for exaction] of this money, just as if he had lost a final court decision to Praxikles in (before) the umpire city in accordance with the *symbolon*, and let this money not be to the credit of the city toward the repayment of the loan. And if any injury or expense arises in the exaction of the money, let this be (the responsibility) of the city of the Arkesineans, and let the city pay back this money along with the rest of the loan.

The Arkesineans agree that nothing shall have precedence over this contract, neither law nor decree nor resolution nor *strategos* nor any other magistrate who renders a decision at odds with what is written in this contract nor anything else at all by any device or under any pretext whatsoever, but that this contract is to be valid wherever the lender or those acting on his behalf produce (it).

The Arkesineans agree to have this contract inscribed at Arkesine in the public archive [and in the] sanctuary of Hera on a stone stele within sixty days from the time when the *daneistai* announce, otherwise they are to owe..., in accordance with the contract deposited with Eurykles [and] Prax[ikles].

[Witnesses]: Eury[kles], Ateisides, [...A]ntipappos, Th[eon], Aristodemos, Niko[sth]e[nes], ...os, Eualk[ides], [Th]eopompos, An...os, Ei...mei[d]a[s], Thorax, Ky..., ...nome[nes], Ant...os, ..., Herakleides.

61. THE DELIANS HONOR PHILOKLES, KING OF THE SIDONIANS

*Syll.*³ 391   ca. 280

The temple of Apollo on Delos, the funds of which were regularly put out at interest (cf. no. 130) to individuals as well as to larger public bodies, had lent a sum to the League of the Islanders. In order to secure repayment, about which there had apparently arisen some question, the Delians appealed to Philokles, Ptolemy II's man in the Aegean, and thus, at least indirectly, to Ptolemy himself. Their *démarche* bore fruit, which is indicative of Ptolemy's relation to the League and, not least, of his desire to maintain order and his own influence in the area.

Resolved by the *boule* and the *demos*; Mnesalkos, son of Teles[archides] spoke: Whereas Philokles, King of the Sidonians, has in former times continually displayed all good-will and zeal towards the sanctuary and the Delians, and now, after an embassy was dispatched to him about the money which the Islanders owed to the Delians, he took all care that the Delians should recover the loans, [just as King] Ptolemy ordered, and that there should be no [delays and postponements] of the repayment (of the money) to the Delians ——— (to) [Bacch]on the nesiarch: so in order that all who come [to Delos] may know that the *demos* of the Delians knows how [to return] thanks to those who benefit the sanctuary and the Delians, [be it resolved by the *demos*] to praise Philokles, King of the Sidonians, [on account of his piety towards the temple] and his virtue [towards the *demos* of the Delians, and] to crown him with a gold crown [of 1000 drachmas, and] for the sacred herald to proclaim in the theater at the (festival of the) Apollonia that the *demos* of the Delians crowns Philokles, King of the Sidonians, with a gold crown of 1000 drachmas, on account of his piety towards the sanctuary and his virtue towards [the] *demos* of the Delians; and to [sacrifice] the savior- offerings on behalf of Philokles in Delos to Apollo [and Artemis and Leto] and Zeus the Savior and Athena the Savior; and for the treasurer to provide [the] expense out of the revenues ———.

62. ATHENS HONORS HERAKLEIDES OF CYPRIAN SALAMIS

*Syll.*³ 304   325/4

Besides giving an indication of the importance for Athens of imported grain, particularly that from the Black Sea area, this decree provides some insight into the workings of the Athenian council and assembly. The dossier here contains five distinct elements, passed in the following order (but inscribed in the order in which they are translated below). (A) is a decree of the assembly instructing the council to prepare and to submit to the assembly a proposal for honoring Herakleides. (B) is the council's response to this instruction. (C) is the decree then passed by the assembly, providing for the honorific crown as well as for the embassy to Herakleia. (A), (B), and (C) together constitute a set of resolutions adopted after Herakleides' provision of grain at a reduced rate in 330/29 but prior to his contribution of money for grain in 328/7. (D) is the council's *probouleuma* issued in response to this later gesture, and (E) is the corresponding and all-embracing resolution of the assembly, which adds designation as *proxenos* and benefactor to the honorific crown and also provides for the recording on stone of the whole dossier.

E.

Gods. In the archonship of Antikles;[188] in the fifth prytany, that of (the tribe) Aigeis, for which Antiphon son of Koroibos, of (the deme) Eleusis was secretary, on the eleventh (of the month), the thirty-fourth (day) of the prytany; of the *prohedroi* Philyllos of (the deme) Eleusis put the question to the vote; Demosthenes son of Demokles, of (the deme) Lamptrai spoke: Whereas Herakleides of Salamis continues to act out of love of honor towards the *demos* of the Athenians and to do whatever good he can, and previously, during the grain shortage, he gave 3000 *medimnoi* of wheat at five drachmas (the *medimnos*),[189] the first of the merchants who sailed in; and then, when the contributions were being made, he contributed 3000 drachmas for the purchase of grain,[190] and in other respects he continues to act with good-will and love of honor towards the *demos*, be it resolved by the *demos*: to praise Herakleides son of Charikleides, of Salamis, and to crown him with a gold crown for his good-will and zeal towards the *demos* of the Athenians; and for him to be a *proxenos* and benefactor of the *demos* of the Athenians, both himself and his descendants, and for them to have the right of owning land and house according to the law; and for them to serve on campaigns and pay the property-tax levies along with the Athenians. (Resolved) for the secretary of the prytany to have this decree and the other praises he has received inscribed on a stone stele and to have it set up on the Acropolis; and for the treasurer to provide thirty drachmas for the inscription of the stele from the (monies) spent by the *demos* for decree-related matters.

C.

Telemachos son of Theangelos, of (the deme) Acharnai spoke: Whereas Herakleides of Salamis gave grain to the *demos* at five drachmas (the *medimnos*), the first of the merchants who sailed in, in the archonship of Aristophon,[191] be it decreed by the *demos*: to praise Herakleides son of Charikleides, of Salamis, and to crown him with a gold crown for his zeal towards the *demos* of the Athenians; whereas he was forced to land by the Herakleotai, as he was sailing to Athens, and had his sails taken away by them, (resolved) to choose one man from all the Athenians as ambassador to go to Herakleia and Dionysios[192] and ask that he return Herakleides' sails and that, for the future, he do wrong to none of those sailing to Athens, and (to say that) in doing this he will do what is right and will not fail to obtain anything of what is right from the *demos* [of the Athenians]; and (resolved) for the treasurer of the *demos* to give to the ambassador chosen travelling expenses of fifty drachmas from the monies spent by the *demos* for decree-related matters. Chosen as ambassador was Thebagenes of (the deme) Eleusis.

A.

Telemachos son of Theangelos, of (the deme) Acharnai spoke: Be it decreed by the *demos*: that the *boule* form a *probouleuma* and introduce it at the next assembly, concerning Herakleides, in what manner he will receive such good as he can at the hands of the *demos* of the Athenians.

B.

Kephisodotos son of Eucharides, of (the deme) Acharnai, spoke: Concerning the matters about which the *demos* has enjoined the *boule* to form a *probouleuma* about Herakleides the Salaminian, be it resolved by the *boule*: Whereas Herakleides, having sailed into Athens with a cargo of grain, gave 3000 *medimnoi* to the *demos* at five drachmas each, the *prohedroi* to whom it falls by lot to preside at the next assembly are to bring Herakleides before the *demos* and deal with the matter, and they are to put before the *demos* a proposal of the *boule*, (namely) that the *boule* resolves: To praise Herakleides son of Charikleides, of Salamis, and to crown him with a gold crown of 500 drachmas; and that it be possible for him to receive such good as he can at the hands of the *demos*, in order that others as well will act from love of honor, knowing that the *boule* honors and crowns those who do.

D.

Phyleus son of Pausanias, of (the deme) Oinoi, spoke: Whereas Herakleides of Salamis, having sailed into Athens with a cargo of grain in the archonship of Aristophon, gave to the *demos* 3000 *medimnoi* at five drachmas (the *medimnos*), and for this reason the *demos* voted that the *boule* was to form a *probouleuma* and bring it before the *demos*, as to how he may receive such good as he can from the hands of the *demos* of the Athenians, and then, in the archonship of Euthykritos,[193] he contributed to the *demos* 3000 drachmas for the purchase of grain, be it resolved by the *boule*: That the *prohedroi* to whom it falls by lot to preside at the statutory assembly are to bring Herakleides before the *demos* and deal with the matter and they are to put before the *demos* the proposal of the *boule*, (namely) that the *boule* resolves: To praise Herakleides son of Charikleides, of Salamis, and to crown him with a gold crown of 500 drachmas; and for it to be possible for him to receive from the *demos* such good as he seems to be worthy of, in order that others as well may wish [readily to benefit the] *boule* and the *demos*, seeing that those who act from love of honor [. . .toward the *boule* and the] *demos* [————].

63. A SAMIAN GRAIN LAW

*Syll.*³ 976   2nd century

This decree of the island city of Samos gives the detailed arrangements for the administration of a grain fund set up by the contributions of numerous citizens of the city. Overall direction was placed in the hands of a board of two wealthy men ("those elected to be in charge of the grain supply"). The money for the fund was collected by the curators, of which one was elected by each of the *chiliastyes* (the units into which the two Samian tribes were divided), and the curators (also wealthy men: the words with which the surviving portion of the inscription opens refer to the candidates for this position) were responsible for lending out this money and paying the proceeds over to the board of two. The latter then turned the accumulated proceeds over to the elected grain-buyer (another wealthy man), who actually purchased the grain. The grain bought was then distributed *gratis*, under the supervision of the board of two, at the rate of two measures a month for each citizen for as many months as the grain thus acquired lasted. Such, in outline, is the procedure laid down. The decree provides also for the appointment of the relevant officials as well as for various sanctions against financial misconduct at the different stages of the process. (Cf. in general, Hands, *Charities and Social Aid* 89-115, and particularly 95 ff.)

———— of the wealthiest. Let them make the appointment in the month Kronion at the second of the assemblies. Let the *prytaneis* convoke the assembly [in the] theater, and let them order those attending the assembly to sit by *chiliastys*, making signs and setting off a place for each of the *chiliastyes*. Whosoever disobeys and does not sit with his own *chiliastys*, let them fine him a native stater. If he says he has been unjustly fined, let him register a plea, and let the judgment take place in the city court within twenty days. Let both the putting forward (of names) and the election be done by the members of the *chiliastyes* themselves. At this assembly let the *chiliastyes* examine also the securities and the guarantors: and let the *prytaneis* enter in the public records whatever securites and whichever guarantors they approve. Similarly, let them enter in the public records the curators who are appointed. When the voting is about to take place, let the city's herald utter a prayer, that it may be well for those who vote for the ones who they believe will best supervise the funds. Let the ones appointed exact the interest from the borrowers, and let them make it over to the men elected to be in charge of the grain supply. And let the latter buy the grain deriving from the five per cent tax levied from the district of Anaia,[194] paying to the goddess a price not less than the five (drachmas) and two obols that the *demos* formerly assigned. The money left over, if the *demos* does not resolve to buy grain, they are to keep until others have been appointed to be in charge of the grain supply; then they are to make it over to them. If the *demos* does resolve to buy grain, let them make the money over immediately to the grain-buyer who has been elected. Let the latter buy the grain from the land of Anaiitis in whatever way he believes will turn out most profitably for the city, unless it seems to the *demos* more profitable to buy the grain from somewhere else. Otherwise, let the matter be handled in whatever way the *demos* resolves. Every year let the *prytaneis* in office for the month Artemision bring this matter forward, giving public notice beforehand. Let the *demos* every year, at the first of the elections after the appointment of the elected magistrates, designate two men, one from each tribe, to be in charge of the grain supply, each of these having property worth not less than three talents. Let these, after receiving the interest from the curators, pay the price of the grain and any other expense that may arise, and let them also measure out the grain. And let the *demos* at the same assembly appoint a grain-buyer, having property worth not less than two talents. And, if it seems good, let the money from the interest be lent out, if any wish, after giving sufficiently valuable securities and providing guarantors, to buy earlier and arrange the grain supply more profitably. Let the men elected to be in charge of the grain supply accept the guarantors at their own risk. Let them measure out all the purchased grain to the resident citizens by *chiliastys*, giving to each two measures a month as a gift. Let them begin the distribution in the month Pelusion, and thereafter let them measure out for as many months as the grain holds out. Let them not measure out grain to one on behalf of another, unless someone is ill. Let them conduct the distribution from the first to the tenth (of the month), but until the thirtieth for those who are abroad, if they come. Let them render an account each month to the office of the public auditor of those who received grain, recording it by *chiliastys* and adding the names of the recipients. Let the members of the *chiliastyes* have the power to appoint the same curator for five years in succession. If any of the borrowers does not pay back the money, either the whole sum or a part of it, let the *chiliastys* surrender the security; and if there is a surplus, let the *chiliastys* pay it to the one who gave the security. If there is a deficiency, let the *chiliastys* exact it from the guarantor. Let the *chiliastys* give the interest accruing to those elected to be in charge of the grain supply. If it does not pay, let the members of the *chiliastys* not receive the grain distribution due to them until they fulfil their obligation. If any of the elected curators, after taking the money which he is supposed to put out at interest, does not put it out at interest but wrongfully holds it himself, let him owe to the city (a fine of) 10,000 drachmas; similarly, if he does not pay the interest to the men elected to be in charge of the grain supply, let him owe an equal amount as penalty and let the public auditors register his property as forfeit to the *chiliastys* against the money which he ought to have paid; and, besides the penalty, let him be registered as *atimos*,[195] and let him be *atimos* until he pays. And let the members of the *chiliastys*, who appointed the curator who did not pay the money, not receive the grain distribution due to them. If [the] members of the *chiliastys* wish to pay the money, either all of them or some of them in proportion, which the curator or the borrower did not pay to the city, let them have the power to do so, and when they have paid let them receive their grain distribution from the time they paid. Let no one have the power to use this money or the interest deriving from it for any purpose other than the free distribution of grain. If any *prytanis* brings forward a measure, or any speaker proposes, or any *epistates* puts the question, to the effect that it should be used or transferred for any other purpose, let each one (of them) owe (a fine of) 10,000 drachmas; similarly, if any treasurer or curator or any of those elected to be in charge of the grain supply or any grain-buyer gives or lends it for any purpose other than the free distribution (of grain).

(There follows here a long list [occupying 128 lines] of those who provided money for the grain fund with an indication of the amount given by each. The individual contributions were from 50 to 1000 drachmas.)

64.   DECREE FOR BOULAGORAS OF SAMOS

SEG I 366   ca. 240

This honorific decree from Samos gives fair indication of the fragility of the public finances of Greek cities and of the extent to which they could, and did, become precariously dependent for their welfare upon their most wealthy citizens (cf. in this connection no. 13). Besides assuming responsibilities within the city, which required time and money, Boulagoras provided the money needed for a *theoria* to Alexandria and effectively constituted by himself the city's grain fund (cf. no. 63), as well as providing a source of interest-free loans to some of the less fortunate. He undertook, moreover, an embassy to King Antiochus (most likely Antiochus II, although Hierax has been suggested), who had made gifts of Samian properties in the Anaiitis to some of his high-ranking subordinates. This area was of the greatest importance to Samos (cf. its rôle as a source of grain in no. 63), and foreign control there likely accounts for much of the financial and alimentary difficulty experienced by the city. Later, when possession of the Anaitis was secure, it was possible to establish the permanent mechanism for bringing grain to the city which is set out in no. 63.

Resolved by the *boule* and the *demos*, proposal of the *prytaneis*, concerning [(the matters) which] Hippodamas son of Pantonaktides initially raised, (namely) that Boulagoras son of Alexis, having rendered many services to the *demos* as a whole and individually to many of the citizens, might be praised and crowned as the *boule* and *demos* may decide: Whereas Boulagoras, in previous times, when properties were commandeered in the territory of Anaiitis, which was then subject to Antiochus the king, and the citizens who had their holdings taken away had recourse to the *demos* and requested an embassy to Antiochus, in order that they might retrieve what was theirs, appointed ambassador, and going initially to Ephesus and when Antiochus marched off accompanying him as far as Sardis, exercised all eagerness and zeal — standing against, during his embassy, the most illustrious of Antiochus' friends, who happened to be in possession of the commandeered (properties) — that the *demos*, recovering the holdings commandeered at that time, might restore them to those from whom they had been taken away; and he brought letters about these matters from Antiochus to our city and to his garrison-commander in Anaia and to the *dioiketes*, thanks to which those who were then deprived regained possession of their own property and no one in Antiochus' service subsequently undertook to commandeer the property of citizens; and, often chosen by the *demos* as *proegoros* in the public court cases, he was constantly vigorous and zealous and brought about many useful and beneficial things for the city; and, elected director of the gymnasium[196] by the people according to the law, on account of the deficiency of the gymnasiarch, he supervised the good-conduct of the ephebes and the youths fairly and nobly; and in the present year, when it was time for the dispatch of the *theoroi* to Alexandria, knowing that the *demos* set the greatest importance by the honors of King Ptolemy and his sister Queen Berenike,[197] since limited funds were available for their crowns and for the sacrifices, which the *theoroi* must needs perform in Alexandria, while for the travelling expenses of the *architheoros* and the *theoroi*, by whom the crown had to be delivered and the sacrifices performed, there was no (money) at all nor any place whence at the time it might be got, wishing that nothing be lacking from the honors previously decreed for the king and the queen and their parents and ancestors, he promised to advance the money required for these things from his own resources, (a sum) not much less than 6000 drachmas; and when a shortage of grain beset the city and the citizens, due to the urgency of the need, appointed three commissions to buy grain,[198] he showed no lack of zeal and love of honor, but in the case of the first commission he advanced all the money to be put out at interest, according to what the *demos* decreed, in the case of the second he promised the same amount as those who contributed the most, and in the case of the third he not only provided all the money to be lent out from his own resources, but also, when the grain was brought into the city and the grain-buyer had contracted a loan on it, he came before the assembly and promised, since there was no source whence the money would be repaid, to pay off the loan for the city as well as the interest and all the other expenses, and he did this quickly and reimbursed the lender without making any contract with the city for this money or requiring guarantors to be appointed for him,[199] but considering more important the common good and that the *demos* might live in prosperity; and in all other matters he continues to show himself zealous and kind both to the *demos* in general and individually to each of the citizens, [giving] the best [counsel] and reconciling those with differences and lending without interest from his own resources to many of those who are in difficulties; in order, then, that we may be clear in honoring good men and in urging many of the citizens to the same attitude, be it resolved by the *demos*: to praise Boulagoras son of Alexis for his virtue and his good-will toward the citizens, and to crown him with a gold crown at the tragedies during the Dionysia, and for the *agonothetes* to look after the announcement; and for the *exetastai* to have this decree inscribed on a stone stele and set up in the sanctuary of Hera; and for the treasurer of the sacred funds to provide the expense from the money he has on hand from fines. Present were Hyblesios, Herodotos, Monimos, Demetrios.

65. POLYTHROOS PROVIDES FOR EDUCATION AT TEOS

*Syll.*³ 578   2nd century

The city of Teos here deals with a gift made for the purpose of education in essentially the same way as Miletos dealt with Eudemos' gift in *Syll.*³ 577. Some differences, however, are apparent. Besides the greater variety of instructors to be hired, it may be particularly noted that the education of girls is here provided for and that a wider range of children's ages is apparently at issue than was the case at Miletos. The oldest of them share at least part of the ephebes' curriculum, and indeed some of the income from the gift is to be used to pay certain instructors of the ephebes.

[Resolved ——— and, after the] selection of [the] gymnasiarch, for a *paidonomos* to be appointed not less than 40 [years] of age; and, in order that the freeborn children may be educated as Polythroos, son of Onesimos, taking forethought, announced to the *demos* and gave for this purpose 34,000 drachmas, establishing a most noble reminder of his love of glory, for there to be appointed each year at the elections of magistrates, after the selection of the secretaries, three grammar-masters to teach the boys and the girls; to pay to the one elected for the first level 600 drachmas a year, to the one for the second level 550 drachmas, to the one for the third level 500 drachmas; for two gymnastics-masters to be appointed, and for wages of 500 drachmas a year to be given to each of them; for a lyre- or harp-player to be apointed and for the one elected to be paid a wage of 700 drachmas a year; he will teach music and lyre- or harp-playing to the children fit to be chosen for the first level [and] to the ones a year younger than these, and music to the ephebes; let the *paidonomos* decide as to the ages of these children;[200] and, if we have an intercalary month, to pay the wage that falls due for the month; let the *paidonomos* and the gymnasiarch pay the arms-instructor and the instructor in archery and spear-throwing, after referring (the matter) to the *demos*;[201] let these teach the ephebes and the ones for whom instruction in music is (here) scheduled; let pay of 250 drachmas be given to the instructor in archery and spear-throwing, and 300 drachmas to the arms-instructor; the arms-instructor will teach for a period of not less than two months; in order that the children and the ephebes may be carefully trained in their lessons, for the *paidonomos* and the gymnasiarch to supervise carefully as is laid down for each of them according to the laws; if the grammar-masters dispute among themselves about the number of children, let the *paidonomos* decide (the matter), and, as he arranges, let them obey; for the grammar-masters to hold the recitations that are to take place in the gymnasium, and the music-instructor (those that are to take place) in the *bouleuterion*; [———] if they do not pay the fine, let it be permitted [to compel] them; regarding the arms-master and the instructor in archery and spear-throwing let it be done as is written above; if the treasurer now in office or those in office at any time (in the future) do not pay the money according to what is written, or anyone else, whether magistrate or private citizen, speaks or acts or proposes or puts to the vote or proposes a law contrary to this or cancels this law in any way or on any pretext whatsoever, to the effect that the money should be touched or expenditure not made from it for the purposes directed by this law or that it be allocated for [any] other (purpose) and not for what is enjoined in this law, let such actions be invalid and let the treasurers next in office allocate to the account (set up) according to this law an equal sum of money from the revenues of the city, and in other respects let it be carried out according to this law; may he be utterly ruined, himself and his entire family, who says or does anything contrary to this law, and let him be (regarded as) a temple-robber, and let there be carried out against him all that is written in the laws about the temple-robber; and let each of those who does anything against this law about this money, or who fails to do what is enjoined, owe to the city 10,000 drachmas; let anyone who wishes bring a case against him, both by private and by public action, both after the presentation of the monthly account and at any time he wishes; let it not be possible to dismiss one of these cases by reference to the required period of time[202] or by any other means whatsoever; let the one convicted pay a fine of double (the sum involved), and let half of this belong to the city, sacred to Hermes and Herakles and the Muses, and let it be deposited in the aforementioned account, and let half belong to the one who obtains the conviction; let the public examiners see to the completion of these cases, as of the other public cases; let the *timouchoi*, whoever are in office, proclaim, in addition to the (regular) imprecation, that he is to be utterly ruined, himself and his entire family, who touches the money given by Poolythroos son of Onesimos for the education of the freeborn children in any way or on any pretext whatsoever, or who assigns (the money) for anyting else and not for what is provided for in the law, or who does not carry out what is prescribed by the law; if the treasurers do not lend out the money according to the written provisions or do not pay what [according to this] law is due to those elected to be in charge of the lessons, let each of them owe to the city 2000 drachmas; let anyone who wishes bring a case against him———let the one convicted pay a fine of double (the sum involved), and———.

66. ILION HONORS THE PHYSICIAN OF ANTIOCHUS I

Ilion 34 (*OGIS* 220)   275-268/7

This decree of the city of Ilion was prompted by two letters addressed to the city, one from Antiochus himself and one from Antiochus' deputy in Asia Minor, Meleager (cf. no. 18). There must be presumed to have been also a third, sent by Antiochus to Meleager. All of this suggests that Metrodoros was to be rewarded for healing the king (saving his life?) in a good many cities of the Seleucid realm.

Whereas King Antiochus has sent to us (to say) that, having been wounded in the neck in the battle, he was safely healed by Metrodoros the physician, (and whereas) Meleager the *strategos*,[203] thinking of what is in the interest of the city, has also sent (to us) about him, be it resolved by the *boule* and the *demos* to praise Metrodoros son of Timokles, of Amphipolis, for his virtue and his good-will towards the Kings Antiochus and Seleucus[204] and towards the *demos*, and for him to be (declared) *proxenos* and benefactor of the city; and for there to be granted to him citizenship and the right of owning land and the right to approach the *boule* and the *demos* first after the sacred matters; and to permit him to [enter into] whatever tribe and phratry he may wish ———.

67. EUMENES I AND PERGAMON

RC 23 (*OGIS* 267 I) and *OGIS* 267 II   ca. 260-245

This inscription contains a letter addressed by Eumenes to the city of Pergamon and the Pergamene decree passed in direct response. The city clearly maintained itself institutionally as a democracy, but its relation to the ruler is equally clear, particularly from the Pergamene decree. A board of five *strategoi* constituted the chief magistracy — the wide extent of their competence emerges from the Pergamene resolution — and these five were appointed each year by Eumenes. The Pergamene decree indicates the existence at Pergamon of a cult in honor of Eumenes, with the epithet Euergetes ("the benefactor").

RC 23

[Eumenes son of Philetairos to the *demos* of the Pergamenes], greeting. [Palamandros, Skymnos, Metrodoros, Theotimos, Phil]iskos, the *strategoi* [who served in the year when...was priest], appear [to have filled] their office [well on all occasions]. They have performed justly [the other duties of the office and in the matter of finance they have not only] managed profitably for the *demos* and for the gods [all the] city's and the sacred revenues of their year but they have sought out obligations overlooked by the previous magistrates and by sparing no one who had held back anything they have restored (these sums) to the city. They have cared also for the repair of the offerings in the temples. As they have brought these matters into good order, future *strategoi* also following their example may easily manage the common affairs. Considering then that it is not just to slight such officials, so that those subsequently appointed may try to preside properly over the *demos*, we have ourselves determined to crown them at the Panathenaia and we thought it best to write you about them, so that in the intervening time you might consider the matter and honor them as you think they deserve. Farewell.

OGIS 267 II

The *demos* decided; Archestratos son of Hermippos spoke: Whereas the *strategoi* appointed by Eumenes — Palamandros, Skymnos, Metrodoros, Theotimos, Philiskos — have conducted their office well, be it resolved by the *demos*: to praise Eumenes on account of the fact that on every occasion he takes thought for what is good for the *demos* and honors and crowns those of the citizens who join him in contributing to these things, wishing to make the magistrates appointed more eager to take thought for sacred and civic affairs. And in order that the *demos* may be clear in its support for Eumenes with regard to these men, be it resolved by the *demos*: to crown them at the Panathenaia with a gold crown on account of their virtue and their good-will toward Eumenes and the *demos*; and let the treasurers appointed for a year always give them a sheep at the Eumeneia, and let them take it and sacrifice it to Eumenes Euergetes, in order that the *demos* may be clear to all in its gratitude. (Resolved also) to have the letter from Eumenes and the decree inscribed on a stone stele and set up in the *agora*, and for the treasurers in office during the priesthood of Arkeon to provide the expense for the stele and the inscription.

IV

THE BUREAUCRACY OF

PTOLEMAIC EGYPT

68. APPOINTMENT OF A *KOMOGRAMMATEUS*

P. Teb. I 9-10[205]   119

These documents are (a) a memorandum from Menches undertaking to pay a large amount of produce in return for renewal of his appointment as village scribe, and (b) a notification from a higher official to the *topogrammateus* of Menches' reappointment on condition of his cultivating some unproductive land. The latter promise was a frequent condition of holding office, but the former was not, and these payments, and in particular those by Dorion, perhaps a dependant of Menches paying for protection, may well have been illegal and meant as bribes.

9

From Menches, *komogrammateus* of Kerkeosiris. On being appointed to the post of *komogrammateus* previously held by me I will pay at the village 50 artabas of wheat and 50 artabas of pulse,[206] namely 20 artabas of lentils, 10 of bruised beans, 10 of peas, 6 of mixed seeds, 3 of mustard, 1 of parched pulse, total 50; total, 100 artabas. Year 51, Pachon 6. And Dorion will pay 50 artabas of wheat and 10 of pulse, namely 3 of bruised beans, 3 of peas, 3 of mixed seeds, 1 of mustard, total 10, total 60.

10

Asklepiades to Marres, greeting. Menches having been appointed *komogrammateus* of Kerkeosiris by the *dioiketes* on the understanding that he shall cultivate at his own expense 10 arouras of the land in the neighborhood of the village which has been reported as unproductive[207] at a rent of 50 artabas, which he shall pay annually from the 52nd year to the crown in full or shall measure out the deficiency from his private means, give to him the papers of his office and take care that the terms of his agreement are fulfilled. Farewell. Year 51, Mesore 3. (Address) To Marres, *topogrammateus*.

69. OATH OF OFFICE

P. Fuad. Univ. Cat. 3-4   246-222

This oath of the Egyptian assistant to the agent of a royal banker stationed in the chief town of a subdivision of the Herakleopolite Nome shows both the typical form of an oath by the gods, the sovereigns and others, and the duties of his office, which consist of keeping accurate records of his receipts and depositing them in the bank unless he is ordered specifically to make a disbursement on the spot. As is typical, the bureaucrat is to be personally responsible for any financial losses to the crown through his actions. Noteworthy also is the pledge to refrain from the not uncommon practice of seeking sanctuary from justice.

In the reign of Ptolemy the son of Ptolemy and Arsinoe, the Brother and Sister Gods, year..., [208] Epeiph 20. the oath which Semtheus son of Teos, of Herakleopolis, one of the assistants, who is also called Herakleodoros, swore and signed:

I swear by King Ptolemy, the son of King Ptolemy, and by Queen Berenike and by the Brother and Sister Gods and by the Benefactor Gods (error for Savior Gods) their ancestors and by Isis and Sarapis and all the other gods and goddesses of the country: to perform my official duties under Klitarchos the agent of Asklepiades the banker in charge of the accounting office in Phebichis of the Koite (toparchy); and to report correctly and justly all payments to the crown treasury and the cash which I receive from Klitarchos separately from what I receive myself; and to deposit these in the bank in Herakleopolis unless I am instructed to disburse any outlay locally; and to give to Klitarchos an account of all payments, both of income and of expense, and the receipts for whatever I disburse.

And if I owe anything to the administration I shall pay it to the royal bank in five days, and the right of execution shall be against me and all my property, and I swear not to alienate any of my property or the agreement shall be against me, and to remain accessible to Klitarchos and his agents outside any temple, altar, sacred precinct, or any sanctuary.

If I keep this oath, may it be well with me, but if I break it I am to be guilty of impiety.

70. LETTER OF MARRES TO MENCHES

P. Teb. I 23   ca. 119 or 114

Marres, Menches' superior, complains to him here that one of the higher official's relatives has been harmed by Menches' conduct; he orders the village official to remember his place.

Marres to Menches, greeting. My kinsman Melas has appealed to me concerning an alleged injury from you obliging him to complain to Demetrios son of Niboitas. I am exceedingly vexed that he should have gained no special consideration from you on my account and should therefore have asked assistance from Demetrios; and I consider that you have acted badly in not having been careful that he should be independent of others owing to my superior rank. Therefore will you now please endeavor more earnestly to correct your behavior towards him, abandoning your previous state of ignorance. If you have any grievance against him apply together with him to me. Farewell.
(Address) To Menches, *komogrammateus*.

71. ACCOUNT OF A POSTAL STATION

P. Hib. I 110 verso   ca. 255

This account contains eight days' entries from the daybook of the operator of a royal postal station, recording the arrival and dispatch of rolls (of accounts and official documents, probably) and letters to and from the king, the *dioiketes* Apollonios, and other persons in Alexandria and in the country. It appears that courtiers stayed mostly near their home bases, shuttling back and forth between that station and the next in either direction, where a new person took the mail. See F. Preisigke, *Klio* 7 (1907) 241-277, and *W. Chr.* 435, introduction, with the remarks of E. Van 't Dack, *Cd'E* 37 (1962) 338-41.

———— [delivered] to Alexander 6 [rolls]; of these 1 roll was for King Ptolemy, 1 roll for Apollonios the *dioiketes* and two letters which were received in addition to the roll, 1 roll for Antiochos the Cretan, 1 roll for Menodoros, 1 roll contained in another (?) for Chel..., and Alexander delivered them to Nikodemos.

The 17th, at an early hour, Phoinix the younger, son of Herakleitos, Macedonian holding 100 arouras, delivered to Aminon 1 roll and the price (?) for Phanias;[209] and Aminon delivered it to Theochrestos.

The 18th, 1st hour, Theochrestos delivered to Dinias 3 rolls from the upper country, of which 2 rolls were for King Ptolemy and 1 for Apollonios the *dioiketes*, and Dinias delivered them to Hippolysos.

The 18th, 6th hour, Phoinix the elder, son of Herakleitos, Macedonian holding 100 arouras in the Herakleopolite Nome, one of the first company of E..., delivered 1 roll for Phanias, and Aminon delivered it to Timokrates.

The 19th, 11th hour, Nikodemos delivered from the lower country to Alexander [—] rolls, from King Ptolemy for Antiochos in the

Herakleopolite Nome 1 roll, for Demetrios, the officer in charge of supplies for the elephants, in the Thebaid 1 roll, for Hippoteles the agent of Antiochos (against?) Andronikos (?) at Apollonopolis Magna, 1 roll, from King Ptolemy to Theogenes the money-carrier 1 roll, for Herakleodoros in the Thebaid [1 roll,] for Zoilos, banker of the Hermopolite Nome, [1], for Dionysios, *oikonomos* in the Arsinoite Nome, 1 [roll].

The 20th,...hour, Lykokles delivered to Aminon 3 rolls, of which 1 roll was for King Ptolemy from the elephant-country below Th..., 1 roll for Apollonios the *dioiketes*, 1 roll for Hermippos, member of the staff of workmen (?), and Aminon delivered them to Hippolysos. The 21st, 6th hour,...delivered two letters from the lower country for Phanias...and Horos delivered them to Dionysios ———

The 22nd, 1st hour, A...delivered [to Dinias] 16 rolls, of which [—] rolls were for King Ptolemy from the elephant-country below Th..., 4 rolls for Apollonios the *dioiketes*, 4 rolls for Antiochos the Cretan, and Dinias delivered them to Nikodemos.

The 22nd, 12th hour, Leon delivered to Aminon from the upper country [— rolls] for King Ptolemy, and Aminon delivered them to Hippolysos.

The 23rd, at an early hour, Timokrates delivered to [Alexander —] rolls, of which [—] rolls were for King Ptolemy, 1 roll for [Apollonios] the *dioiketes*, 1 roll for P... the money-carrier, [—] roll for Par..., and Alexander delivered them to ————.

72. ANNOUNCEMENT OF A GOVERNMENT AUCTION

P. Eleph. 14[210]   ca. 223

The regulations governing an auction of property, probably mostly confiscated by the crown for default, are set out here, including priestly offices with their privileges and incomes, vineyards, and ordinary arable farmland. The regulations for each class of property differ somewhat, mainly in the type of ownership conferred.

We offer (the properties) for sale on the following terms. The successful bidders shall pay annually to the Crown in the case of the vineyards the proper money taxes and the *apomoira* due to (Arsinoe) Philadelphos, and for the arable land the rents in kind which have been imposed upon it and [whatever other payment is required] in respect of such land.[211] They shall pay the price of that which [concerns(?)] the crown to the royal bank, and of that which concerns any of the [temples (?) of its own (?)] banker, in 3 years, the 4th part of the whole price of the priestly offices in gold or silver of the new coinage and the remainder in copper with the customary discount at the rate of 10 drachmas, 2⅓ obols on the mina,[212] and the price of the other landed property in copper with the customary carriage (of the copper) three obols per mina and the proper 1/60th and as crier's fee on the whole purchase 1/1000th. The purchaser shall receive the due revenues of the priestly offices as soon as the first instalment has been paid to the Crown, and he shall be owner of the land and of its produce, if it has been sown by the former owners, and if it has been leased, those who cultivated it shall pay the rent to the purchaser in accordance with the contracts made with the cultivators. The purchasers shall pay the 4th part of the price immediately and the remainder in 3 years beginning from year 25, paying annually in Epeiph and Mesore the amount which falls due, and on cattle and implements they shall pay immediately the taxes of. . .and 1/90th. They shall own the properties in the same way as those who formerly possessed them. Whoever wishes shall be permitted to raise the bid, by as much as he pleases while the auction-ring is still open, but only by ten per cent after the auction is ended and until the 1st instalment has been paid; and (if there is no purchaser) the objects offered shall be classed as unsold after the 6(?) days prescribed by the ordinance.

73.   AVOIDING A LITURGY

P. Mich. I 23   257

In this letter a citizen of an unnamed Greek city asks Zenon to assist his messenger in getting to see Apollonios to ask the latter to intervene to secure cancellation of the author's nomination for liturgical service as his city's commissary in charge of securing a grain supply. Edgar suggests that the city is probably Alexandria, but it seems to us that the tone of the letter and the relative locations of the persons (Zenon in Arsinoe is to help gain admittance to Apollonios, probably in Alexandria) suggest rather an overseas location for the author, Aristeides. The supply of grain to Greek cities was often uncertain and fluctuating, and numerous inscriptions of the period display the gratitude of a city to a prominent citizen who has secured grain for it. Cf. for the grain supply nos. 2, 3, 63, and 64.

Aristeides to Zenon, greeting. If you are well and everything else is to your mind, I would give much thanks to the gods. I too am well. I have had the misfortune to be proposed by the citizens as grain-buyer though I am not yet of the right age nor due for that burden, but [have been proposed by] certain persons out of jealousy. I and my brother Theronides have therefore sent Dromon to explain these things to Apollonios, in order that he may help us and release me from that commission. You would do me a favor then by immediately admitting Dromon to Apollonios' presence and assisting him to have speech with Apollonios as soon as possible and seeing that he sends him back to us immediately after settling everything. And write yourself if ever you need anything from here, in order that we may do all that you want. Farewell.

(Address) To Zenon. (Docket) Aristeides about himself and the charge of supplying grain. Year 29, Panemos 1, in Arsinoe.

74. A LETTER TO ZENON FROM KAUNIANS SEEKING HELP

P. Col. Zen. I 11   257

Zenon was a native of Kaunos in Caria, and after his entry into Ptolemaic service he maintained his family and social ties to this city and others in Caria, all of which were under Ptolemaic control at this period. Three Kaunians, in Egypt on some unofficial political errand, solicit Zenon's help in getting the assistance of his master Apollonios, who — whatever official power he had over Caria — was the most influential royal official of the time. The informal nature of the inner workings of the Ptolemaic bureaucracy is shown clearly here.

Zenon, Protogenes and Apollonides to Zenon, greeting. Hearing of the good-will which you have towards all your fellow-citizens, we commend you; and we would gladly have met you beforehand, desiring to chat with you concerning matters of advantage to the city and about ourselves. Since it has not come about that you were able to (receive?) the three of us, believing that it behooves you as it does the rest of our townsmen whose public life is on a high plane to give thought to these things, we beg you, along with Pyrrhias and Apollonides, to present to Apollonios the letter which we have given to Apollonides, [a letter] which is useful to us all. And if you are in any other way able to work with us so that we may obtain consideration, [we request you to do so] with the full knowledge that when we return to our own city we shall not be unmindful of these things, but will in turn disclose them to the assembly so that it is clear to you [that we are not unmindful]. And we will personally, also, try to return the favor. Farewell. (Address) To Zenon.
(Docket) Zenon, Protogenes, Apollonides. Year 29, Xandikos. In Memphis.

75. LETTER TO ZENON ABOUT A PETITIONER

P. Ryl. IV 563   249[213]

A functionary attempts to enlist the services of Zenon and of Apollonios' interpreter (obviously a man of importance to such a petitioner) to foil the plans of an Egyptian soldier to complain in person to Apollonios about a situation that is not explained in much detail. The solidarity of the Greek subordinates of the *dioiketes* against this Egyptian is interesting.

Pataikion[214] to Zenon, greeting. I assigned to the possession of Aristodemos a house of Sokeus son of Nechauis, a native soldier, in Aueria, and I have heard that he has sailed down to present a petition to Apollonios about me, ignoring both the seller and the buyer, with the idea that he will discomfit me if he appeals to Apollonios. If, therefore, you have an opportunity and if it be practicable, will you please take action against the fellow, in order that I may not be discredited by the rest of them. I have written also to Apollonios the interpreter requesting him also to do the man as much damage as he can. Farewell. Year 36, Pharmouthi 1. (Addressed) To Zenon. (Docketed by sender) The one from Philadelphia.

76. ZENON PETITIONS THE KING

*P. Cair. Zen.*V 59832   ca. 246-240

Soon after the beginning of the reign of Ptolemy III, the new king removed from office Apollonios, who had served Ptolemy II as finance minister for many years. Apollonios lost his "gift" estate at Philadelphia in the Fayum and very possibly his life. This petition[215] from Zenon, Apollonios' former manager on this estate, forms a part of what was obviously a complex process, the winding up of the affairs of the estate. Zenon had been dismissed by Apollonios just before the end of Philadelphos' reign, and unlike his former master he survived and prospered well into the next reign. For this period of Zenon's life, see M. Rostovtzeff. *A Large Estate in Egypt* (Madison 1922) 158-64, and R.S. Bagnall in *Greek, Roman and Byz. Studies* 15 (1974) 215-220.

To King Ptolemy from Zenon, greeting. I was in charge of the gift-estate in Philadelphia belonging to Apollonios the former *dioiketes*, until year 38[216] when I was dismissed by him. I was included in the announcement concerning the rendering of accounts, because I owed...the produce of the fields in my charge and that of my assistants...Therefore, because it has been announced that if anyone owes anything to Apollonios or those who managed his property he should make a declaration, I ask that everything that I demonstrate to have been received by the agents of Apollonios with respect to the crops in my charge and that of my assistants be deducted from what I still owe; and likewise all that my own debtors have been able to declare; so that I may be able to pay the debt and that it may not happen to me to fall under the proclamation[217] for want of being able to pay the debt because these sums were not credited to me.

126

77. PETITION ABOUT ASSESSMENT

P. Cair. Zen. II 59236 254-253

This petition tells us that the basis for taxation on vineyards was a three-year average; the officials had excluded the earliest of the last three years on Stratippos' vineyard on the grounds that the vineyard was not fully in production then, and the latter two years yielded a higher average. The owner's son seeks to have this perfectly reasonable decision overruled, probably with Zenon's intercession. On the wine trade and production see J.A.S. Evans, *Journal of Juristic Papyrology* 7-8 (1953-54) 53-70; on this document, p. 63, n. 69.

To Diotimos the *dioiketes*[218] from Neoptolemos, Macedonian of the cleruchs in Philadelphia, greeting. My father Stratippos is wronged by Theokles, the former *oikonomos* of the Aphroditopolite Nome and by Petosiris the *basilikos grammateus*. For in making an assessment-list for vineyards, taking (as a base) the produce from the (last) three years, they assessed it at a third of the amount; but for my father they made an assessment from two years, claiming that it was newly planted. I therefore ask you, if it seems right to you, to look into this matter, and if these things are true, since they also made the assessment for the others from three years, to give an order for my benefit to Hermolaos and Petosiris that they should make the assessment for my father too from three years, whether they wish to make it from the twenty-ninth year or from the thirtieth year, for we have already made wine from it for four years; and to have credited to him (my father) the silver paid into the bank by the retail wine-sellers from the wine which they brought from the vineyard, so that he may receive justice from you.[219] Farewell. (Docket) Neoptolemos, a petition to Diotimos about a vineyard.

78. DECLARATION OF HOUSE-PROPERTY

W. Chr. 221 (*UPZ* 116) 210-183[220]

The mechanics of declaration for purposes of tax assessment are shown by this document, in which a resident of Memphis declares his home and bakery, which were apparently located across a street from one another at a T-intersection of that street with another (diagram in *UPZ* I, p. 539).

To Metrodoros, *epimeletes*, from Apynchis son of Inarous, Hellenomemphite.[221] I declare, in accordance with the proclamation that has been issued, the house and courtyard belonging to me in the Hellenion[222] in the place Imensthotieion, of which the dimensions of the house are 21 cubits by 13 cubits,[223] and of the courtyard 4 cubits by 13 cubits, the boundaries being on the south the house of Tampsois son of Phanos, on the north that of Pasis son of Arianis, and the road between, on the west my bakery and the road between, on the east (the house of) Pokaus son of Petepoinis. I value this at 4000 drachmas. And another house, in which they make bread, and a courtyard, of which the measurements are, for the house, 21 cubits by 13 cubits and of the courtyard 4 cubits by 13 cubits, the boundaries being (on the south) the house of Onnophris son of Horos, on the north that of Pasis son of Arianis, and the street between, on the west (the house of) Nephergeris son of Pachrates, on the east the afore-mentioned house and street between. This I value at 2000 bronze drachmas. Total, 1 talent.

79.   LETTER ABOUT COLLECTION OF TAXES

P. Hib. I 66   228

The tax-farmer here requests the banker in part of the Herakleopolite Nome to collect a tax for which he has contracted, stating that he will make it worth his while.

Protarchos to Kleitarchos, greeting. I have contracted for the 1½ per cent (tax) with the managers of the *dorea*.[224] Since the 5 per cent tax is paid to you in your district, please order your agents to collect the other taxes too, as Asklepiades has also written to you; and as soon as I arrive from the delivery (?) of the copper I will have a conversation with you, so that you shall not oblige me to no purpose. Farewell. Year 19, Pachons 14.
(Address) To Kleitarchos, banker of the Koite (district).

80.   LETTER ABOUT PROTECTION OF TAX-FARMER

P. Teb. I 40   117

The development of a patron-client type of protection within the bureaucratic structure is well-illustrated by this text; see no. 68 for Menches' involvement in this pervasive and pernicious network.

(Docket of Menches) Received in the 53rd year, Tybi 15. To Ammeneus, *basilikos grammateus*, from Pnepheros son of Paous, contractor for the taxes on beer and natron at Kerkeosiris in the division of Polemon for the 53rd year. Having received certain information that the inhabitants of the

village are with one accord claiming your protection, and being myself anxious to belong to your house because it devolves upon you before all others to watch over the interests of the crown, I beg you to order a letter to be sent to Demetrios the *epistates* of the village and Nikanor the chief of police and Menches the *komogrammateus* and the elders of the cultivators, with instructions to compel the inhabitants to follow the ancient traditions, in order that I may be enabled to pay my dues regularly. Farewell.
(Order of Ammeneus) To Menches, *komogrammateus*. Let justice be done to the taxpayer in accordance with the traditions of the village. Year 53, Tybi 13. (Address) To Menches.

81. RECEIPT FOR MEDICAL AND POLICE TAXES

P. Hib. I 103[225]   231

This receipt acknowledges payment of olyra for two taxes, one for medical services, one for police services; these taxes fell apparently on the military settlers in the country.

Year 17, Phaophi 2: 14 (artabas) of olyra. Apollophanes to Theophilos, greeting. We have had measured out to us by Stratios on behalf of Diodoros son of Kephallen, decurion of Zoilos' troop, through the *komogrammateus* Eupolis for the 17th year, 5 (artabas) of olyra as the medical-tax and nine (artabas) of olyra as the police-tax; total, 14 (artabas) of olyra. Farewell. Year 17, Phaophi 2.

82. LETTER TO ZENON ABOUT WAX

P. Cair. Zen. V 59823   253

The author of this lively and well-written letter was a banker and businessman at Mendes in the Delta. It is interesting that in this very managed economy the price of wax varied sufficiently that it was worth paying an internal customs charge to order some from another nome.

Promethion to Zenon, greeting. You have written to me about the wax to say that the cost per talent, including the toll at Memphis, comes to 44 drachmas, whereas you are told that with us it costs 40 drachmas. Now do not listen to the nonsense that people talk; for it is selling here at 48 drachmas. You will therefore do well to send me as much as you can. Following your instructions I have given your agent Aigyptos 500 drachmas of silver towards the price of the wax, and the remainder, whatever it may be, I will pay immediately to whomever you tell me to. And of honey also let 5 *metretai* be procured for me. I appreciate the kindness and willingness which you always show to me, and if you yourself have need of anything here, do not hesitate to write. Farewell. Year 33, Pharmouthi 19. (Address) To Zenon.[226]

83. TAX-FARMER'S PETITION FOR RELIEF

P. Teb. III 772   236

The contractor for the tax of a sixth on vineyards notifies the nomarch that damage from locusts had caused the owners of the vineyards to refuse to pay the tax to him from the meager remains. When he was in turn unable to pay it to the crown, he was arrested.[227] He asks for an inquiry by all of the chief officials of the nome and for the crop of one vineyard to be impounded pending its outcome. On the sixth of Arsinoe, see no. 95.

To Asklepiades, nomarch, from Nechembes. After I had contracted for the tax of the sixth of Arsinoe Philadelphos in the division of Herakleides for the 10th year, an incursion of locusts fell (on the crop) and destroyed everything, what was saved being carried off by the owners without the payment of the sixth. I have consequently been wrongfully arrested for this. You will therefore do well, if it please you, to join in session Asklepiades[228] and the *antigrapheus* and the *strategos* so that my case against the owners of the vineyards may be heard pending the arrival of Theodoros, for the sum of money is no small one, in order that nothing of this may be lost and that you may also instruct your agent Theokles to impound the crops of the vineyard of Dion which is held by Teisikrates at Tanis. For I have previously taken this man before the *strategos*, and written instructions were issued by him: he wrote that all the produce of this vineyard was to be impounded, and it has been impounded up to now. I beg you, therefore, if it please you, to send written orders to impound the. . .in order that the king may suffer no loss. Farewell. Year 10, Pauni 5. To Asklepiades.

V

THE ROYAL ECONOMY OF EGYPT

84. LETTER TO APOLLONIOS ABOUT REMINTING COINS

P. Cair. Zen. I 59021[229]   258

Demetrios, probably head of the royal mint in Alexandria, writes to Apollonios the *dioiketes* about problems in the application of a recent royal decree ordering all gold and silver coinage to be brought in and reminted. With standard Ptolemaic coinage there was apparently no problem, but the majority of the money could not be reminted for lack, it seems, of means at the disposal of the mint for assaying foreign money or badly worn currency which could not be accepted at face value. The decree has evidently established the new currency as the only legitimate one for internal use, thus rendering it difficult to use the old money and practically paralyzing trade. Demetrios emphasizes the Ptolemies' need to import a maximum amount of gold to keep the currency sound.

To Apollonios greeting from Demetrios. If you are in good health and your affairs are to your mind, it is well. As for me, I am attending to the work as you wrote to me to do, and I have received in gold 57,000 pieces, which I minted and returned. We might have received many times as much, but as I wrote to you once before, the foreigners who come here by sea and the merchants and middlemen and others bring both their local money[230] of unalloyed metal and the gold pentadrachms, to be made into new money for them in accordance with the decree which orders us to receive and remint, but as Philaretos (?) does not allow me to accept, not knowing to whom we can appeal on this subject we are compelled not to accept ———; and the men grumble because their gold is not accepted either by the banks or by us for..., nor are they able to send it into the country to buy goods, but their gold, they say, is lying idle and they are suffering no little loss, having sent for it from abroad and being unable to dispose of it easily to other persons even at a reduced price. Again, all the residents in the city find it difficult to make use of their worn gold. For none of them knows to what authority he can refer and on paying something extra receive in exchange either good gold or silver. Now things being as they are at present, I see that the revenues of the king are also suffering no little damage. I have therefore written these remarks to you in order that you may be informed and, if you think fit, write to the king about the matter and tell me to whom I am to refer on this subject. For I take it to be an advantage if as much gold as possible be imported from abroad and the king's coinage be always good and new without any expense falling on him. Now as regards the way in which certain persons are treating me it is as well not to write, but as soon as you arrive you will hear ————. And write to me about these matters so that I may act accordingly. Farewell. Year 28, Gorpiaios 15. (Address) To Apollonios. (Docket) From Demetrios.

85. INSTRUCTIONS OF THE *DIOIKETES* TO AN *OIKONOMOS*

P. Teb. III 703   Late Third Century

This papyrus is a copy of a long memorandum evidently written by the *dioiketes*, outlining the duties of an official who can only be the *oikonomos*. These consist primarily of the supervision of crops and of the royal monopolies and revenues, in dealing with which the *oikonomos* is to cooperate with other officials and above all to safeguard the crown from loss. It is evident that this is the copy given to one *oikonomos* of what was a standard text for junior bureaucrats; Rostovtzeff (in his introduction to the papyrus) traces older Egyptian parallels in the Middle and New Kingdoms, particularly in the Eighteenth Dynasty. The remarks are general; they do not cover all aspects of the competence of the *oikonomos*, and certainly they have no specific reference to the conditions in the Arsinoite Nome where the papyrus was found.

The date of the papyrus is uncertain; references in the latter part suggest a period of civil disturbance probably connected with a war in the not too distant past (and, indeed, vague as these are, they give the only specific context for the document). The aftermath of either the Third (246-241) or Fourth (219-217) Syrian War would be appropriate; it is unlikely on many grounds that the papyrus can be later than this. On this text see Cl. Préaux, *L'économie royale des Lagides, passim* and A.E. Samuel in *Studi in onore di E. Volterra* II (Roma 1969) 451-460.

(Canals) [You must inspect]... and the water-conduits which run through the fields and from which the peasants are accustomed to lead water on the land cultivated by each of them, and see whether the water-intakes into them have the prescribed depth and whether there is sufficient room in them; and similarly the said cuttings from which the intakes pass into the above-mentioned conduits, whether they have been made strong and the entries into them from the river are thoroughly cleaned and whether in general they are in a sound state.

(Protection of cultivators) In your tours of inspection try in going from place to place to cheer everybody up and to put them in better heart; and not only should you do this by words but also, if any of them complain of the *komogrammateus* or the komarchs about any matter touching agricultural work, you should make inquiry and put a stop to such doings as far as possible.[231]

(Inspection of crops) When the sowing has been completed it would be no bad thing if you were to make a careful round of inspection; for thus you will get an accurate view of the sprouting of the crops and will easily notice the lands which are badly sown or are not sown at all, and you will thus know those who have neglected their duty and will become aware [if any] have used the seed for other purposes.

(Sowing of crops) You must regard it as one of your most indispensable duties to see that the nome be sown with the kinds of crops prescribed by the sowing schedule.[232] And if there be any who are hard pressed by their rents or are completely exhausted, you must not leave it unexamined.

(Registration of cattle) Make a list of the cattle employed in cultivation, both the royal and the private, and take the utmost possible care that the progeny of the royal cattle, when old enough to eat hay, be consigned to the calf-byres.

(Transportation) Take care that the grain in the nomes, with the exception of that expended on the spot for seed and of that which cannot be transported by water, be brought down[233] —— It will thus be [easy] to load the grain on the first [ships] presenting themselves; and devote yourself to such business in no cursory fashion —— Take care also that the prescribed supplies of grain, of which I send you a list, are brought down to Alexandria punctually, not only correct in amount but also tested and fit for use.

(Weaving) Visit also the weaving houses[234] in which the linen is woven, and do your utmost to have the largest possible number of looms in operation, the weavers supplying the full amount of embroidered stuffs prescribed for the nome. If any of them are in arrears with the pieces ordered, let the prices fixed by the ordinance for each kind be exacted from them. Take special care, too, that the linen is good and has the prescribed number of weft-threads. Visit also the washing-houses where the flax is washed and the —— Make a list, and report so that there may always be a supply of castor-oil and natron for washing. [Book?] always the monthly quantity [of pieces of linen] in the actual month and the quantity [of the next month] in the next, in order that the [corresponding amounts may be apportioned (?)] to the accounts of the revenues and the contractors. If there is any surplus over what is booked in the first month, let the surplus be booked in the next month as part of the monthly quantity. Let all the looms which are idle be transported to the metropolis of the nome, deposited in the store-house, and sealed up.

(Auditing accounts) Audit the revenue accounts, if possible, village by village — and we think it not to be impossible, if you devote yourself zealously to the business — if not, by toparchies, passing in the audit nothing but payments to the bank in the case of money taxes, and in the case of grain dues or oil-bearing produce, only deliveries to the sitologoi. If there be any deficit in these, compel the toparchs and the tax-farmers to pay into the banks, for the arrears in grain the values assigned in the ordinances, for those in oil-bearing produce according to the liquid product for each kind.

(Oil production) It behoves you to bestow care on all the points mentioned in the memorandum, but especially those which refer to the oil-factories. For if you duly give heed to them you will increase not a little the sale in the nome, and the thefts will be stopped. This you would achieve by scrutinizing on each occasion the local factories and the store-houses for the produce both dry and liquid, and by sealing them. Be sure that the amounts delivered to the oil-makers do not exceed what is about to be used in the presses which exist in the factories. Take pains to let all the oil-presses be in operation if possible; or if not, most of them, and keep as close a watch as you can on the rest. —— The supernumerary implements of those presses which are not in operation must be collected and sealed up in the store-houses. If you are [neglectful (?)] in this...be sure that besides the payments...you will fall into no ordinary contempt, which you will not be able easily to remove. If you neglect your duty as regards this, [your honor will in no way increase].

(Pasturage) Since the revenue from the pasturage dues,[235] too, is one of the most important, it will most readily be increased if you carry out the registration (of cattle) in the best possible way. The most favorable season for one so engaged is about the month of Mesore; for the [whole] country in this month being covered with water, it happens that cattle-breeders send their flocks to the highest places, being unable to scatter them on other places.

(Retail prices) See to it, too, that the goods for sale be not sold at prices higher than those prescribed. Make also a careful investigation of those goods which have no fixed prices and on which the dealers may put what prices they like; and after having put a fair markup on the wares being sold, make the dealers dispose of them.[236]

(Calf-raising) Take care to inspect the calf-byres also, and do your best to ensure that the grain be supplied in them until the time of the green food, and the quantity prescribed daily be used for the calves, and that the grain be delivered regularly in full, both that from the locality and, if they need in addition an imported supply, from other villages as well.

(Trees and wood) Take care also that of the local trees the planting of the mature ones be done at the right season, namely for willows and mulberry-trees, and that of acacia-trees and tamarisk about the month of Choiak. Of these the rest must be planted in beds in order to have all possible attention during the [time] of watering, and when it is the proper time for planting, then let them...set them on the royal embankments. The guarding of them must be done by the contractors in order that the plants suffer no damage from sheep or any other cause. In your further tours of inspection notice also whether any cut trees are left on the embankments or in the fields and make a list of them.[237]

(Houses and gardens) Make also a list of the royal houses and the gardens belonging to them, stating what attention each one of these requires, and report to us.

(Deserting soldiers and sailors) Take care, too, that the matter of the native soldiers be arranged according to the memorandum which we compiled on the men who absconded from their work and the...sailors, in order that... (all?) those men who fall into your hands may be kept together until they are sent to Alexandria.[238]

(Honesty and security) Take particular care that no peculation or any other wrong takes place. For everyone resident in the country must clearly understand and believe that all acts of this kind have been stopped and that they are freed from the bad conditions of the past, no one having a right to do what he likes, but everything being managed in the best way; you will (thus) make the countryside secure and [will increase] the revenue in no small measure.

(Correspondence) Now to comprise everything and to deliver it to you in memoranda is not easy, owing to the variety of circumstances in consequence of the present situation. Be careful to see that nothing of what I have ordered in my memorandum is neglected, as far as possible, and likewise inform me concerning contingencies, in order that...for since all our business is necessarily conducted by correspondence...you should arrange for them to write about each of the injunctions sent, if possible ——— otherwise, certifying the reasons, in order that ——— and that nothing of what has been specified be neglected ———. If you act thus, you will fulfill your official duty and your own safety will be assured.

(General advice) But enough now on this subject. I thought it well to write down for you in this memorandum what I told you in sending you to the nome. I considered that your prime duty is to act with peculiar care, honestly, and in the best possible way ———; and your next duty is to behave well and be upright in your district, to keep clear of bad company, to avoid all base collusion, to believe that, if you are without reproach in this, you will be held deserving of higher functions, to keep the instructions in your hand, and to report on everything as has been ordered.

86. PLANS FOR RECLAMATION WORK

P. Lille 1[239]   259

This remarkable papyrus describes a square of land in the Arsinoite Nome designated for extensive reclamation works. There were already some dikes, canals and cultivators, but it is proposed here to rework entirely the area with a grid plan of dikes and canals. On these 10,000-aroura estates see L. Criscuolo, *Aegyptus* 57 (1977) 109-22; she rejects Rostovtzeff's thesis that the papyrus concerns Apollonios' estate around Philadelphia.

Stothoetis, checking clerk, to Apollonios. Year 27 and the same by Egyptian (reckoning), in the month of Phaophi. . . Diodoros countersigning (?).

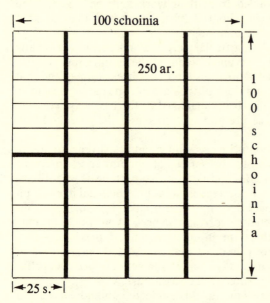

The perimeter of the ten thousand arouras[240] is 400 schoinia, there are 4 dikes, and in the middle (running from South to North) are 3 dikes at a distance of 25 schoinia from each other, and 9 others running across from East to West, ten schoinia distant from each other; in the 10,000 arouras (there are) 40 dike-enclosed areas of 250 arouras each, whose measurements are 25 to 10 (schoinia); the total number of dikes is 16, each 100 schoinia in length, for a total of 1600, which it is necessary to dig out.

The width of the ditch is 4 cubits, the depth 2, for we conclude that a ditch of this size will give dikes of the stated size; the total per schoinion is thus 86 naubia, and for the 1600 (schoinia) 137,600 naubia. And it is necessary for another four water-channels to be made in addition to the existing ones, at 100 schoinia each, a total of 400 schoinia, at 86 (naubia) a total of 34,000, or a grand total of 172,000.

If the works are carried to completion during the winter, we estimate that it will be done at 70 (naubia) to the stater, so that makes 1 talent 3834 dr.[241] 1 dr. per aroura is added for damage (?), besides the fields on a slope, for which it is necessary to add further work on dikes since it is necessary that the dikes be level. That is what we will indicate on the contract as the amount of the land and the extra expense. As to the already existing dikes in the cross-sections, all those that are usable for the projected establishment of the dikes will be deducted from the contractors' expenses; likewise if some canals are suited for the dikes in this way.

If the works are not completed before the harvest,[242] they will be completed at the rate of 50 (naubia per stater), that is, 2 tal. 1760 dr., that is, 1 dr. 2½ ob. per aroura (?).[243] And for the sloping areas it will be necessary to add the difference of the neighboring dikes. This will be on the contract, when we know the amount of earth and the length of the schoinion in those parts. Some places will be suitable and hollowed out, about...per 1000, so that they are surrounded with dikes by the relief of the land itself, for which the expense will fall short, so that in place of it that extra work will be covered. As for the pre-existing dikes, as many as are usable by the farmers, they will be deducted from the price paid to them. They shall follow the existing dikes so that nothing of them shall be without use. Likewise of the ditches that exist in the subdivision, if they are suitable for the dikes.

As for the expenses toward the pre-existent canals and dikes those that are customarily repaired annually, it will be necessary to go and inspect them with the engineers and the *basilikoi grammateis* and render an account of their condition; for some ——.

Later, after inspecting the enclosure dike he[244] has decided to make his dikes the width of the ditch, that is, 3 naubia instead of 4, that is a total of 64 ½ to the schoinion, for 4 dr. per 60 (naubia). Apollonios left the 7th of Hathyr, and I[245] sailed back with him as far as Phylake and disembarked there, and on the 8th I came to Touphis, on the 9th to Syron Kome, on the 10th to Ptolemais, on the 11th to the Labyrinth, and there I found the secretaries, and they took the letter and I returned to the city.

87. CORRESPONDENCE ABOUT THE SOWING SCHEDULE

P. Yale 36   232

Each year after it was possible to gauge the inundation of the Nile the bureaucracy compiled a detailed schedule of what crops were to be sown on what land after the water receded. Acting on general instructions from the central administration, the officials at the levels first of the village, then the district, then the nome, compiled a detailed schedule, which was sent to Alexandria for revision and approval before being sent back to the local officials for implementation. P. Vidal-Naquet, *Le Bordereau d'ensemencement dans l'Egypte ptolémaïque (Pap. Brux.* 5: Bruxelles 1967) provides the soundest and most thorough discussion of the Schedule and documents relating to it, including this one.

Apollonios to Leon, greeting. A copy of the letter from Athenodoros, the *dioiketes*, is appended for you below. Accordingly, having prepared the sowing schedule with the usual persons in compliance with the instructions, hold it in readiness, so that we may personally hand it over to Leukippos, the chief of police, before the stipulated time; knowing that if a delay

140

occurs, you will be sent down to the *dioiketes*. Farewell. Year 15, Mesore (?)...

Athenodoros to Apollonios, greeting. Concerning the sowing schedule of the [...] land for the 16th year, having prepared it with the [...] *grammateus*[246] and the other customary persons, send it by all means sooner, but at the latest by the...of Mesore, (arranged) by cultivator and by village and in summary, to Leukippos, the chief of police. For we have instructed him, whenever up to this date you give him the documents, to send them off to the city to us, sending along with them persons who will bring them back. Year 15, Epeiph...

(Address) To Leon. (Docket) Year 15, Mesore 9. Apollonios, copy of the letter from Athenodoros the *dioiketes*, concerning the sowing schedule for the 16th year.

88. RECEIPT FOR SEED-GRAIN

P. Hib. I 85   261

The government officials issued each year at sowing time the proper amount of seed for sowing the royal peasant's field with the crops required in the Sowing Schedule, in the form of a loan to be repaid from the harvest. In effect, the state kept custody of the seed, preventing the farmers from eating it in bad times, and so assuring an orderly planting of the necessary crops.

In the reign of Ptolemy son of Ptolemy and his son Ptolemy, year 24, the priest of Alexander and the Brother and Sister Gods being Aristonikos son of Perilaos, the canephore of Arsinoe Philadelphos being Charea daughter of Apios, in the month of Mesore. Pasis, son of..., priest, has received from Paris son of Sisybaios, agent of Harimouthes the nomarch from the lower toparchy,[247] as seed for the 25th year, being included in the lists of receipts and expenditures, for the royal holding of Philoxenos of the (troop) of Telestes[248] 40 artabas of wheat, 38 ⅓ of barley which are equivalent to 23 of wheat, and 67 ½ of olyra which are equivalent to 27 of wheat, making a total of 90 artabas of wheat, in grain pure and unadulterated in any way, according to just measurement by the 29-choinix measure on the bronze standard. Pasis shall deliver at the royal granaries in the 25th year the rent of the land for which he has received the seed, in accordance with the terms of the lease, in full, making no deduction for unwatered land; and he shall return the seed, which he has received, before the rent, from the new crops.

(Signed in Demotic) I, P... son of..., have received the stock above written.

89. FLOODING OF A FIELD

P. Enteux. 60   218

Royal officials had to solve many problems concerned with keeping the land in good condition both before and after sowing, in order that the crops might be produced as in the schedule. Here a lessee complains that neighbors have ruined his crop by flooding his land with water accidentally discharged from a holding basin, of the sort used to retain some of the Nile's flood waters for later purposes of irrigation.

To King Ptolemy greeting from Idomeneus, one of the farmers from the gift-estate of Chrysermos,[249] from the village of Kaminoi. I am wronged by Petobastis son of Taos and Horos son of Kelesis, from the same village. For after I leased two arouras from the gift estate of Chrysermos and sowed the land with *arakos*[250] the aforementioned Petobastis and Horos flooded my sown field, so that my *arakos* became lost and I cannot even pay the expenses I have accrued on the land. I beg of you therefore, O king, if it seems right to you, to order Diophanes the strategos to write to Hephaistion the *epistates* to send the accused Petobastis and Horos to Crocodilopolis so that we may be judged before Diophanes and, if I show that they have flooded my sown field, to compel them to take over my sown land and pay the rent on it, and to give me an equal amount from the land which they cultivate in place of that which they have flooded. If this is done, by fleeing to you, O king, I shall be able to pay the rent to Chrysermos, and I shall have experienced kindness at your hands. Farewell.

(*Strategos'* note) To Hephaistion. If possible reconcile them; if not, send them to _____[251] after the 10th of Choiach, so that they may be judged before the proper court. Year 4, Daisios 27, Hathyr 29.

(Docket) Year 4, Daisios 27, Hathyr 29. Idomeneus, farmer of the gift-estate of Chrysermos, against Petobastis and Horos about flooding of land.

90. LOSS OF WATER SUPPLY

P. Teb. I 50   112/1

Agriculture was more often impeded by insufficient water than by too much. This petitioner accuses a neighbor of wrongfully damming up a royal canal and avoiding compliance with an earlier order of the *komogrammateus* and other officials to clear it; he asks for intervention to correct the situation and for payment of his past losses.

To Menches, *komogrammateus* of Kerkeosiris, from Pasis son of Petesouchos, cultivator of crown land from the same village. It is an old-

142

established custom to water the royal land belonging to me in the neighborhood of the said village by means of the royal conduit which passes through the adjacent crown and temple land of Lykos son of Zopyrion, and others. Now in the 2nd year during my absence from home on pressing business for Asklepiades[252] the (king's) kinsman, the aforesaid Lykos, thinking that he had a favorable opportunity, dammed up that part of the above-mentioned conduit which lay on his own land. The result of this was that I missed the right season for the irrigation of the land, and incurred a loss amounting of to 30 artabas of wheat besides 3 talents of copper for the expenses of other irrigation works. I therefore at the time took you and Horos the komarch and the elders of the cultivators and pointed out the damage and the dammed-up conduit, and you decided that the aforesaid Lykos should dig out his part and that I should use it for irrigation according to custom, as is my right. Up to the present time, however, he has not done so, but procrastinates, causing me every year to miss the proper season for irrigating and watering the crops, and involving me in the aforesaid loss in wheat and money, the total of which is from the 2nd to the 6th year 150 artabas of wheat and 15 talents of copper.[253] Wherefore, because my crops did not meet my expectations I was impoverished; and I make this complaint to you in order that you may subscribe to my statements and further forward a copy of the petition to the proper officials, so that the accused Lykos having been made to appear may be compelled first of all to dig out the conduit as it was before and to forfeit the damage foresaid, the 150 artabas of wheat and the 15 talents of copper. I shall then be enabled to pay without hindrance the rent of the land and no loss will result to the king. Farewell.

91. PROTECTION OF THE CROPS

P. Teb. I 27[254]   113

The core of this series of letters is one from the *dioiketes* Eirenaios to Hermias, a superintendent of revenues, reprimanding him in very harsh terms for his insufficient attention to the protection and collection of crops and his practice of appointing bad subordinates. A copy and cover letter go to another superintendent, Asklepiades, and a copy of both plus a cover letter to Horos, the *basilikos grammateus* of the district. He in turn sends a copy of the whole file to his subordinates with a cover circular asking for cooperation in the specific matter of nominating suitable persons to guard the crops, both during growing and after the harvest.

(Docket of Menches) Received in the 4th year, Mecheir 10.
Horos to the *topogrammateis* and *komogrammateis*, greeting. Appended is a copy of the letter from Eirenaios, the (king's) kinsman and *dioiketes*, concerning the persons to be made to undertake the custody of the crops.

You will therefore send us the lists of individuals in your district who are conspicuous for honesty and steadiness and live in the neighborhood, with a statement of the extent of their several holdings and other property, so that the other arrangements may be made in accordance with the instructions. Farewell. Year 4, Mecheir 10.

Eirenaios to Horos, greeting. Appended is a copy of the letter to Asklepiades. Give him therefore a list of persons who can be made to undertake the custody of the crops, and apply due zeal to the end that the other requirements may be carried out in accordance with the directions below, understanding that you too will be held responsible for any neglect in this matter. Year 4, Peritios 23, Choiach 23.

To Asklepiades. Appended is a copy of the letter to Hermias, the overseer of the revenues... Regarding [therefore] the same instructions as issued to yourself also, take care that persons of repute are appointed to the posts of *oikonomos* and chief of police by you also; and that the protection of crops be managed in the manner directed, and the collection of dues for the treasury take place more punctually, and so no debts be incurred.

To Hermias.[255] Harnemgotes, who is in the office of Horos the *basilikos grammateus*, after having submitted to me what he wrote to you, and having also specified what was written to Theodotos, the official discharging the duties of *oikonomos* and chief of police — in which it was stated to be necessary that the *dekanoi* of the police in the villages should be summoned to a general meeting, and that declarations on oath by the sovereigns as suggested by him should be taken with the approval of Theodotos concerning the protection of the annual crops — he began to be much astonished that after the severest treatment at the inquiry instituted against you for not having provided at the proper time for the sale of the green stuffs and the other second crops, nor for the custody of the produce, and for not even using men of repute for the offices of *oikonomos* and chief of police, but without exception evil and worthless persons, you still continue in the same miserable course with no improvement whatever in your improper procedure. But be sure that you are liable to accusation; and, before it is too late, believing that you will receive no pardon for any neglect, see that suitable persons are appointed to the aforesaid offices, and display unremitting zeal in what tends to increase the revenue; and procure from the *komogrammateis* the list of those who can be made to undertake the custody of the produce from those in the army and the other inhabitants of the district who are living in the neighborhood and are conspicuous for honesty and steadiness, and appoint those fit to the posts in the villages; take from them and the policemen in each village two declarations upon oath by the sovereigns that they will provide in the best possible manner for the guardianship; and will allow none of the cultivators of crown land or released land to touch the green stuffs and the other second crops except those intended for the fodder of the animals used in agriculture, which shall be supplied with the approval of the *komogrammateis*, and except amounts to be sold for which the prices and securities shall be paid and deposited at the banks to meet the dues to the treasury in accordance with the regulations previously issued; and will take care that all else is rightly done in the summer, and will convey the produce to the appointed places, and let nothing go until the proclamation concerning the release of crops is published, and unless everything has been duly delivered and the demands for previous years paid up...Similar declarations are (secondly) to be made by you or those set in charge of ———— office of *oikonomos* and from the *basilikoi grammateis*, that those coming to receive the surplus produce are not in debt, and that there is no lien upon it for other charges or causes, and that care is being taken in order that all may pay the crown dues as soon as possible; and (thirdly) by the holders of posts as chiefs of police, that they will take care that this is accomplished in the manner aforesaid. Then deposit one copy of the declarations at the royal bank, and send the other to us; and make it your aim that proclamations are published in the villages to the effect that no one shall let loose animals upon land sown with grass and similar produce, or shall touch the other second crops without giving security as set forth above and that the animals of those who disobey shall be confiscated to meet the rents. Above all be vigilant that the collection of all revenues be carried out more punctually and that it may not again occur to you to be involved in similar difficulties. In general consider how great an impulse attention to the matters indicated gives to business, and deem it an essential that there should be no lapse in anything that is expedient, and that by the continual invention of further improvements everything should proceed according to the method prescribed by us. For we will not accept as an excuse either force or anything else whatever, and any losses will be rigorously exacted from you. Whichever day you receive this letter give notice of the fact.

92. ORDER FOR DELIVERY OF GRAIN

P. Hib. I 39   265

Grain paid as rent for taxes into the granary was, except for what was needed locally for expenses or seed grain, ultimately shipped to Alexandria for the purposes of supplying that city and for export. Xanthos here orders Euphranor to have the grain from certain properties delivered to a royal vessel, together with a sealed sample of the grain, as was usual to protect against contamination of the shipment to the profit of someone other than the government.

Xanthos to Euphranor, greeting. Give orders for the measurement through Killes to Horos on the royal barge, of which the master and pilot is the said Horos, of the grain levied upon the holding of Alexandros and Bromenos and that of Nikostratos and Pausanias; and let Killes or the ship-master write you a receipt and seal a sample, and you bring them to me. Farewell. Year 21, Thoth 10. (Address) To Euphranor.

93. RECEIPT FOR EMBARKATION OF GRAIN

P. Hib. I 98[256]   251

After the grain was loaded on the boat for shipment to Alexandria, the master of the boat gave the land officials a receipt which in effect discharged their obligations to the crown for that quantity of grain.

[Year] 34, Mesore [24, Dionysios], ship-master, acknowledges that he has embarked through Nechthembes the agent of the *basilikoi grammateis* on the boat of Xenodokos and Alexandros 4800 artabas of barley.

In the reign of Ptolemy the son of Ptolemy Soter, year 24, the priest of Alexander and the Brother and Sister Gods being Neoptolemos son of Kraisis, the canephore of Arsinoe Philadelphos being Arsinoe daughter of Nikolaos, the 24th of the month Mesore. Dionysios, ship-master, acknowledges that he has embarked on the boat of Xenodokos and Alexandros, the pilot on which is Ekteuris son of Pasis, of Memphis, through Nechthembes the agent of the *basilikoi grammateis*, for transport to the royal (granary) at Alexandria, with a sample, four thousand eight hundred artabas [of barley], being pure, unadulterated and sifted grain, by the measure and smoothing-rod which he himself brought from Alexandria, with just measurement, and I make no complaint.

94. LEASE OF A VINEYARD

P. Ryl. IV 583   170

This lease (in a standard two-copy format), even in its fragmentary form, shows many details about the operation of a vineyard in the Fayum. The lessee receives only a third of the pressed grape juice, but he must pay all labor costs except treading the grapes, and keep the vineyard in good condition.

In the reign of Ptolemy and Ptolemy the brother and Cleopatra,[257] children of Ptolemy and Cleopatra, the Manifest Gods, in the first year, the priest of Alexander and the Savior Gods and the Brother and Sister Gods and the Benefactor Gods and the Fatherloving Gods and the Gods Manifest and the Motherloving Gods and the athlophore of Berenike Euergetis and the canephore of Arsinoe Philadelphos and the priestess of Arsinoe Philopator being those in office in Alexandria,[258] in the month of Xandikos the ninth, Phaophi ninth,[259] in Philadelphia of the Arsinoite Nome. Nichomachos son of Ph...ades the Halikarnassian, successor of his paternal allotment, has leased to Apollonios son of Apollonios, Persian of the Epigone, the somewhat sandy vineyard situated near the same Philadelphia, belonging to Krates son of Pheidimos, from Arsinoe in Lycia, paymaster of the Pamphylians in their command, which is of six arouras, or however many they be, for the first year for a third part of all the fruit and crops that grow in the vineyard (on the terms that) when all the crops have been made into wine and the *apomoira* due to the crown has been deducted along with the wages for the treaders, hire of a winepress and a contribution [in the month of the vintage (?)] of a half-kados to the agricultural guild, dividing the must remaining into three parts, Nichomachos shall take two parts, and Apollonios the third. Each shall provide jars for himself and as required for the *apomoira* according to the proportions of the lease, and each shall carry down the jars for himself to the winepress, and carry up the must by himself, while the *apomoira* ———.

(Lines 13 ff.) Monthly wages (?) are to be paid at his own expense by Apollonios from the time stated until termination of the lease, as is best for the land and the vine; Apollonios is to prune the vine moderately and exactly, to keep the ground of the property clear of weedy growth and rush and reed and quake grass and *kinaios* reed and all other tangle of roots except for the dry ground inside the cross-trench, and is to maintain the cross-trenches dug and clean and the property fenced; he is to clear out the drains and fence the conduit facing the...and lead it through for the watering; and when the lease has expired, he is to deliver the ground of the property in clean condition and the cross-trenches clean, as is presently stated. If he fails to deliver it or to perform each of the tasks at the proper time, or if he abandons the lease, he is to pay the assessed wage with a 50 per cent surcharge for every task he fails to perform, and a fine of two silver talents for any damage that may be due at the time of his abandoning the lease. Apollonios is to shift 50 rows of vines to the uncultivated ground at his own expense and to transplant in the same year at the proper (time) ———.[260]

95. REVENUE LAWS OF PTOLEMY PHILADELPHOS

P. Rev. 259

This long and remarkable papyrus contains the detailed regulations governing various aspects of the royal economy and administration of Egypt in the time of Ptolemy II. The best preserved portions are divided into three main sections, concerned with the rules governing tax-farming (columns 1-22), the supervision of vineyards and orchards and of their products, mainly wine (23-27), and the royal monopoly on the production and distribution of vegetable oils for all purposes (38-72). Even these sections are full of gaps, and their interpretation is often obscure. Despite this, the "Revenue Laws" are the fullest systematic source of information about these aspects of Ptolemaic Egypt in the third century that we have.

Even a brief discussion of the contents of the papyrus would go far beyond the scope of this introduction, and the reader is referred to the works cited below for the systematic exposition of these subjects. One observes above all the concern of the Ptolemies to provide a degree of security and stability for their revenues through the guarantees, mutual suspicion, and checks of the tax-farmers and the bureaucrats that are inherent in the system of contracting out the taxes and manufactures.

The text used here is that of J. Bingen, *SB* Beiheft 1 (1952), where a selected bibliography about this document is given. The fullest exposition of the contents is Cl. Préaux's *L'Économie royale des Lagides* (Bruxelles 1938), with detailed bibliography. The same scholar has provided a bibliographical supplement in *Proc. IX Intern. Congress of Papyrology* 200-232. The best general exposition in English of these topics is to be found in M. Rostovtzeff, *Social and Economic History of the Hellenistic World* (Oxford 1941). The translation of columns 38-56 here is based on that of *Sel. Pap.* 203.

(1-2) In the reign of Ptolemy, son of Ptolemy Soter [and his son] Ptolemy. —— If. . . wishes to purchase. . . any of the contracts being sold ———.

(3) The *antigrapheis* appointed by the *oikonomos* shall take charge of the revenue pertaining to the contracts ———.

(4) ——— reckoning by count of days within 30 days. But [if] they render accounts in more than thirty days ———.

(5) If they are discovered to be in debt to the Crown, those who secured their condemnation shall have a share in exacting the payment.

(6) It shall [not] be lawful for the tax-farmers to receive payments from those who collected the arrears, even if it be within the 30 [days].

(7) [(The one copy shall be sealed and contain the names of the. . .)] and of the witnesses, the other shall be unsealed; and they shall enter in their books the names of the persons employed, with their fathers' names and ethnic designations and the nature of each person's employment———.

(8) But if these persons did not connive at it, they shall exact the payment from the outgoing tax-farmers. Let the tax-farmers bring an action, if they have any complaints to make against the collectors of arrears or their subordinates in matters connected with the [contract in the nome] in which they were engaged in buying the [tax———].

(9) Within ten days from that on which they take up the contract, let the collectors in the market be announced in the customs-house, writing the law of the [contract] in Greek and in Egyptian, and if there is any public notice [about the things pertaining] to the contract, let it be written ———.

(10-11) They shall appoint a guard for the inspectors, the tax-collectors and the guardians of the vouchers, and for those occupied in any other way concerning the sale and the scrutiny of the revenue pertaining to the sale———[The tax collectors] and the inspectors and the others employed

148

in connection with the contract, if they [collect any of the taxes (?) or] take something else without the *antigrapheis,* or after collecting it do not report it to the *antigrapheus,* shall pay fifty-fold to the Crown————.

(12) If the *oikonomos* and *antigrapheus* discover any person employed in farming the taxes whose name has not been entered in the list, they shall bring him to the king before————anyone by him.

————in [each] nome to the collectors or their subordinates and [all others?] let it be done from the accounts. The salary to the collectors [shall be] for each, thirty drachmas [per month], to their subordinates, twenty [drachmas per month], to the guardians of the receipts, fifteen drachmas each], to one inspector. . . each month one hundred drachmas.

(13) A list of all the collectors required for each contract, and their subordinates and the guardians of the receipts, shall be drawn up by the *oikonomos* and the *antigrapheus* acting in conjunction with the chief farmer————. Whoever commits any of these offenses shall pay 5 talents to the Crown and shall be kept under arrest until the king decides his case.

(14) Registration of chief tax-farmers: those who wish to become chief tax-farmers shall register themselves with the official who holds the auction————whoever, contrary to these provisions, buys, gives a share, or shares, shall be fined thirty minas————.

(15) Those ineligible for becoming either chief tax-farmers or associates, or sureties: crown officials, the *chrematistai,* their clerk————.

Exaction of taxes: the tax-farmers shall exact from those who are subject to taxation all the [taxes] in accordance with the laws. If they disobey this rule in any particular way, they shall pay a fine of 3 talents to the Crown, and the taxes————unless they enter them in their books within 30 [days].

(16) Balancing of accounts: the *oikonomos* and the *antigrapheus* shall hold a balancing of accounts with the tax-farmers every month before the 10th [with reference to the] sums received during the [previous] month. ————They shall not add the sums received in the current [month] to the installment belonging to the preceding month, nor take sums which belong to one installment and credit them to another, and even if one of the tax-farmers or their subordinates pays back a sum which he has received from the revenue of the contract, this shall not be credited to his separate account. But when the next balancing of accounts takes place, they shall add to the revenue of the month the amount which was left over from the previous balancing, making clear the amount of the sum left over from the previous period.

(17) But if the previous period had produced a deficit, while the next month produces a surplus, and the *oikonomos* receives in full that portion of the deficit in the farm which was not covered by surety. . . from the surplus. . . But if subsequently a deficit occurs in the contract which produced the surplus, (the *oikonomos*) shall exact (payment) of the surplus which had been transferred from the sureties inscribed on the register of the contract to which the surplus was transferred; but first. . . let him restore the

surplus (?) which was transferred to another contract, back to the contract from which it was transferred.

(18) Copies of all the balancings of accounts held by the *oikonomos* with the tax-farmers shall be sealed by him and given at once to each of the associates and witnesses (?), and the *oikonomos* also shall have copies which have been sealed by all those who took part in the balancing————, and he shall send copies of the balancings every month to the *dioiketes* and *eklogistes*.

When the period for which the tax was sold expires, the tax-farmers shall all come to the *oikonomos* before the tenth day of the following month, and he shall hold a general balancing of accounts with them, in which he shall state both the value of the [revenue received, and] the balance which they still have to pay, together with the sums which have [already] been reported as paid and the dates of the payment, and whether from the sub-letting of the contract or other quarters any debts are owing of which it is the duty of the *oikonomos* to exact payment, (19) and the remainder, if they should owe anything, and how much is each tax-farmer's share of the debt; and underneath the share of the debt he shall write the amount which he has received separately from them or the surety, with the dates of the payments and the remainder still due; but if there is a surplus the *oikonomos* shall set it down (to the credit of the tax-farmers)————.

(The *oikonomos*) shall report. . . to the *dioiketes* and [to the] *eklogistes*; and the *dioiketes* shall examine his books to see whether there is a surplus in the receipts from the other [contracts]; and if there is a surplus due from him to other contracts, he shall balance the arrears against the surplus, but if there is nothing due from him to other contracts, he shall order the *oikonomos* to exact the arrears and pay them over to him when the collection of arrears takes place. The *oikonomos* shall pay the arrears within three days, or, if he fails to pay them over [on demand], he shall be fined three times the amount, and the *dioiketes* shall exact the payment (from the *oikonomos*)————.

(20) Any tax-farmers who fail to balance their accounts with the *oikonomos*, when he desires them to do so and summons them, shall pay 30 minas to the Crown and the *oikonomos* shall at the same time compel them (to balance the account). ————The *oikonomos* shall also give [to each] of the sureties an account of his balance, stating that the surety has paid what he owed. If the *oikonomos* when asked fails to give the account on the same day or the one following, he shall render himself liable to proceedings for wrongful exaction. Balancings of accounts shall be held in the same manner by all officials who shall put up to auction any of the crown revenues.

[Concerning] contracts: with respect to all contracts made by the *oikonomoi* or *antigrapheis*, or their agents, being officials of the Crown, in matters connected with the contracts, the officials shall not exact any payments from the tax-farmers (21) for the contracts or receipts.

————the appointed (*antigrapheis*) shall pay on behalf of them————

but the additional penalties which have been decreed shall be exacted from the outgoing tax-farmers, unless the officials are discovered to have connived at the fraud with them.

Time for appeal. When disputes arise out of the laws concerning tax-farming, it shall be allowed to bring an action about. . . when they choose, but when other disputes arise out of the laws concerning tax-farming, and a different time for appeal has been appointed in each law, it shall be allowed to bring an action, both in the period for which the revenues have been sold (22) and in the next three months, unless one of the associates or subordinates connected with the tax-farming is discovered after the three months. But if any of these————.

(23) ————of Apollonios the *dioiketes*.

(24) In the reign of Ptolemy, son of Ptolemy and his son Ptolemy, year 27————. (They shall receive for the tax on vineyards from). . . the sixth part of the wine produced, but from the cleruchs who are soldiers and planted their [own] plots, and from land in the Thebaid which requires special irrigation, as much as. . . the tenth part (of the wine). On orchards valued [yearly] in silver the sixth part————.

Concerning the gathering and collection (of the vintage). Let the cultivators gather the produce when the season comes, (25) and when they begin to gather it, let them give notice to the manager (of the farm) or tax-farmer, and if he wishes to inspect the vineyards, let them exhibit to him————.

When the cultivators wish to make wine, they shall summon the tax-farmer in the presence of the *oikonomos* and *antigrapheus* or their agent, and when the tax-farmer comes, let the cultivator make wine, and measure it by the measures in use at each place, after they have been tested and sealed by the *oikonomos* and *antigrapheus*; and in accordance with the result of the measuring let him pay the tax. If the cultivators fail to do any of the foregoing according to the law, they shall pay the tax-farmers twice the amount of the tax.

(26) Those persons who already possess instruments for making wine shall register themselves before the tax-farmer, when————[and when] they intend to make wine, they [shall exhibit] the seal which has been stamped upon the instruments, unbroken. Any person who fails to register himself, or produce his instruments for inspection as the law requires, or to bring them to be sealed up when the tax-farmer wishes to seal them, or to exhibit the seal stamped upon them, shall pay the tax-farmers the amount of the loss which the tax-farmers consider at the moment that they have incurred.

If the cultivators gather the vintage and make wine before the tax-farmer comes, [let them keep (?)] the wine at the vats or————and when they hear (?) the first notice of the auction announced in the town or village in which they live, they shall register themselves on the same day [or the one] following, and shall exhibit the wine which they have made, and the vineyard from which they have gathered the crop prematurely.

(27) Agreements: ————he shall seal the copy of the agreement and give

it to the cultivator. In the agreement the tax-farmer shall declare under royal oath that he has entered in the agreement the full amount of the produce, including all wine made prematurely and reported to him by the cultivator, and has not misappropriated any of it, nor let it out of his possession. The other agreement with the cultivator's seal shall be kept by the *oikonomos* or his representative; and (in this agreement) the cultivator shall declare under royal oath that he has exhibited all the produce, and reported all the wine made before the proper time, and has honestly entered in the agreement the due amount of the tax. And there shall be in addition unsealed copies of both agreements.

(28) [But if] they dispute (about the produce) whether it is more or less, the *oikonomos* and the *antigrapheus* shall decide the question, and the agreements shall be sealed in accordance with his decision. If the tax-farmer fails to make an agreement with the cultivator, when the cultivator wishes him to do so, he shall not have the right to exact payment of the tax. But the *oikonomos* and *antigrapheus* shall make an agreement with the cultivator, and having conveyed the requisite amount of wine to the royal repository, shall enter it as having been received, but shall not put down the value of it to the credit of the tax-farmers———.

(29) Owners of [orchards] shall register themselves before the tax-farmer and [the agent of] the *oikonomos* and *antigrapheus* in charge locally, stating their names, the village in which they live, and the sum at which they assess the revenue (from the produce) in their orchard. If the tax-farmer consents, they shall make a double agreement with him, sealed, as the law requires, and the *oikonomos* shall exact the sixth in accordance with the terms of it. But if the tax-farmer objects to the assessment, he shall be allowed to seize the crop, and shall pay the cultivator by installments from what is sold from day to day; and when the cultivator has recovered the amount at which he assessed his crop, the surplus shall belong to the tax-farmer, and the cultivator shall pay the sixth to the *oikonomos*. On the other hand, if the crop when sold does not reach the amount of the assessment, the *oikonomos* shall exact the deficit from the tax-farmer and———.

(30) If the tax-farmers fail either to carry out duly all the requirements of the law, or [in any other way] hinder the cultivators when giving notice, or summoning the tax-farmer, or paying the tax in accordance with the law, the cultivator shall be allowed in the presence of the agent of the *oikonomos* and *antigrapheus*, as the law prescribes the presence of these two officials when payments are made, full power of action, without incurring any penalty by so doing. But when the tax-farmer comes, they shall show him [the produce and] bring evidence at once to prove that they have done all that was required, and the agent of the *oikonomos* and the *antigrapheus* shall give the tax-farmer a written account both of the produce and of the tax, cultivator by cultivator.

Transport of the tax. The cultivators [(shall transport)] the due amount of wine———. (31) [(if any of them fail to do so)] he shall pay to the tax-

farmer the value of the tax which he owes them: in Libya, the Saite,
...polite, Prosopite, Athribite, Menelaite Nomes and the Delta,
...drachmas for each *metretes* of eight choes; in the Sebynnite, Busirite,
[Mendesian], Leontopolite, Sethroite, Pharbaithite Nomes, Arabia, the
Bubastite Nome and Bubastos, the Tanite, the Memphite Nome, with Memphis, the Letopolite, Hermopolite, Oxyrhynchite and Kynopolite Nomes,
the Lake District, the Herakleopolite and Aphroditopolite Nomes, six
drachmas (for each *metretes*); and the Thebaid, five drachmas. The
oikonomos shall exact the values from the cultivators and pay them over to
the Crown to the credit of the tax-contract.

Stamping of receipts. The *oikonomos* shall establish repositories for the
wine in each village, and shall himself give a stamped receipt for what is
brought, to the [cultivator (?)]. ———The *oikonomos* shall transport the
wine from the [vats (?)]———.

(32) [The cultivator] shall provide [pottery] for the repository, and wax.
And the pottery shall consist of water-tight jars which have been tested and
are sufficient for the wine payable [for the] tax-contract. The *oikonomos*
and the *antigrapheus* shall [...days] before the cultivators gather the crops,
give them the price of the pottery which each cultivator has to provide for
the tax in wine upon his own produce; this price shall be fixed by the
dioiketes, who shall pay it (to the *oikonomos* and *antigrapheus*) through the
royal bank in the nome; the cultivator, on receiving the price, shall provide
pottery of the best quality; and if he does not receive the price, he shall
nevertheless provide the pottery, but shall recover the price of it from the
tax which he has to pay in money, [receiving a price for the] wine of
...drachmas] per 8-chous [*metretes*]———.

(33) The [*oikonomos*] shall examine the [wine], as much as remains, and
taking with him the tax-farmer, the *antigrapheus* and his agent, shall jointly
with them sell the wine, giving the [tax-farmers (?)] time in which to settle
their accounts, and exacting payment of the [amounts] he shall put them
down in the account of the tax-contract to the credit of the tax-farmers.

The *basilikoi grammateis* shall, within ten days from the day on which
they proclaim the auction, notify to the tax-farmers how many vineyards or
orchards there are in each nome, with the number of arouras (which they
contain), and how many vineyards or orchards belonging to persons on the
tribute list paid the tax to the temples before the twenty-second year. If they
fail to make out the list, or if they are discovered to have made it out incorrectly, if convicted in a suit, they shall pay to the tax-farmers for every
mistake of which they are convicted 600 drachmas and twice the amount of
the loss (incurred by them). All owners of vineyards or gardens on the
tribute list who paid the sixth to the temples before the twenty-first year,
shall henceforth pay it [to (Arsinoe) Philadelphos (?)]———.

(34) The tax-farmers shall within thirty days from [the day on which]
they purchase the tax, appoint sureties for a sum greater by one-twentieth
(than the price agreed upon for the tax) and they shall deposit (?) the prop-

erty which they mortgage, in monthly installments from Dios to———.

The value of the wine which is received from them (the tax-farmers) for the Crown shall be credited in the installments [due from them].

Balancing of accounts. When all the crops of the contract have been sold, the *oikonomos* shall take with him the chief tax-farmer and his associates and the *antigrapheus* and shall balance the accounts with the chief tax-farmer and his associates. If there is a surplus left over, he shall pay to the chief tax-farmer and his associates through the royal bank the share of the surplus due to each member of the company. But if there proves to be a deficit, he shall exact from the chief tax-farmer and his associates and the sureties the amount due from each and he shall exact the payment within the first three months of the following year.

(36) ———[so that] it may be in accord with what is written above. Farewell. Year 23, Daisios 5.

The *basilikoi grammateis* of the [nomes] throughout the country shall, each for the nome of which he is secretary, register both the number of arouras comprised by vineyards and orchards and the amount of the produce from them, cultivator by cultivator, beginning with the twenty-second year, and shall separate the land belonging to the temples and the produce from it so that the rest of the land may [be determined], from which the sixth is to be paid to (Arsinoe) Philadelphos, and they shall give a written account of the details to the agents of [Satyros]. Similarly, both the cleruchs who possess vineyards or orchards in the allotments which they have received from the king, and all other persons who own vineyards or orchards or hold them in grants or cultivate them on any terms whatever shall, each for himself, register both the extent of his land and the produce and shall give the sixth part of the produce to Arsinoe Philadelphos for sacrifices and libations———.

(37) King Ptolemy to [all] *strategoi*, [hipparchs], commanders, nomarchs, toparchs, *oikonomoi, antigrapheis, basilikoi grammateis*, libyarchs, and chiefs of police, greetings. I have sent you copies of my proclamation, which ordains the payment of the sixth to (Arsinoe) Philadelphos. Take heed therefore that my instructions are carried into effect. Farewell. Year 23, Dios 2-.

All owners of vineyards or orchards, in whatever manner, shall give to the agents of Satyros and the accountants who have been appointed agents of Dionysodoros, in each nome, a written statement, (which statement shall be given by) themselves in person or by the manager or cultivators of their estates from the 18th to the [21st year], (and shall contain) both the amount of produce and the name of the temple to which they used to pay the sixth due, together with the amount in each year. Similarly the priests also shall report from what property they severally derived a revenue, and the amount of the tax in each year, paid in wine or in silver. Likewise the *basilikoi grammateis* shall send in a written statement of all these details———.

(38) Year 27, Loios 10. I corrected (this) in the office of Apollonios the

154

dioiketes.

(39) [The persons authorized shall buy the produce from the cultivators at the following rates:] for each artaba [of sesame] containing thirty choinikes, clean for grinding, [8] drachmas: for each artaba of kroton containing thirty choinikes, clean for grinding, 4 drachmas; for each artaba of cnecus, clean for grinding, 1 drachma 2 obols; for each artaba of colocynth, 4 obols; of linseed, 3 obols.

If the cultivator does not wish to deliver (his produce) clean for grinding, he shall measure it out from the threshing-floor after cleaning it with a sieve, and against the further purification for grinding he shall add in the case of sesame 7 artabas to every 100, in the case of kroton the same, and in the case of cnecus, 8 artabas.

They shall receive from the cultivators for the (tax of) two drachmas levied on sesame and the (tax of) one drachma on kroton payment in sesame and kroton at the price prescribed in the tariff, and shall not exact payment in silver.

The cultivators shall not be allowed to sell either sesame or kroton to any other person.

(40) ———, and they shall give to the komarch a sealed receipt for what they received from each cultivator. If they fail to give the sealed receipt, the komarch shall not allow the produce to leave the village; otherwise he shall forfeit 1000 drachmas to the Crown, and five times the amount of whatever loss is incurred by the contract through his action.

They shall seal the oil in the country at the rate of 48 drachmas in copper for a *metretes* of sesame oil or cnecus oil containing 12 choes, and at the rate of 30 drachmas for a *metretes* of castor oil, colocynth oil, or lamp oil. (*Altered to*...both sesame and cnecus oil and castor oil, colocynth oil and lamp oil at the rate of 48 drachmas in copper for a *metretes* of 12 choes and 2 obols for a cotyla.)

In Alexandria and in the whole of Libya they shall sell it at the rate of 48 drachmas for a *metretes* of sesame oil and 48 drachmas for a *metretes* of castor oil. (*Altered to*...48 drachmas for a *metretes* of sesame oil or castor oil, and 2 obols for a cotyla.) And they shall provide an amount sufficient for the demands of purchasers, selling it throughout the country in all the cities and villages by...measures which have been tested by [the *oikonomos* and the] *antigrapheus*———.

(41) They shall exhibit the land sown to the director of the contract with the *oikonomos* and the *antigrapheus*, and if after measuring it they find that the right number of arouras has not been sown, the nomarch and the toparch and the *oikonomos* and the *antigrapheus* shall, each who is responsible, forfeit to the Crown 2 talents, and to the holders of the contract, for each artaba of sesame which they ought to have received 2 drachmas, and for each artaba of kroton 1 drachma, together with the profit which would have been made on the sesame oil and the castor oil. The *dioiketes* shall exact the payment from them. See over (a brief and damaged note is

on the reverse).

Before the season arrives for sowing the sesame and the kroton, the *oikonomos* shall give to the nomarch or toparch who is in charge of the nome, if he so desires, for the sowing of each aroura of sesame 4 drachmas, and for each aroura of kroton 2 [drachmas], and he shall receive from the threshing-floor in return for [these payments]———.

(42) When it is time to harvest the sesame and the kroton and cnecus, the cultivators shall give notice to the nomarch and the toparch or, where there are no nomarchs or toparchs, to the *oikonomos*, and these officials shall summon the holder of the contract, and the director of the contract shall visit the acreage with them and make an assessment.

The [natives] and the other cultivators shall assess their own crops severally by kind before they harvest them, and they shall make a duplicate sealed agreement with the contractor concerning the assessment, and the natives shall each write down on oath the amount of land which he has sown by the kind of seed, and the amount of his assessment, and shall seal the agreement, and the agent sent by the nomarch or toparch shall also seal it———.

(43) ———measure in the presence of the cultivators. See over. (On the reverse:) The *oikonomos* and the *antigrapheus* shall assess the sesame and kroton schedule to be sown in other nomes, and they shall receive the sesame and kroton from the cultivators.

The nomarch or the official in charge in the nome shall report the number of arouras sown, cultivator by cultivator, sixty days before the crop is harvested. If he fails to report or to show that the cultivators have sown the amount of land scheduled,[261] he shall forfeit to the purchaser of the contract the prescribed penalty, and shall himself exact payment from the disobedient cultivators.

All persons throughout the country who are exempt from taxation or hold villages and land in gift or as a subsidy shall measure out all the sesame and kroton grown by them, and the other kinds of produce included in the oil monopoly leaving themselves a sufficient quantity for seed, and shall receive the value in copper at the rate of 6 drachmas for an artaba of sesame, 3 drachmas 2 obols for an artaba of kroton, and 1 drachma for an artaba of cnecus. If they do not measure out all the sesame———.

(44) ———to be a factory, and they shall signify their approval by stamping it.

In none of the villages which are held in gift shall they set up any oil factory.

They shall deposit in each factory an adequate amount of sesame and kroton and cnecus.

They shall not allow the oil-makers appointed in each nome to migrate to another nome. Any oil-maker who goes elsewhere shall be subject to arrest by the director of the contract and *oikonomos* and the *antigrapheus*. No one shall harbor oil-makers (from another nome). If anyone does so knowingly or fails to bring them back when ordered, he shall forfeit for each oil-maker 3000 drachmas, and the oil-maker shall be liable to arrest.

(45)———and from the surplus of the oil that is manufactured he shall distribute to the oil-makers for every *metretes* containing 12 choes, 2 drachmas 3 obols. Of this sum the oil-maker and the pounders shall receive 1 drachma 4 obols, and the purchasers of the contract 5 obols.

If the *oikonomos* or his representative fails to pay the oil-makers their wages or their share in the profits from the sale, he shall forfeit to the Crown 3000 drachmas, and to the oil-makers their pay, and twice the amount of any loss incurred by the contract on account of the workmen.

If they fail to set up oil factories in accordance with these regulations, or to deposit a sufficient quantity of produce, and in consequence the contract suffers a loss, the *oikonomos* and the *antigrapheus* shall forfeit the amount of the deficit thus caused, and shall pay to the purchasers of the contract twice the amount of their loss.

The *oikonomos* and the *antigrapheus* shall provide [the plant] in every factory———.

(46) When he comes down to pay wages, he shall not obstruct the work in any way to the damage of the contract.

If he fails to provide plant or causes any damage to the contract, he shall be judged before the *dioiketes*, and if he is found guilty, he shall forfeit 2 talents of silver and twice the amount of the damage.

The contractors and the *antigrapheus* appointed by the *oikonomos* and the *antigrapheus* shall have authority over all the oil-makers in the district and over the factories and the plant, and shall seal up the implements during the time when there is no work.

They shall compel the oil-makers to work every day and shall stay beside them, and they shall make each day into oil not less than 1 artaba of sesame at each mortar, and 4 artabas of kroton, and 1 of cnecus, and they shall pay [as wages for crushing] 4 [artabas] of sesame [... drachmas, and for ...] artabas of kroton, 4 drachmas, and for [... artabas] of cnecus, 8 drachmas———.

(47) Neither the *oikonomos* nor the manager of the contract shall make an arrangement with the oil-makers concerning the flow of the oil on any pretext, nor shall they leave the implements in the factories unsealed during the time when there is no work. If they arrange with any of the oil-makers or leave the implements unsealed, each of the guilty parties shall forfeit 1 talent of silver to the Crown and make good any deficit incurred by the contract.

The agent appointed by the *oikonomos* and the *antigrapheus* shall register the names of the dealers in each city and of the retailers, and together with the managers of the contract arrange with them how much oil and castor oil they are to take and sell from day to day; and in Alexandria they shall arrange with the traders; and they shall make a written agreement with each of them, with those in the country every month, with those in

Alexandria———.

(48) Whatever quantity of oil and castor oil the dealers and retailers in each village agree to dispose of, the *oikonomos* and the *antigrapheus* shall convey the full quantity of each kind to each village before the beginning of the month, and they shall measure it out to the dealers and retailers every five days, and shall receive the price, if possible, on the same day, but if not, before the expiry of the five days, and shall pay it into the royal bank, debiting the contract with the cost of transport.

The quantity which they arrange for in each case shall be put up to auction ten days before the beginning of the month, and they shall publish in writing the latest bid for ten days both in the metropolis and in the village, and shall make an agreement for the finally approved sum.

(49) ———nor [shall they take away (?)] mortars or presses or any other implement used in this industry on any pretext; otherwise they shall forfeit to the Crown 5 talents, and to the purchasers of the contract five times the damage. Persons who already possess any of these implements shall make a declaration before the director of the contract and the agent of the *oikonomos* and the *antigrapheus* within thirty days and shall exhibit their mortars and presses; and the holders of the contract and the agent of the *oikonomos* and *antigrapheus* shall transfer them to the royal factories.

If anyone is detected manufacturing oil from sesame or kroton or cnecus in any manner whatsoever, or buying sesame oil or cnecus oil or castor oil from any quarter except from the contractors, the king shall decide his punishment, but he shall forfeit to the contractors 3000 drachmas and be deprived of the oil and the produce; and payment of the penalty shall be exacted by the *oikonomos* and the *antigrapheus*, and if he is without means, he shall hand himself over———.

(50) ———on any [pretext], nor bring oil into Alexandria apart from the crown supply. If any persons bring in more than they are likely to use for their own consumption in three days, they shall be deprived both of the goods and of the means of transport, and shall in addition forfeit 100 drachmas for each *metretes*, and for more or less in proportion.

The butchers shall use up the lard every day in the presence of the oil contractor, and shall not sell it separately to any person on any pretext nor melt it down nor store it up; otherwise both the seller and the buyer shall each forfeit to the oil contractor for every piece that is bought 50 drachmas.

Those who make oil in the temples throughout the country shall declare before the manager of the contract and the agent of the *oikonomos* and *antigrapheus* the number of the oil work-shops (51) in each temple and of the mortars and presses in each workshop, and shall exhibit the workshops, and deliver the mortars and presses to be sealed up———. If they fail to make the declaration or to exhibit (the workshops) or to deliver (the implements) to be sealed up, the persons in charge of the temples shall, each of them who is guilty, forfeit to the Crown 3 talents, and to the contractors five times the amount at which the latter estimate the damage. When they wish to manufacture sesame oil in the temples, they shall call in the manager of the contract and the agent of the *oikonomos* and *antigrapheus* and make the oil in their presence; and they shall manufacture within two months the amount which they declared that they would consume in the year. But the castor oil which they use they shall obtain from the contractors at the fixed price.

The *oikonomos* and the *antigrapheus* shall write down the amounts of castor oil and sesame oil used by each temple and send the list to the king, and shall also give one to the *dioiketes*. It shall not be lawful to sell to any person any of (52) the oil manufactured for the temples; whoever does so shall be deprived [of the oil], and shall in addition forfeit [100 drachmas] for each *metretes*, and for more or less in proportion———.

[It shall not be lawful] to bring [foreign oil] into the country for sale, either from Alexandria or Pelusium or any other place. Whoever does so shall be deprived of the oil, and shall in addition pay a fine of 100 drachmas for each *metretes*, and for more or less in proportion.

If any persons carry with them foreign oil for their personal use, those who bring it from Alexandria shall declare it in Alexandria, and shall pay down 12 drachmas for each *metretes*, and for more or less in proportion, and shall obtain a receipt before they bring it inland.

Those who bring it from Pelusium shall pay the tax in Pelusium and obtain a receipt.

The collectors in Alexandria and Pelusium shall place the tax to the credit of the nome to which the oil is brought.

If any persons bringing such oil for their personal use fail to pay the tax or to carry with them the receipt, they shall be deprived of the oil, and shall forfeit in addition 100 drachmas for each *metretes*. All merchants who carry foreign or Syrian oil from Pelusium across the country to Alexandria shall be exempt from the tax, but shall carry a receipt from the collector stationed at Pelusium and the *oikonomos*, as is prescribed in the law; likewise for [oil which is brought from...] to Alexandria (53)———and they shall get a receipt from the...; but otherwise———they shall be deprived of the oil.

The [contractors] shall receive the sesame and kroton announced at the auction [as stored up] for each nome within three days from when they take [the contract]...up to the 27th year and for the sesame and kroton and cnecus the price prescribed in the *diagramma* issued in the 27th year.

If those laying down the contract leave behind more, they shall receive from the *oikonomos* the value, 29 dr., 3 ob. per *metretes* of sesame oil, 20 drachmas per *metretes* of castor oil, 17 drachmas 1 obol per *metretes* of cnecus oil; 8 drachmas per artaba of sesame, 4 drachmas per artaba of kroton, 1 drachmas 2 obols per artaba of cnecus.

However much oil they announce that they will receive from each nome for the storehouse in Alexandria, we shall receive from them in the nome 19 drachmas 2 obols per *metretes* of castor oil, and the value shall be set to the credit of the contractors for the next report. The *oikonomos* shall exhaust first the value of the produce and the wages and the expenses.

(54)———They shall have [no authority] to import on any pretext. If they are caught importing, they shall be deprived of the oil. If they do not render an account or show that they have imported all the oil to Alexandria, they shall have exacted from them the value of the oil that they cannot show that they have imported, and each of the lessees of the village shall in addition forfeit 3 talents. The confiscated material shall belong to the Crown and it shall be set to the credit of the oil monopoly in the country.

The contractors shall also appoint *antigrapheis* at Alexandria and Pelusium (to check) the oil which is dispatched from Syria to Pelusium and Alexandria, and these shall keep the storehouses under seal and check the oil as it is issued.

The *antigrapheus* of the oil contract appointed by the *oikonomos* shall hold a balancing of accounts with the contractor every month in the presence of the *antigrapheus*, and he shall write in his books the amount which he has received of (55) each kind of produce and the amount of oil which he has manufactured and sold [at the prices] prescribed in the tariff, [except] the oil which is set apart, and the price of the produce [received] as prescribed in the tariff,———together with the price of the jars and the other expenses, namely 1 drachma for each artaba of sesame,...for kroton, 2 obols for cnecus,...[for colocynth,...for linseed, and for each...artabas made into sesame oil,...drachmas], for each 5 artabas [made into castor oil] 1 drachma 1 obol, for each 8 artabas made into cnecus oil..., for each 7 artabas made into lamp oil 1 drachma, for each 12 artabas made into colocynth oil 1 drachma 1 obol, and the amount out of the profits which is the appointed share of the oil-maker and the contractor, and the expenses, whatever they may be, of the transport of the produce.

The contractors shall receive their pay from the allotted portion of the profits. In Alexandria the wages for making sesame oil and the brokerage and the contractors' pay shall be given in accordance with the proclamation made at the auction.

Search. If the contractors or their subordinates wish to make a search, stating that certain persons are in possession of contraband oil or of oil presses, they shall hold a search in the presence of the agent of the *oikonomos* or the agent of the *antigrapheus*. If the agent of the *oikonomos* or *antigrapheus* when summoned fails to accompany them or to remain until the search is completed, he shall forfeit to the contractors twice the amount of the latter's valuation of the contraband, and the contractors shall be allowed to make the search [within...] days———.

(56) ———If the searcher does not find what he professed to be looking for, the person whose property is searched shall have the right to make him swear an oath in a temple that he made the search for no other than its declared object and the interests of the oil contract.

If he fails to take the oath the same day or the day after, he shall forfeit to the person who exacts the oath twice the amount at which he valued the contraband before making the search.

The contractors shall present sureties for a sum exceeding their liabilities by one-twentieth, and the taxes which they collected they shall pay into the bank from day to day, and the installment for each month before the middle of the month following.

(57) Revision of the [law] governing the oil monopoly. We sell the oil monopoly for the country from the month of Gorpiaios of the [27th(?) year], Mesore of the Egyptian calendar, for 2 years [according to the proclamation] that follows————the tax on sesame and kroton shall belong to the incoming contractors.

If the number of arouras which we designate as sown is less than the number announced at the auction in each nome, we will furnish from other nomes the deficient amount of sesame and kroton, and the tax on the sesame and kroton provided of 2 drachmas per artaba of sesame and 1 drachma for kroton will belong to them. From the nome from which we export sesame or kroton beyond the amount announced, they shall not collect the tax from the sesame and kroton.

However much (sesame or kroton) we do not give, we shall manufacture through the *oikonomos* and measure out colocynth oil toward the deficient sesame and oil; and from the colocynth oil we shall take the equal surplus, as much as (they took) from the sesame oil and the sesame; for the castor, we will manufacture through the *oikonomos* and measure out colocynth oil and linseed oil; from these we shall take the equal surplus, as much as they took from the castor and from the kroton. The contractors shall accompany the manufacturers and keep it under seal.

(58) On the sesame or kroton which [we supply] from each nome, either sesame oil or castor or colocynth [toward the deficit], the contractors of the oil monopoly for the nome from which [we export the surplus shall not exact] any tax.

The *oikonomos* shall receive the sesame and kroton sown in the separate land and shall furnish it to the oil factory in Alexandria.

We sell the contract for copper and we will take twenty-four obols for a stater. If the yield comes out greater than this, the excess will belong to the Crown.

(59-60.17 repeat 57-68. 60-72 contain a nome by nome breakdown of the number of arouras to be devoted to the production of each oil-bearing crop, sesame and kroton. The section is in parts badly damaged. 73-78 contain ordinances about banks, very fragmentarily preserved. 70-107 held further fragmentary texts concerning other aspects of the royal revenues and monopolies.)

96. ASSAULT ON AN OIL-CONTRACTOR

P. Teb. I 39²⁶²   114

Oilmaking was a profitable enterprise, and the government monopoly inevitably tempted black-market operators; in this petition a hapless oil-contractor recounts the self-defense of one such illegal producer.

To Menches, *komogrammateus* of Kerkeosiris, from Apollodoros, con-tractor for the distribution of and the tax upon oil²⁶³ at the said village for the 4th year. I have already reported to Polemon, the *epistates* of the village, about my having heard on the 27th of Phaophi that there was at the house of Sisois son of Senapynchis in the shrine of Thoeris²⁶⁴ here some contraband oil. When I immediately took Trychambos, the agent of the *oikonomos* who had been sent for the payment, since you and the other officials did not wish to come with me, to the house alluded to, and descended on it with him, the aforesaid Sisois and his wife Tausiris set upon me and gave me many blows; and having driven us out they shut the door of the temple and of the house. Therefore when on the 4th of Hathyr I en-countered Sisois near the temple of Zeus here, and I wished to arrest him, Ineilos the swordbearer and Trychambos being present, Pausiris the brother of Sisois, a porter, and Belles and Demas and Maron son of Takonnos with others whose names I do not know hurled themselves upon us and over-powered us, showering blows on us with the cudgels which they carried; and they wounded my wife on the right hand and myself also, the resulting loss to my contract amounting to 10 talents of copper. I accordingly present to you this statement, in order that you may order the proper officials to exact from them———.

97. OVERCHARGING FOR OIL

W.Chr. 300   242²⁶⁵

Horos, probably the *basilikos grammateus* but not in the vicinity at the time of writing, writes to the *topogrammateus* Harmais asking why the superior official has heard nothing from his subordinate about charges coming from travellers from the nome (the Arsinoite) that extortionate prices are being charged for oil, presumably by the contractors from the government. *W.Chr.* 301, probably in connection with the same affair, is a warning letter to oil-sellers that they will be sent to the *dioiketes* for judgment if they are caught overcharging.

Horos to Harmais, greeting. I have heard from many persons who have sailed down from the nome that oil is being sold for a higher price than that prescribed in the ordinance, but you have said nothing to me nor have you reported to Imouthes my son, who is on the spot.[266] Even at this late time, then, inform me how the oil is sold in your district, so that I can report to Theogenes the *dioiketes*. And from now on be careful, if such a thing should happen or the cultivators and the others should suffer extortion or if any other injustice should occur, to write to me or to report to Imouthes my son on the spot, so that it may be sent to me through him and I may report to the *dioiketes*. Farewell. Year 5, Pauni 16. (Address) To Harmais. (On the reverse is the draft of a reply which reads in part: Harmais to Horos greeting. I have read the letter from you, in which you write about oil being sold at an excessive price; I happen to have written to you previously————.)

98. REGULATING THE PRICE OF MYRRH

P. Teb I 35[267]   111

Myrrh, which along with other aromatic substances was produced under government contract as a monopoly, was probably sold at retail by contractors; but like oil it might also be sold by officials when necessary. This circular letter orders the *epistatai* of villages not to charge over 40 drachmas of silver for a mina of myrrh, and a public notice appended instructs purchasers not to pay more than this amount. Thr price is thus fixed, since maximum was also no doubt minimum. It is likely that this sale was an abnormal one, dealing with a supply of myrrh which the retailers were unable for some reason to sell.

Apollonios to the *epistatai* in the division of Polemon and the other officials, greeting. For the myrrh distributed in the villages no one shall exact more than 40 drachmas of silver for a mina-weight, or in copper 3 talents 2000 drachmas, and 200 drachmas on the talent for carriage; which sum shall be paid not later than Pharmouthi 3 to the collector sent for this purpose. Let the following notice be published with the concurrence of the *komogrammateus*, who shall sign below the circular with you. Anyone acting contrary to these orders will render himself liable to accusation. We have therefore also sent the swordbearers.[268] Farewell. Year 6, Pharmouthi 2.

Purchasers of myrrh from the *epistatai* of the various villages and from the other (officials) shall not pay more than 40 drachmas of silver for the mina-weight, or in copper 3 talents 2000 drachmas, and for carriage 200 drachmas on the talent; anyone acting contrary to these orders will render himself liable to accusation.

VI
THE MILITARY AND POLICE
OF PTOLEMAIC EGYPT

99. REIMBURSEMENT OF NAVAL EXPENSES

P.Cair.Zen. I 59036[269]   257

This papyrus concerns a complicated financial arrangment by crown officials in Egypt and Caria; the probable sequence of events is as follows: Xanthippos, trierarch (captain) of a very large Ptolemaic warship, was not on board when his ship needed repairs in Halikarnassos, one of the Ptolemaic-controlled ports in the Aegean (he was probably in Egypt), so his deputy borrowed the money from the *oikonomos* there, Apollodotos, who advanced it from various funds he had accumulated from local taxes. Apollodotos writes to Xanthippos asking him to repay the bulk of the money to Apollonios the *dioiketes* in Alexandria, to whom it would eventually have been transferred anyway. The whole file is sent under cover-letter to Apollodotos' agent Charmides, who is to pay a dunning visit to the trierarch. For detailed discussion, see R.S. Bagnall, *Chronique d'Egypte* 46 (1971) 356-62.

Apollodotos to Charmides, greeting. I have written below for you copies of my letters to Xanthippos. Interview him therefore, and with regard to the 2465 drachmas find out how he wishes to settle, and if he desires to pay the money to you, take it from him and pay to Medeios the sum of 2000 drachmas, which Straton[270] the keeper of the chest at Halikarnassos has given to Antipatros, the agent of Xanthippos, for the ship of which Xanthippos is trierarch, from the proceeds of the medical tax;[271] and send over to me the 465 drachmas 2 obols [2 chalkoi], giving them to someone to carry guaranteed against risk, and with regard to the 3000 drachmas see to it that he pays them to Apollonios as I have sent word to him. Farewell. Year 28, Apellaios 27.

Apollodotos to Xanthippos, greeting. If you are well in body and other things are satisfactory, it would be as I desire. I myself am well. I wrote to you before that I have given, through Perigenes, for the ship of which you are trierarch, 2000 dr. to Antipatros who is sailing in charge of the ship, requesting you therefore either, if it so please you, to pay this sum, together with the 465 dr. 2 ob. 2 ch. given to Hekatonymos for the nine-oar, to Medeios to the account of the medical tax or, if you choose, to write to Hikesios to refund it to me out of the ship's equipment account (?); but as you have sent no word, I thought it better to write to you again about this affair. You will oblige me therefore by sending word how you wish to make the payment, in order that we may enter it accordingly. If you like to pay the money to Charmides my agent who is delivering this letter to you, do so. Farewell.

Apollodotos to Xanthippos greeting. Besides the 2000 dr. of which I have written to you in the other letter, I have given to Antipatros, who is acting for you as trierarch of the nine-oar, a further 3000 dr., which you will have to make good to Apollonios the *dioiketes*. You will oblige me then by giving an order to pay him in accordance with the following note. Farewell.

(Owed by) Xanthippos to Apollonios: the sum of 3000 dr. which Apollodotos paid in Halikarnassos through the bank of Sopolis to Antipatros who is in charge of the nine-oar of Xanthippos, being the sum paid in on Peritios 8 of year 27 by the treasurers of Halikarnassos in the magistracy of Demetrios and forming the crown[272] for the king, for which Apollonios made himself responsible for Epikydes, which sum Xanthippos shall have to pay to Apollonios in Alexandria guaranteed against risk.

(Address) To Charmides. (Docket) copies of the letters to Xanthippos.

100. A LETTER FROM APOLLONIOS ABOUT WOOD FOR THE NAVY

SB VI 9215   250

This papyrus contains instructions from the *dioiketes* Apollonios regarding the cutting of trees to provide wood for royal warships. P.M. Fraser suggested in his commentary to this papyrus (*Chronique d'Egypte* 24 [1949] 289-94) that it is indicative of contemporary attempts by Ptolemy II to reassert naval hegemony in the Aegean, which may be correct, but is not by any means demonstrable. The recipient's position is not recorded, but he was probably a high official in the Oxyrhynchite Nome.

Apollonios to Demetrios, greeting. The king has given instructions that native timber, namely acacia, tamarisk, and willow should be felled to provide the breastwork for the men-of-war. On reading this letter you will therefore take with you the *basilikoi grammateis*, the chiefs of police, the thieves, and the...and [collect] laborers for felling to the number of 500 ———the required contingent on the spot. [Give this matter your attention and] expeditiously complete your quota [by...or], failing that, at the latest by Choiak 15. [See that the wood is...] and serviceable for its purpose. ———The king has ordered in respect of this quota———to make the survey———.

101. PAY FOR ELEPHANT-HUNTERS

P.Eleph. 28²⁷³   223

Elephants were an important part of the Hellenistic army. (Cf. no. 26.) The Ptolemies maintained a corps of elephant-hunters to provide a steady supply; the hunting grounds were in the far south along the coast of Africa, distant from the regular centers of administration. The troops whose pay is directed here had evidently been out of contact for several months.

Mnesarchos to Antipatros, greeting. I have instructed Paniskos to pay from the bank in Arsinoe²⁷⁴ to Demetrios the secretary of the hunters (hired) through Andronikos for the 231 men who set off with Peitholaos, their wages from Artemision through Panemos, 3 months: 2 talents, 1860 dr., subtracting the advance payment for the month of Artemision made to the advance guard, 60 dr., a balance of 2 talents, 1800 dr. Carry this out therefore as has been written. Farewell. Year 25, Thouth 21.
   To Apollonides. Carry this out as has been written. Farewell. Year 25, Thouth 21.²⁷⁵

102. COMPLAINT ABOUT OWNER OF LODGING

P.Enteux. 12   244/3

The complainant here has been dispossessed of part of the quarters assigned to him, evidently by action of the owner of the house. He complains in a petition addressed to the king but in fact directed to the *strategos*.

To King Ptolemy greeting from Bithys, one of the veterans of Kardendos, from Sebennytos of the Arsinoite. I am wronged by Hellanikos. You gave to us, O king, a lodging with the *kleroi* so that we might not be wronged by anyone nor have to pay for lodging; but Hellanikos has forcibly entered the house, demolished the wall of the courtyard, and moved in. I earlier submitted a petition to you, O king, about these matters, which was transmitted to Aphthonetos the *strategos*. But the man is still unwilling to give it to me, and continues to insult me. I beg you therefore, O king, if it seems right to you, to order Aphthonetos the *strategos* to write to ... to send him to Aphthonetos, so that he may be judged in our conflict and that I, by fleeing to you, O king, may obtain justice. Farewell.
(Subscription) Agenor to Timoxenos,²⁷⁶ greeting. I have sent you a copy of the petition that came to me from Aphthonetos. If it was assigned to him, assign to them their shares in accordance with the ordinance.²⁷⁷ Year 4, Panemos 23. (Docket) Year 4, Daisios 23, Bithys against Hellanikos: ordinance of the king.

103. ROYAL ORDINANCES

P.Hib. II 198[278]   ca. 240

This complex and badly preserved papyrus contains royal regulations in various forms concerning the cleruchic system (assignments, control of *stathmoi* and *kleroi*), matters of internal security (particularly for water traffic), administration (licensing), and judicial procedure (security forfeiture and sale, court disputes). The emphasis on these areas suggests that this collection of legislation was made for the use of a nome *strategos*, during a critical period in which the powers of this official were expanding at the expense of other bureaucrats. See R.S. Bagnall, *Bull. Amer. Soc. Papyrologists* 6 (1969) 73-118 for the date and purpose of the document, and N. Lewis, *American Journal of Philology* 89 (1968) 465-9 on the sailors.

———and he does not return (him), let him be liable to the same penalty as the brigand. Likewise, let the guards in the localities keep watch for the sailors bearing the brand[279]...from the fleet. As many as are caught, let them be sent up to the man in charge of the guardposts. If they do not send them up, upon conviction they themselves shall be sent to the ships. And let those harboring the sailors be liable for theft from the crown. Let brigands and other malefactors and royal sailors be subject to seizure everywhere, and let no one hinder them, or let the one interfering himself be subject to the same penalties as the brigand and the man who leaves the ship. Likewise, let those harboring them themselves, be liable to the same penalties———, it is written———. Let no one hinder them or let him be liable———let them make a search, taking the...of the *epistates* and the crown investigator———but at night let no one go———.

Let the judges to whom it is appointed to judge brigands judge [them].

Let those sailing toward the river to anchor give notice [during the day] at the appointed places; but at night[280]———. But if any, being driven by a storm [are not able] to anchor on the promontory when they come to the [harbor and its] appurtenances, let them announce to the police the reason and the place in which they have anchored. To those who have reported, the chief of police shall send a [guard] adequate to protect them while they are moored, [so that no] violence may be done. And if any sent from...sailing in haste and wish [to sail] at night, they shall provide them an escort and———.

By decree of the king: Officials in the royal administration [or acting on the king's business] and tax-farmers or their checking-clerks are not to...nor to grant tax-exemptions nor to allow any goods to be carried down river unless licenses are presented, and they are those issued by Epikydes, copies of which are deposited with Herakleides.[281] Otherwise these documents are to be null and void. Year 14, Artemisios.

By decree of the king:[282] In the case of persons concerning whom an inquiry is held as being accomplices in the debt of the Crown, if one side (i.e. the debtors to the Crown) accuses the other of owing money to themselves and wishes to bring the other party into court when the debt is disputed, they are to be summoned before the appointed court, and if they pay it they are not to be penalized; but if they deny it, they are to pay the indicated amount————the private individual's fine, while the debt to the Crown————.

But those who bring charges against. . ., or those against whom the latter bring charges are to obtain justice before the appointed court. They are to be judged on [these] charges in conformity with the ordinances before the courts which concern [them] in each district. Should any dispute arise about————as is prescribed in the *diagramma*————the *strategos* in each [nome] will act as judge conjointly with the nomarch and. . . Year 5, Peritios.

VII
THE PTOLEMAIC LEGAL AND
JUDICIAL SYSTEM

104. EXTRACTS FROM THE CITY LAWS OF ALEXANDRIA AND ROYAL ORDINANCES

P.Hal. 1[283]   mid-third century

Ptolemaic royal legislation is known from a comparatively large number of documents, some long, some short, a number of them translated in this book.[284] The civic laws and institutions of Alexandria and the other Greek cities of Egypt, on the other hand, are poorly known; this papyrus provides the only really extensive selection from the Alexandrian city laws.[285] It apparently constituted the *dikaiomata* for a court case, the legal texts called upon to support one side, and it ranges over a number of subjects in the extracts. There are also some passages from royal decrees, which would have supplemented (and in cases of conflict supplanted) the civic laws.

About perjury. Anyone challenging testimony shall challenge it at the point when the information is read out by the *dikastai* or *diaitetai* or *kritai*, and he shall challenge all those who have testified to the same effect, and, taking copies of the testimony if he wishes, he shall bring the charge on that day or the next for an amount of one and a half times the value of that which is in the complaint. He shall also be able to challenge a part of the testimony, in which case he shall make it clear in his complaint what part he is challenging. But if anyone cannot find the persons who have given testimony, the charge shall be transferred to the one who called them as witnesses. If anyone acts contrary to these regulations, his complaint shall be inadmissible.

The proof-texts of a case,[286] in which someone is challenging testimony, shall be produced in a case of false testimony from the *dikasterion* by the clerk, from the *diaitetai* by the appointee of the *nomophylax*, and in the *kriteria* by scribes, insofar as they are available.

If anyone, when the case is decided against him, challenges the witnesses, he shall file his complaint in accord with the ordinance, and the *praktor* or his assistant shall take sureties for his presence from him, but shall not carry out the execution (on his pledges) until the case of perjury is brought to an end. And if he defeats the witnesses, he shall be released from the damages and the agreement of surety shall be invalid, but the witnesses shall have the penalty fully exacted from them. But if he is defeated, the *praktor* or his assistant shall carry out the exaction.

If anyone after the case has been decided for him challenges the witnesses

and after laying a charge of perjury is successful, the witnesses shall have
the damages exacted from them in accordance with the ordinance and the
one who called them shall pay the winner the amount at stake in the case in
which the latter was acquitted, and for which he furnished the witnesses,
and an additional tenth or fifteenth.

But if both parties to the suit challenge the witnesses and are convicted of
perjury, the witnesses shall have the damages exacted from them in accordance with the ordinance, but the judgment from the original case shall be
legally valid unless it is appealed.[287]

The person who called the witnesses shall be permitted to defend them.

Those who call testimony from non-residents or from those on behalf of
whom others take the oath, shall be liable to accusation themselves for perjury and the parties opposing them shall file their suits against those who
called the witnesses.[288] If anyone in a case before the *dikasterion* or before a
kriterion furnishes testimony sworn by someone in another place————.

From the city law about planting, building, and excavation. If anyone
builds an embankment [by] the land of another, he shall not cross the
[boundary marker]. If he builds a wall or dwelling outside the city,[289] if a
wall [he shall leave] a foot, [if a dwelling] two feet. If he builds inside the
city he shall————of the expenses or he shall leave half [of what is prescribed to be left by those] building [outside the] city. If he excavates a grave
or [trench], he shall leave [as much as the depth is], and if a cistern, six feet;
in planting an olive tree or [fig tree, he shall plant nine feet from the]
neighbor, and for other trees five feet.

If anyone plants [contrary to these rules, he shall dig it up within five]
days from when the injured party complains, and if he digs it up, he shall
make it level again. But anyone who does not [act according to the] regulations shall be liable to judgment for the damages, and the injured party shall
be allowed to remove the building and plantings and to level out the digging
without penalty————.[290]

[Cutting and cleaning] of graves. If anyone wishes to cut a new grave or
to dig up an old one————to the neighbors of the land and each shall
contribute a share toward the expense, and he shall cast up half of the exca-
vated [earth] on each side. If anyone does not wish to contribute, the person
cutting the grave or digging it up shall cast up [the dirt] for his side onto the
land of whichever one is willing (to contribute), and if successful in a suit he
shall exact twice [the expense].

If a grave on someone's own land [is choked (?)...] they shall contribute
to him for the cleaning of the grave————each according to his share, and
anyone who does not contribute shall be [liable to the person doing the
cleaning] for thrice the expense if he is defeated in a suit.

If anyone [after bringing suit for outrage] or blows is defeated, he shall
pay to [the winner] an additional[291] tenth of the value of the suit and the
praktor or his assistant shall exact it from his property [in accordance with a
court decision]. If he does not completely do this, from his person also.

Anyone who after bringing suit for [assault or] bodily harm is defeated shall pay to the winner an additional fifth of the [value of the suit], and the *praktor* or his assistant shall exact payment from his property in accord with a court decision, [and if he does not completely do this, from his] person as well.

If any persons file suits [against one another] in different courts, an equal number of judges [shall be chosen by lot] from each court for them and there shall not be more than ten of them and their president shall be the one who drew the lot, and the (suit) that draws the first lot shall always be brought into court first———.

No one[292] shall bring into court a suit against persons who have been sent on service by the king,[293] either against themselves or against their sureties, nor shall the collector of debts or his assistants arrest these.

Likewise if any persons bring suits against the dependants (of the absentees) or against their sureties concerning matters of complaint which took place when those who left them behind were still at home, these suits shall not be brought into court, unless it happens that though classed as dependants they have themselves obtained legal satisfaction from others concerning matters of complaint which took place at the said time;[294] if the suit is against such persons, it shall be brought into court.

If any persons claim to belong to the class of dependants, the judges shall decide the point, and if they are recognized to belong to the class and if the matters of complaint are proved to have taken place when those who left them behind were still at home and they have not obtained legal satisfaction from others as stated above, the suits shall be adjourned until those who left them behind return, but the depositors shall recover their cautions of one-tenth or one fifteenth.[295]

All cases in which the dependants are accused by other persons of having wronged them after the departure of those who left them behind or in which the dependants accuse other persons, claiming to have been wronged by them after they had been left, shall be judged before the appointed court.

If any persons after bringing a suit are sent on service by the king before their suits have been brought into court, they shall, if they choose, take back their cautions of one-tenth or one-fifteenth, but the suits shall be adjourned until they return, and they shall not be brought into court [before] those who have recovered their cautions [of one-tenth] or one-fifteenth [deposit them anew].

If persons residing in [the country bring] a suit and are sent on service by the king before it has been brought into court, their suits shall be adjourned in like manner until they come back.

Of persons enrolled in the army all those who have been admitted to the citizenship in Alexandria and bring complaints concerning salaries and grain allowances and the amounts of money or grain credited to them, if their adversaries also are in the army and have been admitted to the citizenship, shall receive and give satisfaction in the courts for foreigners, and execution shall take place in conformity with the ordinance.

King Ptolemy to Antiochos greeting.[296] About the billeting of the soldiers, we hear that some undue violence is used, as they do not receive lodgings from the *oikonomoi*, but themselves break into the houses and ejecting the inhabitants occupy them by force. Give orders therefore that in the future this is not to be done; if possible, let them provide accommodation for themselves, but if indeed it is necessary that quarters should be given to them by the *oikonomoi*, let these give them what they strictly require. And when they depart from their quarters, let them give them up after putting them in order and not leave them as theirs until they return, as we hear that they now do; for it seems that when they go away they let them to others or seal up the rooms before leaving. Be particularly careful about Arsinoe near Apollonopolis, to see that, if soldiers come, none of them shall be billeted there, but that they should reside in Apollonopolis. But if they have any urgent reason for staying in Arsinoe, let them erect for themselves mud huts, as did those who came formerly. Farewell.

Threatening with iron.[297] If a freeman threatens a freeman with iron or copper or stone or . . . or wood, he shall forfeit a hundred drachmas, if he is defeated in the suit. But if a male slave or a female slave does any of these things to a freeman or a freewoman, they shall receive not less than [a hundred] stripes, or else the master of the offender, if he is defeated in the suit, shall forfeit to the injured party twice the amount of the penalty which is prescribed for a freeman.

Injuries done in drunkenness. Whoever commits an injury to the person in drunkenness or by night or in a temple or in the market-place shall forfeit twice the amount of the prescribed penalty.

For a slave striking a freeman. If a male slave or a female slave strikes a freeman or a freewoman, they shall receive not less than a hundred stripes, or else the master, if he acknowledges the fact, shall pay on behalf of his slave twice the amount of the penalty which is prescribed for a freeman. But if he disputes it, the plaintiff shall indict him, claiming [for a blow] a hundred drachmas, and if the master is condemned, he shall forfeit three times that amount without assessment; and for a greater number of blows the plaintiff shall himself assess the injury when he brings the suit, and whatever assessment [is fixed] by the court, the master shall forfeit three times that amount.

Blows between freemen. If a freeman or a freewoman, making an unjust attack, strikes a freeman or a freewoman, they shall forfeit a hundred drachmas without assessment, if they are defeated in the suit. But if they strike more than one blow, the plaintiff in bringing the suit shall himself assess the damage caused by the blows, and whatever assessment is fixed by the court, the accused shall forfeit [twice] that amount. And if anyone strikes one of the magistrates while executing the administrative duties prescribed for the magistracy, he shall pay the penalties trebled, if he is defeated [in the suit].

Outrage. If any person commits against another an outrage not provided for in the code, the injured party shall himself assess the damage in bringing the suit, but he shall further state specifically in what manner he claims to have been outraged and the date on which he was outraged. And the offender if condemned shall pay twice the amount of the assessment fixed by the court.

The legal oath. When anyone administers an oath, the one to whom the oath is administered shall swear in the market-place in the swearing place, pouring out libations on the offerings, and the challenger shall provide the offerings. He shall swear by Zeus, Hera and Poseidon. No one shall be permitted to swear another oath nor to administer one nor to produce his offspring (and swear by them).[298]

About citizens, that they are not to become slaves. An Alexandrian man shall not be a slave to an Alexandrian man [or woman][299] nor an Alexandrian woman to an Alexandrian man or woman.

Summons to testimony. They shall summon (witnesses) to testimony in the presence of two witnesses to the summons, being present and on each point announcing about what it is necessary to testify. The summoner shall write down the testimony[300] on a tablet. The person summoned shall testify before the magistrate and court to the things at which he was present or of which he knows, swearing the legal oath to testify truthfully about the things written on the tablet, and he shall offer no other testimony.

But if he asserts that he was not present or has no knowledge about the matters on which he is ordered to testify, he shall swear the royal oath immediately that he does not know or was not present at the things about which he is summoned to testify. If he says that he knows some of the matters of the requested testimony but not others, he shall testify to what he says he knows and take an oath concerning what he says he has no knowledge of.[301]

Apollonios to Zoilos, greeting. We have released the [teachers] of letters and masters of gymnastic and [performers of] the rites of Dionysos and victors in the [Alexandrian contest] and in the Basileia and Ptolemaia from the tax on salt, them and their [descendants, as the king] has ordered. Farewell. Year———.

105. PETITION ABOUT USURY AND ILLEGAL DETENTION

P.Col.Zen. II 83   245-244

This petition is part of a group of documents about the troubles of Antipatros. His wife for some reason had borrowed from Nikon 70 drachmas at the extraordinary interest rate of 6 per cent per month, which was after some 10⅔ months totalled up in a loan contract for 115 drachmas, in which the petitioner himself was the security. For unexplained reasons apparently not part of this case Antipatros found it advisable to move to Upper Hermopolis, but when Nikon offered a contract for interest-free repayment of the original principal, Antipatros was lured back to Philadelphia. Nikon, however, appeared in Hermopolis and with threats of execution through a *praktor* managed to shut Simon the wife up in some friend's house, her son being detained elsewhere. Simon escaped to Philadelphia, where she and her husband made depositions against Nikon. Whether their case was as sound as they say is uncertain; it may be noted that their son may well have been pledged in the contract, and his freedom might thus be jeopardized. But it is the lack of legal process in Nikon's actions that is at stake in this petition.

To King Ptolemy greeting from Antipatros, resident of Philadephia. I am wronged by Nikon. For having lent seventy silver drachmas to my wife Simon at an interest rate of six drachmas per mina each month and having totalled (the interest) with the principal he drew up a contract of loan with her for 115 drachmas[302] in which I myself was entered as security. After I had gone away from Philadelphia because I was being falsely accused by Artemidoros, agent of Apollonios the *dioiketes*, and had opened a shop in Upper Hermopolis, Nikon wrote a letter to Philadelphia, to a certain Menestratos, our servant, in which he includes the statement, made upon royal oath, that he will draw up an agreement with us for the principal by itself, namely, the seventy drachmas. When Menestratos wrote me at Hermopolis to come to Philadelphia and I sailed down there, Nikon sailed up to Hermopolis and said that he would hand my wife over to the *praktor* in the matter of the loan unless she followed him of her own accord. Simon, impelled by fear, sailed down with Nikon together with her boy, and Nikon led them to Herakleopolis and shut them up with certain persons, apart from each other. Then Simon escaped and came away; but the boy he holds in detention even now. And when we demand that he give him back, sometimes he acknowledges that he has seized him as pledge for the debt, and is still holding him, sometimes he denies it. I beg you therefore, O king, to send my petition to the *chrematistai*, and if I prove that the allegations set forth in the petition are true, I beg that Nikon may meet with fitting punishment both in the matter of the interest which he has contracted for contrary to the ordinance and because by his own authority he has placed in detention and holds (the boy) a free person; and I beg that the boy be restored to me in order that I, having fled to you for help, O king, may meet with justice.

106. LETTER FROM A MAN IN JAIL

P.Mich. I 87   mid-third century

The extensive powers — formal or informal — exercised by Zenon in Philadelphia are seen here in a request from a herdsman and farmer of Zenon who asks the latter to get him out of jail, where he was being held indefinitely and without bail pending trial.

To Zenon greeting from Kalippos. Have [you] fallen asleep, regardless of me in prison? Think of your flocks and herds. Know that if the goats of Demetrios remain here, they will perish; for the road down which he drives them to the pastures is enough to kill them. Think too about the hay already cut in Senaru, that it not be lost; for not small is the profit you will gain from it; I reckon there will be as many as 3000 sheaves. I pray and beseech you, be not unmindful of me in prison. Much loss have I suffered since I was led to jail from the allotment which I leased, trusting in your support. No little loss have you suffered since I was led to jail; and the sheep which I have acquired since I came to you have been carried off by the shepherds since I was led to jail. And if it seems good to you, I will leave my wife in prison to be answerable for me, until you inquire into the matters about which they accuse me. Farewell.

107. CONTRACT FOR SURETIES

P.Hib. I 92   263

Defendants in civil suits or even criminal charges were usually set at liberty until trial provided that they furnished persons acceptable to the court who could guarantee that in case the defendant did not appear they would pay on his behalf the full amount hinging on the trial, plus penalties. This is a contract for two men to offer themselves as such sureties for a defendant, who is evidently the brother of one of them.

In the reign of Ptolemy son of Ptolemy and his son Ptolemy,[303] the twenty-second year, the priest of Alexander and the Brother and Sister Gods being Pelops son of Alexandros,[304] the canephore of Arsinoe Philadelpos being Mnesistrate daughter of Tisarchos, on the fourteenth of the month Xandikos which is Mecheir of the Egyptians, at Mouchinaro in the Oxyrhynchite (Nome), Mnason son of Simos, Thracian of the Epigone, and Hegemon son of. . .imos, Cretan of the Epigone, are sureties for Timokles son of Simos, Thracian of the Epigone, on the condition that they shall deliver him up at Herakleopolis[305] before the *strategos* Krisippos until the decision of the suit in which Apollonios placed him on bail according to the contract for a principal of 300 drachmas and interest of 100 drachmas; and if they do not deliver him up as above written, they shall forfeit the 300 drachmas[306] and the extra tenths and other charges,and Apollonios or any one besides of the attendants of Krisippos or of the collector shall have the right of execution in accordance with the decree.

108. DECREE ABOUT A SURETY

P. Mich. I 70   237

This proclamation of Ptolemy III was issued in response to a request on Zenon's behalf by a military officer named Heniochos[307] for a clarification of a judicial problem: is a surety for the appearance of a defendant to be freed from his bond and excused from tardiness if he produces the defendant after the originally stated time? The answer is affirmative, and the reply to Zenon is then made into a universal rule.

By order of the king, announced by Aischylos agent of Sostratos[308] to Zenon, on behalf of whom Heniochos of the troop of Anthippos, taxiarch, presented a petition. If he has become surety for the appearance of Kallias as defendant against Eukles, on producing his person let him be released from the penalty of exceeding the term (*or*, released from his bond and not debarred from exceeding the term),[309] and in like manner let all who become surety for the appearance of another be on producing his person released from their bond and not debarred from exceeding the term. Year 10, Audnaios.

109. REPORT ON AN INVESTIGATION

P. Teb. I 14[310]   114

Aside from discovering the facts of a case the government sought to ensure the appearance of the defendant and to freeze his assets so that there would be, if he were convicted, a source from which to exact penalties. Menches here reports on the rather small property of an accused murderer.

Menches, *komogrammateus* of Kerkeosiris in the division of Polemon, to Horos,[311] greeting. You wrote to me that I was to give notice to Heras son of Petalos, an inhabitant of the village, who is arraigned on charges of murder and other offenses, to appear in three days' time for the decision to be made concerning these charges, and that until the matter was concluded I was to make a list of his property and arrange for it to be placed in bond, and was to send a report stating the measurements, adjoining areas, and values of it in detail. Accordingly I gave notice to the said Heras in person on the 14th of the current month at Ptolemais Euergetis[312] that he was to appear for the decision upon the aforesaid charges, and I report that he owns the sixth part of the shrine of the Dioskouroi in the village, of which the adjacent areas are on the south and west the free space around the village, on the north and east a canal, and of which the total value is one talent of copper. Farewell. Year 4, Phaophi 14.

110. TRIAL OF HERMIAS AND THE *CHOACHYTAI*

UPZ II 162   117

This text is the culminating document of an archive concerning the house property in Thebes owned by an Egyptian family engaged in the funerary service of the dead: pouring libations, making offerings, maintaining funerary foundations, caring for tombs, and carrying out various other priestly functions. Their ownership of this property was repeatedly challenged in the last decade of Euergetes II's reign by a Greek military officer, Hermias, who lived in another nome.

Here we have the final trial in which Hermias' last effort to assert ownership is completely blocked. It seems that his claim goes back to the reign of Epiphanes, but it is shown that no one of his family had ever lived in the house or, it seems, made claim to it, rented it, or maintained it over the many decades since that time. The Egyptians, on the other hand, have documentation plus occupancy, and Hermias' case is very weak. We find the court giving the decision therefore not to their fellow Greek and military officer — a man of some rank, in fact — but to Egyptians citing Egyptian (Demotic) contracts, who make their living performing a quintessentially Egyptian service to the dead. The papyrus also presents us with a fine example of a complete trial (insofar as it was recorded) before an administrative/judicial tribunal in a time when the bureaucracy is supposed to have been badly out of order; it appears here to good effect. For the general state of the Theban region in this period see A. Bataille, *Chronique d'Egypte* 26 (1951) 325-353.

(1) Year 54, Hathyr 22, in Diospolis Magna[313] before Herakleides, one of the chief bodyguards (of the king) and *epistates* of the Theban Nome and superintendent of revenues of the nome, in the presence also of Polemon of the chief bodyguards, Herakleides of the same and gymnasiarch, Apollonios the son of Apollonios and Hermogenes, of the friends, Pankrates of the *diadochoi*, Komanos of the *hegemones*, Paniskos son of Ammonios of the settlers, and many others.

After Hermias son of Ptolemaios, resident of the Ombite (Nome) stood forth against the *choachytai* from the place (the Theban Nome), Horos and Psenchonsis (and Panas) and Chonopres and their brothers, the memorandum submitted by Hermias to Hermias the kinsman and *strategos* and nomarch, and then sent on to us, and of which the following is a copy, was read:

"To Hermias, kinsman and *strategos* and nomarch, from Hermias the son of Ptolemaios, one of the *diadochoi* at the court and *hegemon* over men. In Mecheir of the 53rd year, when Demetrios the kinsman (of the king) and *epistrategos* came to Diospolis Magna, I delivered a memorandum against Horos the son of Harsiesis and Psenchonsis the son of Teephibis, Panas the son of Pechytis, Chonopres son of Harsiesis and their brothers, who furnished services in the cemetery, called *choachytai*, in which I reported that, there belonging to me ancestral properties in Diospolis, which my ancestors owned for as long as they lived there, the accused, who live in the Memnoneia (where it has been granted to them and their ancestors to live), in the circumstances of the times did not respect me because I lived elsewhere, but came to one of my houses, which is on the south and west of Diospolis, to the north of the road leading to the river of the very great goddess Hera,[314] and to the south of that leading to the sanctuary of Demeter,[315] and which is surrounded by walls, and took possession of it with their own force; (2) they reconstructed the broken-down parts and live in it, occupying it illegally. When I was informed of these happenings, I went to Diospolis in the 45th year and when I had words with them they claimed that they had bought it from Lobais the daughter of Herieus. Therefore, in the same year I submitted a petition to the *chrematistai* in the Thebaid, whose clerk was Dionysios, in the pot set out by them in Diospolis, against Lobais, in order to deprive them of all excuse; and when I brought an action against her to trial in the month of Pachon of the aforesaid 45th year when she learned that she had no secure title, because neither she nor her ancestors had any part of the land, she gave me an agreement in which she stated that she did not have a claim to the house either formerly or now.

"Since things were so, the accused, being utterly crushed by having no legal claim, went away to the Memnoneia, but I, being severely harmed, after a considerable number of days was compelled, since the men did not come to me in person, to go away to my command. And after that as often as I went into Diospolis they continued on every occasion to avoid me.

"But not satisfied with living in my house, they even buried corpses there without paying the fines incumbent on them, and this although the house lies on the road of Hera and Demeter the very great goddesses, to whom dead bodies and those who care for such are unlawful. And even when Aineas the former *strategos* wrote to Ptolemaios, then the *epistates*, to transfer the clan to the Memnoneia as formerly,[316] based on what Tatas the royal physician reported to him that the king had decreed, and Diasthenes the former *strategos* also wrote about the same class to transfer them (and I will deposit copies of these documents for the proceedings);

"And when it was announced to them by the agents of Demetrios to come to the tribunal until our affairs should be settled, they stayed away and did not appear. Since Demetrios had gone away, I asked that the memorandum about their case be handled by you, and I delivered the dispatched document in Latopolis in the month of Phamenoth. And when you wrote to Ptolemaios, who was then *epistates*, to send them up so that our business should be settled, and they were not sent up, in Pauni of the same year (3) when you went to Diospolis with Demetrios for the crossing of the very great god Amun and I gave you the aforesaid memorandum about the persons named, and when it was announced to them to appear before the tribunal, they became fugitives from justice and did not appear, because I had to sail back up to my district with you.

"I ask you therefore to look upon the disaster that has happened to me at the hands of these impious men, and if it seems good to you, to order a letter written to Herakleides, who is in charge of the Theban Nome, to send the culprits and to inquire about these things, so that, if I demonstrate that things are so, they may be compelled to move out of the house and if, having been brought to trial, they confess to having buried corpses in the said house, that they be sent to you, so that they may receive the proper punishment. If this is done I shall have received justice. Farewell. (Subscription of *strategos*): To Herakleides. Year 54, Phaophi 21."

Since this was the state of things, the attorneys for both parties also argued their cases — Philokles for Hermias, Deinon for Horos and his associates — and the proof texts deposited by them were read, as selected by each; Philokles introduced material similar to the information from the memorandum and also read from the appended proof-texts the petition, in connection with which he said that Hermias had deposited it in the pot publicly set out by the *chrematistai* who are concerned with Diospolis Magna, whose clerk was Dionysios, against Lobais the daughter of Herieus, one of those who had sold the house to Horos and his associates; and that Lobais had thus given him an agreement in which, as he said, she stated that she did not formerly and did not now have any claim to the house, in order to leave (Hermias') opponents without pretext and with no claim to legal satisfaction. And he said that in this manner he had driven them out of possession of the house.

And he likewise read out a report of the *basilikos grammateus*, according to which, he said, the trial had been carried on (4) before the *chrematistai* against Harmais son of Nechthmonthes, one of the priests of Ammon from Diospolis, about 20 arouras of grain-producing land, which he stated that Apollonios the son of Damon had sold illegally to Harmais although they were his own ancestral property, and after Apollonios assumed the case on behalf of Harmais, when the report was made to the *chrematistai* by the *basilikos grammateus* on the basis of reports from the *topogrammateus* and *komogrammateus* about the registration of the land in the name of Hermon son of Hermias, the grandfather of Hermias' mother, Apollonios gave him a deed of cession, surrendering the land; he (the attorney) said that in accordance with this decision a great piece of evidence was contributed to the case being pursued at present against Horos and his associates about the house.[317]

And he likewise (read) a copy of a proclamation about the invalidity of unwritten Egyptian contracts, and he said that the contracts produced by Horos and his associates in regard to the house were useless.

And he (read) sections from the native law about disregarding it if anyone produces to the court a contract that has not been guaranteed by oaths, and if anybody produces a false contract it is to be torn up, and a portion from the law of guarantee according to which he said it was necessary for those sued to seek an accounting from those who sold (the property) to them, and other administrative acts of Hermias the kinsman and *strategos* and nomarch, to which was appended the letter written to him by Diasthenes the *strategos*, followed also by the letters sent to him by the priests of Ammon and the report of Pamonthes the former *topogrammateus* and the letter of Aineas the *strategos*, about moving the *taricheutai* from Diospolis to the Memnoneia, and he claimed that from these also a valid right of possession accrued to him.

And he read royal ordinances about statutes of limitations, for which he was waiting...not having acted beyond the past time, and from which he reported and read in his brief; he asked that the defendants be expelled from the house and that it be given back to himself.

(5) Taking the floor, the attorney for Horos and his associates, Deinon, charged that Hermias had idly disturbed Horos and his associates with all the slander and extortion and caused them extraordinary trouble with no reasonable grounds. He said that the house belonged to them, in accordance with the subjoined copies of Egyptian contracts, translated into Greek, one which was made in Pachon of the 28th year of Philometor, in which the father of one of the accused, Psenchonsis and Chonopres, Teephibis, purchased from Helekis and Lobais and Tbaiais and Senerieus and Herieus and Senosorphibis and Sisois also called Herieus, seven in all, seven and a half cubits of building property from the south part of the ten cubits of vacant land belonging to them; and the others, according to which the father of the accused Nechoutes and Asos and another Nechoutes and their sister Nechoutis, Asos, purchased from the same persons two and a half cubits in the same year and month, and another of the 35th year, Mesore, under the same king, by which Pechytes the father of the others, Panas and Patous and Pasemis and Harpchemis and Senamounis, bought from Ammonios and Zbendetis the one-fourth portion that belonged to them of the same house, three and a third cubits, for which the taxes were also paid to the contract of the sales tax...and that they have owned it for thirty-seven years up to the present without any contest or anyone making any disturbance. He also produced sections of the royal amnesty decrees about those who have owned property, that even if they cannot furnish the documentation for it they are to be allowed to keep it.

Then returning to the proof-texts of his opponent, and after reading the previously read petition, he said that although his opponent claimed to the sovereigns that his father had set out from Diospolis with other soldiers to the upper country in the past rebellion under the father of the sovereigns, the Manifest God, and he said, reckoning the time, from Epiphanes, 24 years, Philometor, 35 years, the God Euergetes from the 25th to the 53rd years, 29 years, that the years thus came to 88, so that confessedly by his own testimony he had made it clear that neither he nor his father had lived in Diospolis, nor was there any basis for refutation left to him at all about the house, in making a claim after so many years, and neither he nor his father had had possession or ownership of any landed property from the earliest times up to the present.

(6) And he stated additionally that since Hermias could produce neither a deposit ticket[318] nor any other evidence of ownership, but was without any demonstration of his case, that he had wickedly and knavishly pressed the cession; and since the sellers were nine and Horos and his associates were living in the house and had possession of it, it was necessary first to submit a petition against them, so that they might themselves either defeat Hermias in the suit against them by bringing investigative action against the sellers and defending the case against Hermias, or, turning to the guarantors, start a suit on account of the guarantee, with the legal proceedings open and known to every person and with everybody brought before the tribunal, if he really reckoned by proceeding truthfully on the way according to the laws to bring an action of a direct trial, and not to use stealthy subtleties to carry out some evil scheme, with his opponents kept in ignorance, or to work up some collusion with Lobais alone, who did not have the power to lay claim to the house since she had sold only the seventh part falling to her share of the seven and one-half cubits and the one cubit that belonged to her according to one of the aforesaid contracts.

And he also pointed out, to establish that things were such as he alleged, starting from what Hermias appended about the other suit which he said that he had prosecuted against Harmais and Apollonios, (he said that he [Hermias] had reported about the sale by Apollonios to Harmais, of land which he said that a part was his own, making an accusation not against the seller Apollonios but against the purchaser and owner, Harmias); but Harmias after filing suit against Apollonios, the seller, had yielded the case to him and he (Harmais) had vindicated the case against Hermias from the suit formerly instituted against Harmais the purchaser and owner, that there is no argument left to him about the agreement with Lobais nor are Horos and his associates "completely crushed" by it.

And about the royal decree about registration he remarked that it was no use to him (Hermias), since he agreed in the same petition that Lobais with her brothers and sisters sold the house to Horos and his brothers, and that on receiving (7) this information he filed the petition against her; that the same defense was valid also about the sections which he adduced from the national laws about sworn guarantee of contracts, showing that if they were judged before the *laokritai* by the laws which he cited, he had to prove first that he was the son of Ptolemaios and the mother whom he named and that his ancestors whom they claimed were of the kinsmen, before his claim could be heard at all about any matter,and that after these proofs he could ask for proofs about the house;[319] and that in the same way he had also to give the same proofs according to the common law and the decrees, and to declare his inheritance and pay tax on it or pay ten thousand drachmas and have all the arrangements which he had made be invalid and not be allowed to enter into the property of the deceased;[320]

And that since the very great sovereigns released everyone under their rule from all offenses up to Thouth 19 of the 53rd year,[321] they established that the contracts deposited by him are unassailable and that the possession and ownership of the house are guaranteed for Horos and his associates from the same amnesty and also according to the decrees issued by them and by their ancestors about those who have come to have ownership, even if some-one should establish that they can produce no contracts, even more that they did not produce title-deeds and they claimed the right and amnesty from the decrees, our opponent has introduced no proof himself.

And about the ordinances regarding statutes of limitations which were cited, he said that if one concedes to one's opponent and attacker the right to claim the goods of another, not more than a year or two or three is to be conceded for the grace-period and this by no means to everyone, but to those who have some legal claim, and is not to be given for the entire time since the father of Hermias up to the end of his life and Hermias himself had passed the years and come to extreme old age...and neither of them ever lived in Diospolis at all, so that he has no claim to ownership of any land, making this attack after so many years and furnishing no proof at all.

And he also deposited a subscription, reporting that it had been made on Pauni 8 of the 51st year,[322] in reference to which he said that Hermias was defeated in his suit against them before Ptolemaios, who was *epistates* before us: that he was not to be permitted to harass Horos and his associates constantly on every point, but that they were to be permitted to retain possession.

(8) Returning to what Hermias testified about the suit which Hermias said he had prosecuted against Harmais and Apollonios, he reported that what he had introduced was an entirely different business, and that he was not to be allowed to transfer onto another question the contest between himself and other men about any matter which had no pertinence to him in his suit against Horos and his associates about their house.

And likewise about the administrative documents which he deposited about moving the *taricheutai* from the place to the Memnoneia, he said that these documents were entirely separate, and that it was rather very easy to recognize that he realized that he had no legal claim and had occupied the role of informer and accuser, concluding that his opponents could be easily crushed; but that Horos and his associates were not *taricheutai* but *choachytai*, and did not perform the same tasks, but that their services were different; and that on the public and legally established and named feast-days they brought dust to scatter on the road of Ammon and through the sanctuary and went to the sanctuary of Hera to do the same thing, and in the yearly crossings of Ammon to the Memnoneia they precede the procession to perform the services proper to them and they pour out libations to the dead and they have priestly offices. But the *taricheutai* too have a decree, by which they are to be unmolested. But even if someone should establish that which is not true, that the *taricheutai* have been moved, no one would have any authority, nor would Hermias, to confiscate any land of theirs; and that each of them was master of his own property, and that in selling or ceding it to another he would take the price;

But Hermias, introducing complications that have nothing to do with the present case and are not part of his decision, and like a busybody arrogating to himself the power that belongs to the *strategos*, has made it obvious that since he has no evidence at all he has decided to assume the guise of an informer and to depose the documents concerning the *taricheutai*, and also the documents concerning Harmais and Apollonios and the others as if they had greatly supported his case; and if he really thought he had some legal claim by merit of which he might persuade the court and not to boast of the (9) previously read documents, he would never have had it arranged for other dispositions with no pertinence to him to have been deposited.

Since[323] he had presented a brief along these lines, and more besides, and Hermias had introduced no title deed or other document showing that the disputed house was his ancestral possession, but with arguments and speeches claimed that the house was his,

And since Horos and his associates had deposed that their ancestors had bought the said house from Helekis and Lobais and the others named above, nine in number, in accordance with an Egyptian contract, for which the proper taxes had been paid to the contract of the sales tax, and after they had shown in addition that their ancestors had owned the house from the times of the contracts for the entire time they had been there; and that after their deaths they themselves had possessed it up to the present time with no contest, and no one had made a claim for all of these years, and since they deposed a section of a royal decree issued in the 26th year about amnesty and those who had had possession; and also a copy of the subscription of Ptolemaios who was *epistates* before us pertinent to the suit between them. . . It was ordered, "Do not make a claim";

We also, in accordance with the contracts introduced by them and the decrees of the sovereigns about possession, since no document has been produced against the contracts, give sentence: to Hermias, to refrain from forcible entry; and to Horos and his associates, to have possession as they have had from the beginning.

111. ACTION BEFORE THE *CHREMATISTAI*

P.Mert. 59   154 or 143

This papyrus contains the decisions of the Greek court in Crocodilopolis in the Arsinoite Nome to accept a pre-trial settlement of a suit and counter-suit filed by a separate husband and wife. The woman Antigone had probably left her husband Asklapon, who started action against her in order to be able to keep her dowry; she in turn claimed that the fault was his, and that she should recover not only the dowry but an extra penalty. Evidently neither party had a very good case, for they settled it on the terms of her retention of her dowry, the dissolution of the marriage, and no penalties. The agreement had to be accepted by the court in order to be valid, however; instructions are then given to the *xenikon praktor* to ensure the carrying out of the agreement.

To the *xenikon praktor*[324] of the Arsinoite Nome, the copy of the decision reached is now appended. Year 27, Tybi 17.

Year 27, Tybi 16, at Crocodilopolis in the Arsinoite Nome, the *chrematistai* who hear appeals to the king, Ptolemaios son of Ptolemaios of the Crateraean deme and Aristeus son of Ammonios, judges of cases which concern the crown, the revenues, and the private individual, in view of the fact that the third, Etearchos, has been attacked by a slight seizure (?) — when the case of Asklapon son of Dizaporis against Antigone daughter of Alketas was announced, and the parties had appeared, Alketas son of Menandros being entered as Antigone's guardian, [before] the delivery of the pleas, they presented to us an agreement, of which the following is a copy:

To the *chrematistai*, whose clerk is Artemidoros, from Asklapon son of Dizaporis and from Antigone daughter of Alketas with [Alketas son of] Menandros as her guardian, concerning the case which we have before you, which is concerned with, on the one hand, the return of the trousseau and the [slave-girl called Opora], who is included in the same valuation, and, on the other hand, the thirty talents of bronze, if no [judgment] take the place of the present one (?), (we ask that) judgment be given to the effect that he be released from the terms of the marriage-contract and that she bring no action against him henceforth, on condition that the objects also be restored or their value, forty-six talents four thousand one hundred drachmas.[325] We agree to a settlement with each other on the following conditions: the agreements which we made together on the fifteenth of Tybi in the twenty-seventh year are to be valid, likewise the declaration covering them and attested by the royal oath; Antigone, since she has recovered her dowry, is to bring no action against Asklapon originating from the terms of the marriage contract, but he is to be released from them, and also Antigone from all the charges brought against her by Asklapon in the petition; Asklapon is to meet Antigone's father, Alketas, at Busiris in the Herakleopolite Nome by the thirtieth of the present month, in whose presence — in order to prevent the aforesaid slave-girl Opora from being misrepresented as having run away — he is to produce her alive or, otherwise, to pay to Antigone her value, fifteen talents of bronze; if she is dead, Asklapon is likewise to pay for her the fifteen talents of bronze by the same time; but if, despite Asklapon's readiness to produce the slave-girl alive, Alketas does not meet him at the appointed time, or does meet him and receives her alive, then he (Asklapon) is to be released henceforth (?) from payment of her value; the copy of the agreement is to be sent to Theon, the *xenikon praktor*, so that, if either he does not pay her all that is required or Opora is dead or dies before the thirtieth of Tybi, then he (Theon) may grant [Antigone] right of execution against Asklapon upon the fifteen talents in the time appointed.

Read.

I, Asklapon, agree to the aforewritten.

I, Antigone, agree to the aforewritten.

I, Alketas, am entered as the guardian of Antigone, who agrees to the aforewritten.

We therefore decide that their agreement is to be valid and that a copy of it be sent to the aforementioned *xenikon praktor*, as they have agreed.

Through the clerk Artemidoros son of Isidoros.

112. PROBLEMS WITH A BREWERY

P.Cair.Zen. II 59202   254

The problems of Zenon and Apollonios with their brewery at Philadelphia figure here. The accounts of the previous brewer Ammeneus were being audited, and the audit had evidently resulted in conflicting claims from the auditor and the brewer. Zenon had arrested the former, and Apollonios sends the latter so that they can confront one another before the *chrematistes*. It has often been thought that the conclusion of the text includes a threat to hang Ammeneus (i.e. capital punishment), but E.G. Turner, in *Essays in Honor of C. Bradford Welles* (New Haven 1966) 79-86, argues convincingly that this is wrong.

Apollonios to Zenon, greeting. You have done rightly in arresting the treasurer from the brewery. We have sent to you also Ammeneus the brewer, so that the treasurer may convict him before Peton the *chrematistes* on the matter about which you wrote that he had accused him. Bring both of them before Peton therefore. If it appears that Ammeneus has in fact spoken what you wrote to me, let him be strung up for a whipping with his hands tied behind him. Farewell. Year 31, Dystros 23, Phamenoth 30. (Address) To Zenon. (Docket) Year 32,[326] Pharmouthi 1. Apollonios about the brewer Ammeneus.

VIII
SOCIAL RELATIONS AND PRIVATE LIFE

113. BILINGUALISM

W.Chr. 50[327]   third century

A considerable number of Egyptians — certainly all who wanted economic or political advancement — learned Greek well enough to get along. Fewer Greeks learned Egyptian, but many of those who married Egyptian women must have done so. Here we apparently have one such Greek writing to another and recording his dream in Egyptian, for whatever reason (Wilcken thinks there is a religious motivation; certainly interpretation of such dreams was a specialty of Egyptian religion). The dream concerned the Taunchis mentioned in the letter.

Ptolemaios to Achilleus, greeting. After writing about the..., it seemed good to me to inform you also about the dream, so that you may know in what way the gods know you. I have written below in Egyptian, so that you may understand correctly. Just before I was about to go to sleep, I wrote two letters, one about Taunchis the daughter of Thermouthis, and one about Tetimouthis the daughter of Taues, who is the daughter of Ptolemaios, and————(a long gap) annoint yourself, in which manner I myself passed a fine day. Farewell. Year 2, Phaophi 25 (Here follows a Demotic Egyptian description of the dream).

114. COMPLAINT BY A NON-GREEK ABOUT CONTEMPTUOUS TREATMENT

P.Col. Zen. I 66   ca. 256-255

The writer of this letter was not a Greek (the editors suggest he was an Arab). As a former subordinate of Zenon during the latter's stay in Syria, he had been left behind to work for other agents of Zenon, who did not, however, pay him his promised salary after Zenon left. The reason, the writer alleges, was that the Greeks despised him as a barbarian who did not "know how to act the Hellene." The worst feature of this treatment seems to have been the attempt to pay him in local wine. The "barbarism" that caused the contemptuous treatment was not simply one of language (the letter, though crudely written, is not badly composed) but of manners and customs.

...dab...to Zenon, greeting. You do well if you are healthy. I too am well. You know that you left me in Syria with Krotos and I did everything that was ordered in respect to the camels and was blameless toward you. When you sent an order to give me pay, he gave nothing of what you ordered. When I asked repeatedly that he give me what you ordered and Krotos gave me nothing, but kept telling me to remove myself, I held out for a long time waiting for you; but when I was in want of necessities and could not get anything anywhere, I was compelled to run away into Syria so that I might not perish of hunger. So I wrote you that you might know that Krotos was the cause of it. When you sent me again to Philadelphia to Jason, although I do everything that is ordered, for nine months now he gives me nothing of what you ordered me to have, neither oil nor grain, except at two month periods when he also pays the clothing (allowance). And I am in difficulty both summer and winter. And he orders me to accept ordinary wine for salary. Well, they have treated me with scorn because I am a "barbarian". I beg you therefore, if it seems good to you, to give them orders that I am to obtain what is owing and that in future they pay me in full, in order that I may not perish of hunger because I do not know how to act the Hellene. You, therefore, give attention to me, if you please. I pray to all the gods and to the guardian divinity of the king that you remain well and come to us soon so that you may yourself see that I am blameless. Farewell. (Address) To Zenon.

115. PETITION ABOUT AN ASSAULT

UPZ I 8[328]   161

In the second century, with the increasing tide of Egyptian nationalism and resentment of the superior position of the Greeks, it was sometimes dangerous to be a Greek among Egyptians. An episode of Ptolemaios' stay in the Serapeum of Memphis (cf. introduction to nos. 142-144) illustrates this problem.

To Dionysios one of the friends and *strategos*, from Ptolemaios son of Glaukias, Macedonian, one of those in *katoche* in the great Serapeum in Memphis in my 12th year. Being outrageously wronged and often put in danger of my life by the below-listed cleaners from the sanctuary, I am seeking refuge with you thinking that I shall thus particularly receive justice. For in the 21st year, on Phaophi 8, they came to the Astartieion in the sanctuary, in which I have been in *katoche* for the aforesaid years, some of them holding stones in their hands, others sticks, and tried to force their way in, so that with this opportunity they might plunder the temple and kill me because I am a Greek, attacking me in concerted fashion. And when I made it to the door of the temple before them and shut it with a great crash, and ordered them to go away quietly, they did not depart; but they struck Diphilos, one of the servants compelled to remain by Sarapis,[329] who showed his indignation at the way they were behaving in the sanctuary, robbing him outrageously and attacking him violently and beating him, so that their illegal violence was made obvious to everybody. When the same men did the same things to me in Phaophi of the 19th year,[330] I petitioned you at that time, but because I had no one to wait on you it happened that when they went unwarned they conceived an even greater scorn for me. I ask you, therefore, if it seems good to you, to order them brought before you, so that they may get the proper punishment for all these things. Farewell.

Mys the clothing seller, Psosnaus the yoke-bearer, Imouthes the baker, Harembasnis the grain-seller, Stotoetis the porter, Harchebis the doucher, Po...os the carpet-weaver, and others with them, whose names I do not know.

116. LEARNING EGYPTIAN

UPZ I 148   second century

This fragment of a letter, from a wife to her husband (on the interpretation of Rémondon) apparently deals with a man who has learned Egyptian in order to be able to teach it to Greek slaveboys learning the Egyptian medical skill of *iatroklysteria* from an Egyptian master of the specialty. To Rémondon, such a system indicates a Greek wish to use this Egyptian knowledge for economic gain, rather than any deep-seated growth of social interaction of the races: cf. *Chronique d'Egypte* 39 (1964) 126-46.

Discovering that you are learning Egyptian[331] writing, I am happy for you and for myself, because now when you come to the city you will teach the slave-boys in the establishment of Phalou...the douche-doctor,[332] and you will have a means of support for old age.

117. SCALDING IN THE BATHS

P.Enteux. 82[333]   221

The baths were an important feature of life for the Greeks, but the Egyptian employees of the baths were perhaps not always experienced or adept in handling their jobs. Here one has scalded the petitioner by bringing excessively hot water; she demands his punishment.

To King Ptolemy, greeting from Philista daughter of Lysias, resident in Trikomia. I am wronged by Petechon. For as I was bathing in the baths of the aforesaid village on Tybi 7 of year 1, and had stepped out to soap myself, he being bathman in the women's rotunda and having brought in the jugs of hot water, emptied one (?) over me and scalded my belly and my left thigh down to the knee, so that my life was in danger. On finding him, I gave him into the custody of Nechthosiris the chief policeman of the village in the presence of Simon the *epistates*. I beg you, therefore, O king, if it

please you, as a suppliant who has sought your protection, not to suffer me, who am a working woman, to be thus lawlessly treated, but to order Diophanes to write to Simon the *epistates* and Nechthosiris the policeman that they are to bring Petechon before him in order that Diophanes may inquire into the case, hoping that having sought the protection of you, O king, the common benefactor of all, I may obtain justice. Farewell.
(Response) To Simon, send the accused. Year 1, Gorpiaios 28, Tybi 12.
(Docket) Year 1, Gorpiaios 28, Tybi 12. Philista vs. Petechon, bathman, about having been scalded.

118. ORDINANCE ABOUT SLAVE SALES

P.Col. I (Inv. 480)   ca. 198-197

This papyrus provides extracts from a *diagramma* on the sums due on sales of the various sorts involving slaves. The first three paragraphs (according to the interpretation of F. Pringsheim, *Journal of Juristic Papyrology* 5 [1951] 115-20) deal with the various cases of the sale of a slave through a private auction, while the remainder deal with various forms of legally forced sale.

From the ordinance about slaves:
The contractor of the tax on slaves and the checking-clerk shall collect for the slaves whose sales are recorded before the *agoranomoi*, on the price at which they are recorded, in silver (the following): from the seller, including the one per cent tax formerly collected for the grant to Dikaiarchos,[334] 9 drachmas, 2½ obols per mina, and from the buyer 8 drachmas, 2 [½] obols, making a total of 17 drachmas, 5 obols per mina; and for the city a guarantee-fee from the seller of 4 drachmas, 1 obol per head.
If anyone buys on condition that he will pay all the taxes[335] they shall collect 20 drachmas 1 obol per mina, and for the city, 4 drachmas [1 obol] per head.
If anyone gets possession of a slave through an overbid or counterbid he shall pay to the city another guarantee fee.[336]
Upon those sold through the *praktor xenikon*[337] the purchaser shall pay 19 drachmas per mina, and a one per cent crier's fee of 1 drachma (per mina) and a clerical fee to the grant of 1 drachma per head.
Upon those sold in consequence of debts to the crown, the purchasers shall be charged 16 drachmas 5 obols per mina, and a one per cent crier's fee of 1 drachma (per mina), and a clerical fee to the grant of Dikaiarchos of 1 drachma per head.
Upon debtors who being still free [mortgage (?)] their persons [against] the debt[338] there shall be collected from the lender 5 drachmas 1 obol [per mina] and from the borrowers 5 drachmas 1 obol, [making a total of] 10

drachmas 2 obols per mina, and a clerical fee of 1 drachma per head.

[And if they are sold (?)] to meet the debt, there shall be collected from [the purchaser...drachmas,...] 5 obols, and a one per cent tax of 1 drachma per mina, and a clerical fee of 1 drachma per head (?).

119. PROCEDURAL LAWS ABOUT SLAVES

P. Lille 29[339]   third century

The laws of a Greek city of Egypt concerning slaves in legal proceedings are in part preserved in this text. The city is not Alexandria, where procedures were different (cf. no. 104). Both Ptolemais and Naukratis have found proponents; the reference to export seems to favor the latter and is itself a significant indication of the Ptolemaic opposition to allowing the slave trade to be as extensive as the Greeks would have liked. For discussion see *P.Hal.*, pp. 109-117, and H.J. Wolff, *Die Justizwesen der Ptolemäer* (München 1962) 31-2, n. 2.

If anyone brings suit against the slave of another person because of an injury, as against a free man, and succeeds in convicting him, the master shall be allowed to appeal within 5 days from that on which the judgment is executed, and if he is worsted in his suit, the master shall pay the extra tenth or fifteenth, and the execution shall be carried out according to the laws about slaves, except where the ordinance is in effect.[340]

No one shall be allowed to sell persons for export nor to mark them nor to flog them (?)————.[341] It shall also be permitted for slaves to testify.

When slaves have given evidence the judges shall apply torture to their bodies in the presence of the parties to the suit, unless they are able to render judgment from the proof-texts submitted to them.

Summoning of slaves and execution for those convicting them. Whoever claims to be wronged by a male or female slave shall, announcing the injury to the master in the presence of not fewer than two witnesses, make a written declaration to the *nomophylakes*. He shall be forbidden————.

120. SALE OF A SLAVE-GIRL

P.Cair.Zen. I 59003[342]   259

Phoenicia was one of the chief sources of imported slaves for Greek residents of Egypt. Here Zenon purchases a young girl (who may be later attested spinning wool in the Fayum) from an agent of the powerful Toubiad chieftain of the Transjordan (cf. no. 54), who was on close terms with Apollonios.

[In the reign of] Ptolemy son of Ptolemy and of his son Ptolemy, year 27, [the priest] of Alexander and of the Brother and Sister Gods and the canephore of Arsinoe Philadelphos being those in office in Alexandria,[343] in the month Xandikos, at Birta of the Ammanitis: Nikanor son of Xenokles, Knidian, in the service of Toubias, sold to Zenon son of Agreophon, Kaunian, in the service of Apollonios the *dioiketes*, a Sidonian (?)[344] [slave girl] named Sphragis, about seven years of age, for fifty drachmas. [Guarantor...] son of Ananias, Persian, of the troop of Toubias, cleruch. Witnesses:..., judge; Polemon son of Straton, Macedonian, of the cavalrymen of Toubias, cleruch; Timopolis son of Botes, Milesian, Herakleitos son of Philippos, Athenian, Zenon son of Timarchos, Kolophonian, Demostratos son of Dionysios, Aspendian, all four in the service of Apollonios the *dioiketes*. (Docket) Deed of sale of a slave girl.

121. OFFER OF REWARD FOR ESCAPED SLAVES

UPZ I 121[345]   156

This papyrus is an offer of rewards for two slaves who escaped together, one belonging to a Carian ambassador in Alexandria, the other to an Alexandrian court official (the host of the ambassador?). The amount offered had evidently not led to the capture of the slaves, for a second hand has corrected the papyrus, raising the rewards. The organs of the state issued this proclamation and are prepared to act for the owners, an unusual occurrence in Greek legal procedure.

Year 25, Epeiph 16. A slave of Aristogenes son of Chrysippos, of Alabanda, ambassador, has escaped in Alexandria, by name Hermon also called Neilos, by birth a Syrian from Bambyke,[346] about 18 years old, of medium stature, beardless, with good legs, a dimple on the chin, a mole by the left side of the nose, a scar above the left corner of the mouth, tattooed on the right wrist with two barbaric letters.[347] He has taken with him 3 octadrachmas of coined gold, 10 pearls, an iron ring on which an oil-flask and strigils are represented, and is wearing a cloak and a loincloth. Whoever brings back this slave shall receive 3 talents of copper; but if he has pointed out in a temple, 2 talents;[348] if in the house of a substantial and actionable man, 5 talents. Whoever wishes to give information shall do so to the agents of the *strategos*.

There is also another who has escaped with him, Bion, a slave of Kallikrates, one of the chief stewards at court, short of stature, broad at the shoulders, stout-legged, bright-eyed, who has gone off with an outer garment and a slave's wrap and a woman's dress (?) worth 6 talents 5000 drachmas of copper. Whoever brings back this slave shall receive the same rewards as for the above-mentioned one. Information about this one also is to be given to the agents of the *strategos*.

122. MARRIAGE CONTRACT

P.Eleph. 1[349]   311

This is the earliest dated papyrus in Greek from Ptolemaic Egypt, coming from the years in which Ptolemy I still called himself a satrap for Alexander IV. It is the contract of marriage between two Greeks, Herakleides of Temnos and Demetria of Kos, drawn up in the traditional and purely Greek form of a marriage in which the bride is given by her parents; her father in fact is to have a say in choosing the residence of the couple. These were recent immigrants, and the developments (whether or not under Egyptian influence) that led to the centrality of the dowry and the making of provisions for voluntary divorce are yet to come.

In the reign of Alexander son of Alexander, in the seventh year, in the satrapship of Ptolemy in the fourteenth year, in the month of Daisios. Marriage contract of Herakleides and Demetria. Herakleides (the Temnitan) takes as his lawful wife Demetria the Koan, both being freeborn, from her father Leptines, Koan, and her mother Philotis, bringing clothing and ornaments to the value of 1000 drachmas, and Herakleides shall supply to Demetria all that is proper for a freeborn wife, and we shall live together wherever it seems best to Leptines and Herakleides consulting in common. If Demetria is discovered doing any evil to the shame of her husband Herakleides, she shall be deprived of all that she brought, but Herakleides shall prove whatever he alleges against Demetria before three men whom they both accept. It shall not be lawful for Herakleides to bring home another wife in insult of Demetria nor to have children by another woman nor to do evil against Demetria on any pretext. If Herakleides is discovered doing any of these things and Demetria proves it before three men whom they both accept, Herakleides shall give back to Demetria the dowry of 1000 drachmas which she brought and shall moreover forfeit 1000 drachmas of the silver coinage of Alexander. Demetria and those aiding Demetria to exact payment shall have the right of execution, as derived from a legally decided action, upon the person of Herakleides and upon all the property of Herakleides both on land and on water. This contract shall be valid in every respect, wherever Herakleides may produce it against Demetria, or Demetria and those aiding Demetria to exact payment may produce it against Herakleides, as if the agreement had been made in the place. Herakleides and Demetria shall have the right to keep the contracts severally in their own custody and to produce them against each other. Witnesses: Kleon, Gelan; Antikrates, Temnitan; Lysis, Temnitan; Dionysios, Temnitan; Aristomachos, Cyrenaean; Aristodikos, Koan.

123. REQUEST FOR A GUARDIAN

P.Enteux. 22   218

Greek women normally acted in legal transactions through *kyrioi*, guardians. These were typically male relatives or husbands, but circumstances might dispose otherwise. Here a widow, having lost not only her husband but also his son, asks for the appointment of her late husband's brother-in- law.

To King Ptolemy greeting from Nikaia daughter of Nikias, Persian. My husband Pausanias died in the 23rd year, leaving a will of the same year, of the month of Panemos [...in which] he designated ...naios his son as my guardian. It has now happened that he has died in the 4th year, in the month of Daisios which is Hathyr of the Egyptians, and I have no relative who can be registered as my [guardian. Therefore, so that] the legacy to me from my husband may not be dissipated for that reason, [since I have] no guardian with whom I can make arrangements about these things, I ask you, O king, to order Diophanes the *strategos* to give me as guardian Demetrios the Thracian, a 60-aroura holder of the troop of Ptolemaios son of Eteoneus of the...th hipparchy, to whom Pausanias married his sister, and for the *strategos* to make written records about these things, so that this may be in the official register; and since, being old and getting infirm, I am not able to make the trip to Crocodilopolis, I have sent the aforesaid Demetrios to deliver the petition, for Diophanes to write to Dioskourides the *epistates*, to make a description of me and of the guardian whom I am requesting, and to send them to Diophanes. If this is done, I shall have benefited, O king, from your kindness. Farewell. (Response) To Dioskourides. Taking some of the elders of the village go to Nikaia and if———, their descriptions, and send me a report. Year 4, Daisios 27, Hathyr 29. (Docket) Year 4, Daisios 27, Hathyr 29. Nikaia, daughter of Nikias, Persian, about a request.

124. WILL

P.Eleph. 2³⁵⁰   284

This will was made by two Temnitans living in Elephantine; the man was a witness in no. 122 (311 B.C.), and by 284 their children were clearly of adult age. Like the marriage contract, this document from the first generation of Greek settlers in Egypt is purely Greek in character, particularly in the strong provisions about the support of the parents by the children (cf. no. 126).

In the reign of Ptolemy, year 40, in the month of Gorpiaios, in the priesthood of Menelaos son of Lagos. Contract and agreement. Dionysios,

Temnitan, has made this testamentary pact with his wife Kallista, Temnitan. Should anything happen to Dionysios, he shall leave all his property to Kallista and she shall be owner of all the property so long as she lives. Should anything happen to Kallista while Dionysios is alive, Dionysios shall be owner of the property; and should anything happen to Dionysios, he shall leave the property to all his sons. In like manner Kallista, should anything happen to her, shall leave the property to all the sons, except the portions which Bacchios, Herakleides, and Metrodoros may receive from Dionysios and Kallista for their labors in the lifetime of their father and mother; but if Bacchios, Herakleides and Metrodoros are married and settled, the property of Dionysios and Kallista shall be shared in common by all the sons. If in their lifetime Dionysios or Kallista is in need or in debt, all the sons in common shall support them and contribute to pay their debts. If any one of them refuses to support them or contribute or does not help to bury them, he shall forfeit a thousand drachmas of silver and there shall be right of execution on him who is insubordinate and does not act in the manner stated. If Dionysios or Kallista leaves any debt, it shall be permissible for their sons not to take up the inheritance if they do not wish to after the death of Dionysios and Kallista. This document shall be valid in every respect wherever it is produced, as if the compact had been made there. They have of their own free will placed the contract in the keeping of Herakleitos. Witnesses: Polykrates, Arcadian; Androsthenes, Koan; Noumenios, Cretan; Simonides, Maroneian; Lysis and Herakleitos, Temnitans.

125. PREPARATIONS FOR A FESTIVAL

P.Hib. I 54   ca. 245

A letter of miscellaneous requests, mostly not apparently on official business, from an official to a subordinate. Prominent are the provisions for food and entertainment for a festival.

Demophon to Ptolemaios, greeting. Make every effort to send me the fluteplayer Petoüs with both the Phrygian flutes and the rest; and if any expense is necessary, pay it and you shall recover it from me. Send me also Zenobias the effeminate with a drum and cymbals and castanets, for he is wanted by the women for the sacrifice; and let him wear as fine clothes as possible. Get the kid also from Aristion and send it to me; and if you have arrested the slave, deliver him to Semphtheus to bring to me. Send me as many cheeses as you can, a new jar, vegetables of all kinds, and some delicacies if you have any. Farewell. Put them on board with the guards who will assist in bring the boat. (Address) To Ptolemaios.

202

126. UNGRATEFUL DAUGHTER

P.Enteux. 26[351]   221

In both Egyptian and Greek laws there were obligations of support for aged parents laid on children who had been properly raised and educated; the wronged father here stresses that he had brought his daughter up properly.

To King Ptolemy greeting from Ktesikles. I am wronged by Dionysios and by Nike my daughter. For though I raised her, my own daughter, and educated her and brought her to maturity, when I was stricken with bodily ill-health and was losing my eyesight, she was not minded to furnish me with any of the necessities of life. When I sought to obtain justice from her in Alexandria, she begged my pardon, and in the 18th year she swore me a written royal oath in the temple of Arsinoe Aktia[352] to give me each month twenty drachmas, which she was to earn by her own bodily labor. If she did not do this or transgressed any part of the provisions of the written oath she was to pay me 500 dr. or to be liable for the consequences of the oath. [But now seduced by] Dionysios, who is a *kinaidos*[353] she does not do for me anything of what was in the written oath, despising [my weakness and] ill-health. I beg [you], therefore, O king, not to allow me to be wronged by my daughter and by Dionysios the *kinaidos* who seduced her, but to order Diophanes the *strategos* to summon them and hear us out [and if I am speaking the truth (?)] for Diophanes to treat her seducer as [seems best to him, but] to compel [Nike] my daughter to do justice to me...[If this] is done I shall no longer be wronged but by fleeing to you, O king, [I shall obtain justice. Farewell]. (Note) Euphor...has been sent————. (Docket) Year 1, Gorpiaios 30, Tybi 13. Ktesikles vs. Dionysios and Nike his daughter about a written oath.

IX
RELIGION

A. Greek Sanctuaries and Cities

127. MAGNESIA-ON-THE-MAEANDER AND ARTEMIS LEUKOPHRYENE

*Syll.*³ 557   after 208/7

In 221/0 Artemis Leukophryene appeared at Magnesia-on-the-Maeander. The Magnesians consulted the oracle of Apollo at Delphi and, following what they took to be his advice, began to institute crowned games for those dwelling in Asia in the goddess' honor. The proclamation, including a request to recognize Magnesia itself as sacred and inviolable, was apparently sent out and universally (or at least widely) disregarded. In 208/7 they renewed the attempt and this time met with success. Numerous replies were received from the Greek cities and leagues (see no. 128 for those from the kings) accepting the games and recognizing the city as sacred and inviolable. The present text is what remains of the city's history of the venture, inscribed sometime after the events themselves (the specification of the men's *pankration*, if the restoration is correct, means a date of 200 or after, as the boys' *pankration* was instituted in that year).

———(line 4) the god, by which things they will keep the city sacred. When Artemis Le[ukophryene, after her] brother,³⁵⁴ appeared to [the priestess] Aristo, he gave the following response to [their] inquiry: that it would be more propitious and better for those who revere [Pythian] Apollo and Artemis Leukophryene and who recognize the [city and the] land of the Magnesians on the Maeander as [sacred and inviolable].

When [Artemis] appeared, accepting the oracle in the stephanephorate of Zenodotos — in the archonship of Thrasyph[on] at Athens, when [. . .] the Boeotian was the victorious lyrist [at the Pythian games] in the previous year, and when Hagesidemos the Messenian was victorious, in the following year, in the [men's] *pankration* at the Olympic games in the [one hundred] and fortieth Olympiad³⁵⁵ — they first [set about establishing crowned] games for the inhabitants of Asia, taking this to be the sense of the oracle: [that] they would thus honor Artemis Leukophryene, being otherwise piously disposed [toward] the divine, if, [coming] to the [holy] altar, [they brought] welcome gifts to the mistress, inasmuch as the other games were originally established with money as the prize but later became crowned because of oracles. But after they were disregarded in this undertaking, in the stephanephorate of Moiragoras, who is the four[teenth] from Zenodotos — in whose time they received the oracle — calling to mind ancestral ways (?), they pointed out to others also [their experience]. In the stephanephorate of Moiragoras son of Stephanos, they gave a crown of Pythian rank made from fifty gold pieces, and when the kings accepted[356] and when [all] the other [Greeks] to whom they sent envoys by leagues and by cities [agreed] to honor Artemis Leukophryene and to [recognize as inviolable] the city and land of the Magnesians, on account of the bidding [of the god] and the [friendships and] relationships obtaining from ancestral times between them all and the Magnesians———.

128. ROYAL LETTERS TO MAGNESIA-ON-THE-MAEANDER

RC 31-34 ca. 205

Among the responses to the Magnesian proclamation were letters from Antiochus III, his son Antiochus, Ptolemy IV, and Attalus I of Pergamon. All welcome the provisions about the games, but Attalus and the Seleucids say nothing about recognizing the city as inviolable. Nor, it seems, did Philip V of Macedon (his letter is lost, but the response of Chalkis, which he directed, is silent on the issue). Ptolemy, then, is alone among the kings in acceding to this element of the Magnesians' request, and he, unlike the other rulers, had no territorial interest in the area (cf. *RC*, p. 147).

31

King Antiochus to the *boule* and the *demos* of the Magnesians, greeting. Demophon and Philiskos and Pheres, the *theoroi* sent by you to us to proclaim the games and the other things which the *demos* has voted to perform for the mistress of the city Artemis Leukophryene, met (with us) in Antioch in Persis, and delivered your decree and themselves spoke with enthusiasm in accordance with what was set out in the decree, calling upon (us) to recognize as crowned (and) of Pythian rank the games which you hold in honor of the goddess every four years. Since we have had from the beginning the kindliest feeling for the *demos* because of the good-will which you have shown on all occasions to us and to our state, and since we are anxious to make clear our policy, we give our approval of the honors decreed for the goddess and we propose to aid in furthering them in whatever (ways) you may call upon us or we ourselves think of. We have written also to those in positions of authority so that the cities may also give their approval accordingly. Farewell.

32

King Antiochus to the *boule* and the *demos* of the Magnesians, greeting. Demophon and Philiskos and Pheres, the *theoroi* sent by you to my father to proclaim the games and the other things which the *demos* has voted to perform every four years for the mistress of the city Artemis Leukophryene, delivered the decree addressed to me and spoke with enthusiasm in accordance with what was set out in it, calling upon (me) to recognize as crowned (and) of Pythian rank the games which you hold in honor of the goddess. Since my father has the kindliest feeling toward the *demos* and has approved these things, being anxious myself to follow his policy, I now approve the honors decreed by you for the goddess and [in the future] shall try, following my father's example, to aid you in furthering them [in whatever (ways)] you may call upon (me) or I myself think of. Farewell.

33

King [Ptole]my to the *boule* and the *demos* of the Magnesians, greeting. [The] envoys sent out by you, Diopeithes [. . .] and Ithalides [. . .] delivered [to me] the decree in which [. . .] games of the [Leukophryena which] you celebrate in accordance with the oracle [of the god] in honor of Artemis Leukophryene, [and] about considering [the city and its land] as sacred and [inviolable]; I also [was called upon (?)] to recognize [the games] as crowned (and) of Pythian rank [in honors] as you have proclaimed them to us. [Those] sent [by you] themselves spoke with all zeal [also in accordance with] the other things in [the decree about which they had] instructions. [I have, therefore], recognized as crowned [the games], as you requested, [and———].

34

King Attalus to the *boule* and the *demos* of the [Ma]gnesians, greeting. Pythion and Lykomedes who (came) from you brought to me a decree in accordance with which you call upon me to recognize as crowned (and) of Pythian rank the musical and equestrian and gymnastic games which you celebrate in honor of Artemis Leukophryene; and they spoke themselves according to what was written (in the decree); and they asked that the cities subject to me also grant their approval in the same manner. Seeing that the *demos* is mindful of the favors conferred upon it [by] me, and zealous in the service of the Muses, I recognize the games as you request, and I have ordered a contribution to be made (toward them), and the cities which [obey] me will do likewise, for [I have written] calling upon them (to do so). And [———], as the *demos* [asks], I shall aid in furthering the games [———].

129. LETTER OF KINGS THEODOROS AND AMYNANDER TO TEOS

RC 35   205-201

Near the end of the third century the Teans sought recognition of their city as sacred to Dionysos and thus inviolable and as free from the imposition of tax or tribute. They were widely successful, at least over a period of time (cf. no. 37 for the granting of the request by Rome). The position of Teos on the coast made it par-

210

ticularly vulnerable to pirates, and the Teans were especially anxious for favorable replies from such as the Aetolians (which they received) and the rulers of Athamania.

(From the) Athamanians. King Theodoros[357] and Amynander to the *boule* and the *demos* of the Teans, greeting. Pythagoras and Kleitos, the envoys sent out by you, have both delivered the decree [and themselves] spoken [to us] about its being granted on our part that (the) city and the land be sacred to Dionysos and inviolable and free from tribute; having heard them through with favor we accede to all your requests and consent that your city and the land be sacred and inviolable and free from tribute. This we do both because of our being in fact related to all the Greeks, since there exists a kinship between us and the original himself of the common appellation of the Greeks[358] and also, to no slight extent, because of our having a very friendly feeling toward your city, and still further because we are at the same time about to confer a favor on you who have asked it and, as we think, gain the favor of the god————.

130. ACCOUNTS AND INVENTORIES OF THE TEMPLE OF APOLLO ON DELOS

I.Délos 442   179

The temple of Apollo on Delos was one of the greatest of the panhellenic shrines, and as such it was the recipient of dedications made by kings, cities, commanders, and private individuals from all over the Mediterranean world. It was at the same time an active financial center. Loans at interest (generally 10%) were regularly made from the great wealth of the sanctuary, houses and agricultural land owned by the temple (these often representing property confiscated from religious offenders) were rented out, and the temple itself housed not only the treasure chest of the god but the public chest of the city of Delos as well. The annually appointed officials of the sanctuary, the *hieropoioi*, supervised both the more standard operations of the sanctuary (e.g., sacrifices) and were responsible besides for the accumulated dedications and the various financial transactions. Each year they published their accounts on stone. These contained the records of income and expenditure, first for the god's chest and then for the public chest, and complete inventories of the dedications located in all the temples of the sanctuary. The accounts for 179 are among the best preserved and begin with the statement "Gods. [Account] of the *hieropoioi* who held that office for the year of the archonship of Demares, Amphoteros son of Aristeas (and) Polyxenos son of Parmenion (and) Silenos son of Silenos (and) Philippos son of Akesimbrotos." The selections presented here are as follows. A: the list of the jars of money deposited in the sacred chest during the year (*I. Délos* 442A.38-55; this follows the list of what these *hieropoioi* took over from their predecessors); B: list of monies expended from the sacred chest (442A.55-75; this is followed by the analogous accounting for the public chest); C: from the inventory of dedications in the temple of Apollo (442 B.1-17); D: additions to the lists of monies received (442C — these represent late payments); E: final additions to the list of outstanding debts (442D).

A

The following money also was deposited in the sacred chest during our tenure of office: a jar, on which the inscription "from the (bank) of Philon and Silenos, in (the archonship) of Demares, (the month) Aresion, the *hieropoioi* Polyxenos, Philippos, Amphoteros, Silenos deposited the capital of the loan which Hermon son of Solon paid back, 605 drs. 1½ ob., and the interest he said he owed, 242 drs. 1 ob."; another jar, with the inscription "from the (bank) of Philon and Silenos, in (the archonship) of Demares, (the month) Apatourion, the *hieropoioi* in the archonship of Phokaieus, Krittis, Nikarchos, Synonymos, Hierombrotos deposited in the temple the surplus from the account, 220 drs. 4¼ ob."; another jar, (with the inscription) "from the (bank) of Hellen and Mantineus, in (the archonship) of Demares, (the month) Posideon, the treasurers[359] Menyllos and Phokaieus deposited in the temple, in accordance with the budget, 1000 drs. toward repayment of the city's outstanding loans from the god, and 1350 drs. toward repayment of the amount advanced for the crown for King Philip[360] and King Massinissa[361] and toward the amount still owing on the crowns in the archonship of Telesarchides"; another jar, (with the inscription) "from the (bank) of Philon and Silenos, in (the archonship) of Demares, (the month) Posideon, the treasurers Menyllos and Phokaieus deposited 1303 drs. 3⁷⁄₁₂ ob., proceeds of the market place rents"; another jar, (with the inscription) "from'the (bank) of Philon and Silenos, in (the archonship) of Demares, (the month) Posideon, the treasurers Menyllos and Phokaieus deposited 40 drs., from the tax on boundary markers"; another jar, (with the inscription) "from the bank of Philon and Silenos, in (the archonship) of Demares, (the month) Posideon, the treasurers Menyllos and Phokaieus deposited 486 drs. 4 ob., the choregic fund"; another jar, (with the inscription "from the (bank) of Philon and Silenos, in (the archonship) of Demares, (the month) Posideon, the treasurers Menyllos and Phokaieus deposited 200 drs., from the tax on banks"; another jar, with the inscription "from the (bank) of Nymphodoros and Herakleides in (the archonship) of Demares, (the month) Posideon, the *hieropoioi* in the archonship of Telesarchides, Euboeus and Parmenion, deposited 6998 drs. 4¹¹⁄₁₂ ob., the proceeds from farm rents, house rents, taxes, and interest"; another jar with the inscription "from the (bank) of Philon and Silenus, in (the archonship) of Demares, (the month) Posideon, the *hieropoioi* in the archonship of Telesarchides, Euboeus and Parmenion, deposited in the temple the remaining sum which according to the stele they collected from farm-rents, house rents, taxes and interest, 1600 drs."; another jar, with the inscription "from (the bank) of Nymphodoros and Herakleides, in (the archonship) of Demares, (the month) Posideon, the *hieropoioi* Polyxenos, Silenos, Amphoteros, Philippos deposited 500 drs., the capital of the loan which

Paches paid back on behalf of his father Diogenes and which the latter had borrowed from the *hieropoioi* Euboeus and Parmenion, and 60 drs., the interest he paid, saying that he owed it, for one year and two months"; another jar, with the inscription "in (the archonship) of Demares, (the month) Posideon, Menyllos and Phokaieus deposited in the temple 15 drs. 1 ob., the surplus from the (amount allocated for the Dionysiac) artists". Total of what was deposited during our tenure of office: 14,623 drs., 1¼ ob. Total of what was handed over to us and deposited during our tenure of office, 75,553 drs. ¼₂ ob. And (total) of the copper handed over to us by the treasurers Menyllos and Phokaieus, 3733 drs. 2 ob.

B

In the holy month we withdrew for (expenditure on) works, in the presence of the archon of the city and the secretaries and the monthly *prytaneis*, (the following): a jar, with the inscription "from the (bank) of Nymphodoros and Herakleides, in (the archonship) of Telesarchides, (the month) Posideon, the *hieropoioi* Euboeus and Parmenion deposited, in accordance with the decree of the *demos*, the capital of the loan which Ostakos son of Ktesikles paid back, 500 drs., and the interest he said was outstanding, 20 drs. 5 ob., and the capital of the loan which Boethos son of Orthokles paid back, 500 drs., and the interest he said was outstanding, 20 drs. 5 ob., and the capital of the loan which Kaibon son of Kaibon paid back, 500 drs., and the interest he said was outstanding, 20 drs. 5 ob., and the capital of the loan which Theodoros son of Sosibios paid back, 500 drs., and the interest he said was outstanding, 20 drs. 5 ob." — the whole amount, 2083 drs. 2 ob.

On the twentieth of the month Galaxion we withdrew from a jar with the inscription "from the (bank) of Nymphodoros and Herakleides, the *hieropoioi* in the archonship of Apatourios, Praximenes and Telesarchides, deposited the surplus referred to in the stele, 4349 drs. 2 ob.": from this we withdrew 1350 drs. for the crown for King Philip; the remainder in (the jar) is 2999 drs. 2 ob.; from this we withdrew for works on the fifth of the month Thargelion 2000 drs.; the remainder in the jar is 999 drs. 2 ob. And the following money also we withdrew for works in the month Bouphonion: a jar with the inscription "from the (bank) of Philon and Silenos, in (the archonship) of Phokaieus, (the month) Posideon, the treasurers Kaibon and Mnesikleides deposited in the temple in repayment to the god of what the city borrowed for the crown for King Philip and that for King Eumenes[362] and the one (sent) to Rhodes, 1300 drs." In the month Posideon we withdrew from a jar with the inscription "from the (bank) of Hellen and Mantineus, in (the archonship) of Demares, (the month) Posideon, the treasurers Menyllos and Phokaieus deposited in the temple, in accordance with the budget, 1000 drs. toward repayment of the city's outstanding loans from the god, and 1350 drs. toward repayment of the amount advanced for the crown for King Philip and King Massinissa and toward the amount still owing on the crowns in the archonship of Telesarchides"; from this we, the *hieropoioi* in the archonship of Demares, withdrew 2200 drs. for work on the temple of Artemis, according to the decree of the *demos*; the remainder in the jar is 150 drs. In the month Posideon we withdrew from a jar with the inscription "from the (bank) of Nymphodoros and Herakleides, in (the archonship) of Demares, (the month) Posideon, the *hieropoioi* in the archonship of Telesarchides, Euboeus and Parmenion, deposited 6998 drs. $4^{11}/_{12}$ ob., the proceeds from farm-rents, house-rents, taxes, and interest": from this we the *hieropoioi*, Polyxenos, Amphoteros, Philippos, Silenos withdrew for works in the month Posideon 1120 drs. (4 ob.); the remainder in the jar is 5878 drs. $^1/_{12}$ ob. In the month Posideon we withdrew 500 drs. for the loan to Euboeus, according to the decree of the *demos*, from a jar with the inscription "from the (bank) of Philon and Silenos, in (the archonship) of Demares, (the month) Aresion, the *hieropoioi* Polyxenos, Philippos, Silenos, Amphoteros deposited the capital of the loan which Hermon son of Solon paid back, 605 drs. 1½ ob., and the interest he said he owed, 242 drs. 1 ob."; the remainder in the jar is 347 drs. 2½ ob. Total of what was withdrawn during our tenure of office: 11,553 drs., (2) ob. The rest we turned over to the *hieropoioi* after ourselves, Demetrios and Meilichides, 63,999 drs. 4½ ob. We turned over also to the *hieropoioi* after ourselves the copper which we received from the treasurers Menyllos and Phokaieus, 3733 drs. 2 ob.

C

We received the following items in the temple of Apollo from the *hieropoioi* Krittis son of Nikarchos (and) Synonymos of Hierombrotos, in the presence of the *boule* and the secretary of the city Poseidikos son of Soteles, and the (secretary) of the *hieropoioi* Neokrontides son of Neokrontides, and we turned (these items) over to the *hieropoioi* after ourselves, Demetrios son of Timoxenos (and) Meilichides son of Kritoboulos, in the presence of the *boule* and the secretary of the city Telemnestos son of Antigonos, and the (secretary) of the *hieropoioi* Timoxenos son of Timoxenos: a gold signet, with an image of Apollo in carnelian, which Stratonike[363] dedicated to Leto: weight 10 drs.; a gold necklace set with precious stones, which Stratonike dedicated to Leto, comprising 48 shield-shaped disks, and one (such disk) in two halves, and (two more,) one on either side of the central piece, and 141 pendants: weight 106 drs.; a gold signet, which Stratonike dedicated to Apollo (and) Artemis, with an image of Nike; weight with the ring, 36 drs. 4 ob.; 3 miniature gold crowns, which Stratonike dedicated to the Graces, one without rings or fastenings, in pieces: weight 60 drs. 3 ob.; a gold ingot from the statue of Apollo: weight 98 drs. 3 ob.; another gold ingot from (the statues of) the three (Graces): weight 27 drs. 3 ob.; 3 gold coins of Philip; 1 of Alexander; coin from various places: weight 68 drs.; a gold drinking cup, dedication of Echenike:[364] weight 49 drs. 3 ob.; a gold crown of oak leaves, dedication of Lysander:[365] weight 63 drs. 3 ob.; a gold crown of ivy leaves, dedication of King Ptolemy,[366] in pieces, and five clusters: weight 107 drs.; a gold crown of bay leaves, dedication of King Demetrius:[367] weight 71 drs. 3 ob.; a gold crown of bay leaves, dedication of Polykleitos:[368] weight 65 drs. 3 ob.; a gold crown of bay leaves, dedication

214

of Philokles:[369] weight 77 drs. 3 ob.; a gold crown of ivy leaves, dedication of the Delians, three broken clusters: weight 76 drs.; a gold crown of myrtle, dedicaton of Iomilkos:[370] weight 21 drs. 3 ob.; a gold crown of bay leaves, dedication of King Antigonus: weight 26 drs.; golden snakeweed, dedication of Solon to Asklepios: weight 88 drs.; a gold crown of bay leaves, dedication of King Antigonus; a gold crown of bay leaves, dedication of Antipatros: weight 39 drs. 3 ob.; a gold crown of bay leaves, uninscribed: weight 37 drs.; a gold crown of bay leaves, dedication of Pharax: weight 43 drs.; a gold crown of bay leaves, dedication of Pnytagoras:[371] weight 62 drs.; a new gold crown of bay leaves: weight 61 drs.; a gold ball in a case, dedication of Phila[372] daughter of Theodoros: weight 58 drs.; a gold crown of myrtle, dedication of Xenophantos:[373] weight 48 drs. 3 ob.; 2 tetradrachmas; one part-copper coin of Lysimachus; one coin of Antiochus; a drachma of Alexander; 18 silver signets and a small cup and handle, two with stones, one of iron: weight 34 drs.; 11 gilt iron signets; a partly copper tetradrachm of Lysimachus; 5 *phialai* removed from cases: one a dedication of the Deliades, presented by the *theoroi* and the *architheoros* Kleanax: another a dedication of the Pontic Chersonnetai, another a dedication of the Pontic Chersonnetai, another a dedication of Bacchios of Kolophon, another a dedication of the Pontic Chersonnetai — weight 480 drs.; 7 gold distaffs: weight 12 drs.; a tetradrachm of Lysimachus. (The inventory of the temple of Apollo continues for another 150 lines.)

D

From Charistias son of Antigonos (?), on behalf of his grandfather Nikomachos, the interest on the sacred money which he said his grandfather Nikomachos owed, on the loan he received from the *hieropoioi* Praximenes and Telesarchides, for the year of Demares, 100 drs.; and on behalf of Euthytime daughter of Diodotos, the interest he said he owed on the sacred money for the year of Demares, 39 drs. 1½ ob. From Aristoboulos son of Aristoboulos, on behalf of Orthokles son of Orthokles, the interest, arising from the guarantee made for the sacred money, which he said was his share, 80 drs. From Tlepolemos son of Amnes, the interest he said he owed on the sacred money, 101 drs. 3 ob. From Demochares son of Sotion, on behalf of Antichares son of Authosthenes, the amount (for which) he said his name had been entered by the *hieropoioi* in the archonship of Ariston for the cargo-discharge tax. . . From Diaktorides son of Aristotheos, the interest he said he owed on the sacred money, 11 drs. 4 ob. From Glaukyrios son of Tharsagoras, on behalf of Ktesylis, the interest for the year of Demares, arising from the guarantee made for the sacred money, which he said Ktesylis owed, 9 drs. From Demokritos son of Parmenion, the amount (for which) he said the *hieropoioi* Kineas and Kallias entered his name for interest at one-sixth, 50 drs. From Phokaieus son of Leukinos, on behalf of his mother Aristako, the interest on the sacred money owing in the archonship of Demares———.

E
We enter (the names of these debtors) also: Euphranor and his guarantor Aristeides son of Aristeides, (for) the amount he did not pay for rent on the sacred 'Episthenes' house,...and 24 drs. 2/3 ob.; and Dionysodoros son of Marathonios and his guarantor Demeas son of Phokritos, (for) the amount he did not pay for the ferry-toll to Rheneia, 62 drs.; and Antigonos son of Charistias, (for) the amount he did not pay for the harbor-tax, 19 drs.; and Orthokles son of Orthokles, for interest on the sacred money, one half the principal sum, 80 drs. If we have not entered any who are in debt to the god, we enter them and their guarantors as being in debt to the god.

131. ESTABLISHMENT OF A ROYAL CULT OF LAODIKE, WIFE OF ANTIOCHUS III

RC 36-37 (*OGIS* 224)   193

In the Seleucid kingdom, queens were not as a matter of course included in the royal cult. In 193 Antiochus III set about establishing the official worship throughout his realm of his wife Laodike (although styled "sister" she was in fact his cousin, a daughter of Mithridates of Pontus). This required the establishment of a chief-priestess of the queen in all the satrapies, and indeed the king's letter was sent, with the insertion of the names, to all the governors. The letter here is addressed to the *strategos* of the Carian satrapy, but others have been found elsewhere; one from Nehavend in Iran, indeed, finally settled the question of the date (L.Robert, *Hellenica* 7 [1949] 5 ff.). It is preceded by a covering letter from the governor to the hyparch of the district around Eriza, where the stone was found.

37
[Anaxim]brotos to Dionytas, greeting. Enclosed is the copy of the decree written by the king concerning the appointment of Berenike, the daughter of Ptolemy son of Lysimachus,[374] as chief-priestess of the queen in the satrapy. Carry out (the matter) according to the instructions, just as he enjoins, and see to it that copies, inscribed on a stone stele, are set up in the most conspicuous place. Farewell. Year 119, Artemisios 19.[375]
36
King Antiochus to Anaximbrotos, greeting. As we desire to increase still further the honors of our sister Queen Laodike, and as we think this most important for ourselves because she not only lives with us lovingly and considerately but is also reverently disposed toward the divine, we continue to do lovingly the things which it is fitting and right for her to receive from us and we have decided that just as there are appointed throughout the kingdom chief-priests of us, (so) there are to be established [in] the same districts chief-priestesses of her also, who shall wear golden crowns bearing her [images] and who shall be mentioned in [the] contracts after the chief-

priests of our [ancestors] and of us. Since, therefore, in the districts under your administration Berenike, the daughter of our relative Ptolemy son of Lysimachus, has been appointed, carry everything out according to what has been written above and have copies of the letters, inscribed on stelae, set up in the most conspicuous places, so that both now and in the future there may be evident to all in these matters also our policy toward our sister.

132. ANTIOCHUS III APPOINTS A CHIEF-PRIEST AT DAPHNE

RC 44 (*OGIS* 244)   189

Faithful supporters of a dynasty might be rewarded with land (cf. no. 18), or with comfortable positions. The man whom Antiochus here appoints to supervise the sanctuaries at Daphne had been high in the service of the Seleucids for thirty-five years or more, and it is clear that his new occupation would indeed allow him to live in the quiet he so earnestly requested. This letter was written something less than a year after Antiochus was defeated by the Romans at Magnesia.

————, as he had been in honor and trust with our brother [376] [and] has zealously given many great demonstrations of his attitude toward us and our state, and as he has spared neither his life nor his property in what is beneficial to us, but has performed everything entrusted to him as was fitting and in general conducts himself consistently with his past services in behalf of our state, we wished to keep him still associated with us in our affairs. He often, however, called our attention to the bodily infirmity which had come to him from the incessant hardship, and asked us to allow him to live in quiet in order that he might spend the remaining time of his life without distraction in good bodily health; we have accordingly yielded, wishing to make clear in these matters also the attitude we have toward him. We shall take care that in the future he will receive all that pertains to honor and glory, for as the chief-priesthood of Apollo and Artemis Daittai and of the other sanctuaries whose precincts are at Daphne requires a man who is a friend and competent to fill it in a manner worthy of the interest both our ancestors and ourselves have had in the place[377] and of our reverence toward the divine, we have appointed him chief-priest of these (sanctuaries) in the conviction that the administration of the sanctuaries will be carried on by him as is necessary. Give orders to include him as chief-priest of the specified sanctuaries in legal documents and to honor the man in a manner worthy of our decision; and if he calls upon (anyone) to perform any of the regular duties in these connections, (for all) to assist him, both those who may be connected with the sanctuaries and all others for whom it is proper to obey him — make clear that (we) have given orders to obey him in all matters about which he may write or issue orders. (Give orders) also for the copy of the letter to be inscribed on stelae and set up in the most conspicuous places. Year 124, Dios 14.[378]

B. CULTS IN PTOLEMAIC EGYPT

133. DECREE ABOUT THE DIONYSIAC ARTISTS

BGU VI 1211[379]   ca. 215-205[380]

Ptolemy IV is known to have been particularly interested in the cult of Dionysos. Here he orders all of the *technitai* of Dionysos in Egypt to register in Alexandria, to make known the source of their training, and to submit their copies of the book concerning these mysteries. The purpose of this royal decree is much debated,[381] but it is likely that the desire to exercise control over the activities of this group of performers was predominant.

By decree of the king. Persons who perform the rite of Dionysos in the country shall sail down within 10 days from the day on which the decree is published and those beyond Naukratis within 20 days, and shall register themselves before Aristoboulos at the registration-office within three days from the day on which they arrive, and shall declare forthwith from what persons they have received the transmission of the sacred rites for three generations back and shall hand in the sacred book sealed up, each inscribing thereon his own name.

134. THE *SYNODOS* OF ZEUS HYPSISTOS[382]

SB V 7835   ca. 69-58

This papyrus contains the regulations of an organization calling itself the *Synodos* of Zeus the Highest, made up probably of residents of Philadelphia in the reign of Ptolemy XII Auletes. What we have is probably a somewhat abridged member's copy of the general statutes. The organization was constituted for a year only, and if it was to continue after that a reenactment of the act of incorporation was necessary each year. The members meet in a public temple of Zeus for their banquets, at which they are to offer sacrifices for the king; despite the name of the union, no mention is made of any devotion to Zeus, who merely supplies the meeting place. The features of the organization, including the fact that the only officers are the president (elected for the year) and his assistant, are derived from Egyptian models,[383] although the members of this organization may have been, as the language of the document would suggest, Greek. There is an extensive commentary in the original publication by C.H. Roberts, T.C. Skeat and A.D. Nock in *Harvard Theological Review* 29 (1936) 39-88.

May it be well. The law which those of the association of Zeus the highest made in common, that it should be authoritative. Acting in accordance with its provisions, they first chose as their president Petesouchos the son of Teephbennis, a man of parts, worthy of the place and of the company, for a year from the month and day aforesaid, that he should make for all the contributors one banquet a month in the sanctuary of Zeus, at which they

222

should in a common room pouring libations, pray, and perform the other customary rites on behalf of the god and lord, the king. All are to obey the president and his servant in matters pertaining to the corporation, and they shall be present at all command occasions to be prescribed for them and at meetings and assemblies and outings. It shall not be permissible for any one of them to... or to make factions or to leave the brotherhood of the president for another, or for men to enter into one another's pedigrees at the banquet or to abuse one another at the banquet or to chatter or to indict or to accuse another or to resign for the course of the year or again to bring the drinkings to nought or... to hinder the (leader?)———contributions and other (?) levies and shall each pay... If any of them becomes a father, he shall contribute (?)———.

135. RELEASE ON THE KING'S BIRTHDAY

PSI IV 347   254

The birthday of the king (Dystros 24 in this reign) was apparently no more than a few weeks off when this letter was written, seeking to persuade Apollonios (and Zenon) that the king's birthday was an auspicious time to pardon Epharmostos,[384] whose crimes are unknown.

Epharmostos to Zenon, greeting. I have appended copies of the letter written by me to Apollonios; for I thought it proper to write also to him myself. Please show zeal both for my sake and your own that taking your opportunity on the king's birthday you may petition him with the rest on my behalf. Farewell. Year 31, Phamenoth...
To Apollonios. Please look into my case; for it has now been a year already since I had the misfortune to be handed over to be imprisoned. And the occasion itself affords the chance of an inquiry even on my behalf on the king's birthday. Farewell.

136. THE CANOPUS DECREE

OGIS 56   238

This trilingual inscription (Greek, Egyptian hieroglyphs, Egyptian Demotic), which survives in three variously preserved copies, contains a set of resolutions passed by an assembly of Egyptian priests meeting at Canopus (just to the northeast of Alexandria). It gives indication above all of the care taken by the third Ptolemy in conciliating the native population by way of the Egyptian priesthood. It is not certain whether the document was originally drafted in Greek and then translated into Egyptian or *vice-versa*, but it is clear that there is much less by way of Egyptian influence here (most notably in the titulature) than in the inscription of the Rosetta Stone some forty years later (no. 137).

In the ninth year of the reign of Ptolemy, son of Ptolemy and Arsinoe the Brother-and-Sister Gods, the priest of Alexander and the Brother-and-Sister Gods and the Benefactor Gods[385] being Apollonidas son of Moschion and the canephore[386] of Arsinoe Philadelphos being Menekrateia daughter of Philammon, on the seventh of the month Apellaios, the seventeenth of the Egyptians' (month) Tybi:[387] decree: the chief-priests and the prophets[388] and those who enter the shrine for the adorning of the gods and the feather-bearers and the sacred scribes and the other priests who come together from the temples in the country for the fifth of (the month) Dios, on which day is celebrated the birthday of the king, and for the 25th of the same month, on which day he received the kingdom from his father, (all these) having assembled together on this day in the temple of the Benefactor Gods in Canopus spoke:[389] Whereas King Ptolemy, son of Ptolemy and Arsinoe the Brother-and-Sister Gods, and Queen Berenike, his sister and wife, the Benefactor Gods, continually bestow many and great benefactions on the temples in the country and increase ever more the honors of the gods, and in all respects they exercise concern, with great expense and abundance, for Apis and for Mnevis[390] and for the other renowned sacred beasts of the country; and the king marched out and brought back safe to Egypt the sacred images, which had been carried out from the country by the Persians, and returned them to the temples whence each had originally been taken away;[391] and he has maintained the country in a state of peace, fighting wars on its behalf against many peoples and those who rule among them; and they provide law and order for all those in the country and for the others who are ranged under their rule; and when the river once over-flowed its banks insufficiently and all those in the country were terrified at this happening and were thinking upon the destruction that had taken place under some of the former kings, in whose reign those dwelling in the country met with droughts, exercising provident care over those in the temples and the others inhabiting the country, by exercising much forethought and forgoing not a little of their revenues for the sake of the safety of the people, and by sending for grain for the country from Syria and Phoenicia and Cyprus and many other places at rather high prices they saved the inhabitants of Egypt, leaving behind an immortal benefaction and the greatest record of their virtue both for contemporaries and for future generations; in return for which the gods have granted them their kingdom peacefully established and will give them all the other good things for all time; with good fortune, be it resolved by the priests of the country: To increase the already existing honors (paid) in the temples to King Ptolemy and Queen Berenike, the Benefactor Gods, and to their parents the Brother-and-Sister Gods, and to their grandparents the Savior Gods;[392] and for the priests in each of the temples of the country to be designated also "priests of the Benefactor Gods," and for the priesthood of the Benefactor Gods also to be written into all their documents and for it to be engraved in addition on the rings which they wear; and for there to be constituted, in addition to the now existing four tribes of the group of priests in each temple, also another (tribe), which shall be designated the fifth tribe of the Benefactor Gods, since it has happened with good fortune that the birth of King Ptolemy, son of the Brother-and-Sister Gods, also occurred on the fifth of (the month) Dios, which has also been the beginning of many good things for all men; for there to be enrolled in this tribe those who have become priests since the first year and those who are to be assigned until the month Mesore of the ninth year and their descendants for all time, but for those who were already priests prior to the first year to remain in the same tribes in which they previously were and similarly for their descendants henceforth to be enrolled in the same tribes in which their fathers are; instead of the twenty councillor priests chosen each year from the pre-existing four tribes, of whom five are taken from each tribe, for the councillor priests to be twenty-five, another five being added from the fifth tribe of the Benefactor Gods; and for those of the fifth tribe of the Benefactor Gods also to share in the ceremonies and everything else of those in the temples, and for there to be a phylarch of this (tribe), just as is the case also for the other four tribes. And whereas feasts of the Benefactor Gods are celebrated each month in the temples in accordance with the previously written decree, the first (day) and the ninth and the twenty-fifth, and feasts and public festivals are celebrated each year in honor of the other greatest gods, (be it resolved) for there to be held each year a public festival in the temples and throughout the whole country in honor of King Ptolemy and Queen Berenike, the Benefactor Gods, on the day on which the star of Isis[393] rises, which is reckoned in the sacred writings to be the new year, and which now in the ninth year is observed on the first day of the month Pauni,[394] at which time both the little Boubastia and the great Boubastia are celebrated and the gathering of the crops and the rise of the river takes place; but if, further, it happens that the rising of the star changes to another day in four years,[395] for the festival not to be moved but to be held on the first of Pauni all the same, on which (day) it was originally held in the ninth year, and to celebrate it for five days with the wearing of garlands and with sacrifices and libations and what else that is fitting; and, in order also that the seasons may always do as they should, in accordance with the now existing order of the universe, and that it may not happen that some of the public feasts held in the winter are ever held in the summer, the star changing by one day every four years, and that others of those now held in the summer are held in the winter in future times as has happened in the past and as would be happening now, if the arrangement of the year remained of 360 days plus the five days later brought into usage (be it resolved) for a one-day feast of the Benefactor Gods to be added every four years to the five additional days before the new year,[396] in order that all may know that the former defect in the arrangement of the seasons and the year and in the beliefs about the whole ordering of the heavens has come to be corrected and made good by the Benefactor Gods. And whereas it happened that the daughter born of King Ptolemy and Queen Berenike, the Benefactor Gods, and named Berenike, who was also immediately declared Princess,[397] while still a maiden suddenly passed into the everlasting world, while the priests were still with the King who came to him every year from the country, who straightway made great lamentation at what had befallen and, petitioning the King and the Queen persuaded them to establish the goddess with Osiris in the temple in Canopus, which is not only among the first temples but also among those most honored by the King and by all in the country — and the sacred boat of Osiris is brought to this temple from the temple in the Herakleion every year on the 29th of Choiach, when all those from the first temples perform sacrifices on behalf of each of the first temples upon the altars built by them on both sides of the entry way — and after this they performed magnificently and with care the rites for her deification and for the conclusion of the mourning, as it is customary to do also for Apis and Mnevis, be it resolved: To perform everlasting honors to Berenike, the princess born of the Benefactor Gods, in all the temples in the country, and, since she went to the gods in the month of Tybi, the very month in which also the daughter of Helios, whom her father lovingly called sometimes his crown and sometimes his sight, in the beginning departed from life, and (since) they hold in her honor a feast and a boat-procession in most of the temples of the first rank in this month, in which her apotheosis originally occurred, (be it resolved) to hold in honor of Berenike as well, the princess born of the Benefactor Gods, a feast and boat-procession in the month Tybi in all the temples in the country for four days from the seventeenth, on which day the boat-procession and the conclusion of the mourning for her originally took place; and to fashion a sacred image of her, of gold and precious stones, in each of the first- and second-rank temples and to set it up in the holy place; the prophet or (one) of those who [enter the shrine] for the adorning of the gods shall carry it in his arms, whenever there are processions or festivals of the other gods, in order that, being seen by all it may be honored and obeisance may be done to it, being called (the image) of Berenike Mistress of Maidens; and for the royal crown set upon her image, as distinct from the one set upon the images of her mother Queen Berenike, to consist of two ears of grain, in the middle of which shall be the asp-shaped insignia and behind which a commensurate papyrus-shaped scepter, such as the goddesses are wont to hold in their hands, about which the tail of the (asp-shaped) insignia shall be wound, so that the name of Berenike, in accordance with the symbol of the sacred script, will be signified by the arrangement of her royal crown; and, when the Kikellia are celebrated in the month of Choiach before the boat-procession of Osiris, for the maiden daughters of the priests to fashion another image of Berenike, Mistress of Maidens, to which they shall likewise perform a sacrifice and the other rites performed at this feast; and for it to be permitted in the same way to the other maidens, who so wish, to perform the rites to the goddess; and for her to be hymned by the chosen sacred maidens who are in the service of the gods, when they have put on the individual royal crowns of the goddesses whose priestesses they are accounted as being; and, when the early sowing is at hand, for the sacred maidens to carry up ears of grain to be laid before the image of the goddess; and for the men and women singers to sing to her each day, during the feasts and festivals of the other gods, whatever hymns the sacred scribes write and give to the teacher of songs, of which also copies shall be entered in the sacred books. And whereas provisions are given to the priests from the sacred (revenues) whenever they are brought to the group (of priests in each temple), (be it resolved) for there to be given to the daughters of the priests from the day of their birth food from the sacred revenues, such as shall be determined by the councillor priests in each temple in proportion to the sacred revenues; and for the bread given to the wives of the priests to have its own particular shape and to be called the bread of Berenike. And let the appointed supervisor and chief-priest in each temple and the scribes of the temple inscribe this decree on a stone or bronze stele, in sacred characters[398] and in Egyptian (characters),[399] and in Greek (characters), and let them set it up in the most conspicuous place in the first- and second- and third-rank temples, in order that the priests in the country may be seen to honor the Benefactor Gods and their children, as is just.

137. THE ROSETTA STONE

OGIS 90   196

This trilingual inscription (in Greek and in Egyptian hieroglyphics and Demotic) contains, like the Canopus decree from the reign of Ptolemy III (no. 136), a decree passed by an assembly of native Egyptian priests. The two are in many respects similar, but Egyptian influence is much more prominent in the Rosetta decree (note especially the royal titulature and the fact that the assembly took place at Memphis and not at Canopus). This reflects the increased prominence of the native element in Ptolemaic Egypt, a development fostered not least by the employment, for the first time on a large scale, of Egyptian troops by Ptolemy IV at Raphia in 217. Discovered at Rosetta (Raschid) by Napoleon's French in 1799 and transported to the British Museum in 1802, the inscription has achieved a wider fame than most, for "it was this stone which first gave the key of the ancient language of Egypt to the younger Champollion in 1824, and is thus the foundation upon which the whole of modern Egyptology has been built up" (Bevan, *House of Ptolemy*, 262).

In the reign of the young one[400] — who received the throne from his father — lord of crowns, glorious, the one who established Egypt, and pious towards the gods, superior to his opponents, the one who restored the life of men, lord of the thirty-years' feasts just as Hephaistos the great,[401] king just as Helios the great king of the upper and lower regions,[402] offspring of the Father-Loving Gods, the one whom Hephaistos approved, to whom Helios gave the victory, living image of Zeus son of Helios,[403] Ptolemy Ever-Living, Beloved of Ptah, in the ninth year, the priest of Alexander and the Savior Gods and the Brother-and-Sister Gods and the Benefactor Gods and the Father-Loving Gods and the God Manifest (and) Gracious[404] being Aetos son of Aetos, the athlophore of Berenike Euergetis being Pyrrha daughter of Philinos, the canephore of Arsinoe Philadelphos being Areia daughter of Diogenes,[405] the priestess of Arsinoe Philopator being Eirene daughter of Ptolemy, on the fourth of the month Xandikos, the eighteenth of the Egyptians' (month) Mecheir:[406] decree: The chief-priests and the prophets[407] and those who enter the shrine for the adorning of the gods and the feather-bearers and the sacred scribes and all the other priests who came together from the temples of the country to Memphis to the king for the festival of the assumption of the throne of Ptolemy Ever-Living Beloved of Ptah, God Manifest (and) Gracious, which he received from his father, (all these) having gathered together in the temple at Memphis on this day, spoke:[408] Whereas King Ptolemy Ever-Living Beloved of Ptah, God Manifest (and) Gracious, he born of King Ptolemy and Queen Arsinoe, Father-Loving Gods, has in many ways conferred benefits on the temples and those in them and (on) all those ranged under his rule, being a god born of a god and goddess, just as Horus the son of Isis and Osiris, who avenged his father Osiris, and, being beneficently disposed toward the gods, has dedicated to the temples revenues in both silver and grain, and has undertaken many expenses for the sake of bringing Egypt into a state of prosperity and establishing the temples, and has been generous with all his own means, and of the revenues and tax-collections existing in Egypt he entirely remitted some and others he has lightened, in order that the native people and all the others might be in a state of serenity during his reign, and the royal debts, which both those in Egypt and those in the rest of his kingdom owed and which were many in number, he remitted, and those who had been led off to prisons and those who were since long ago under accusation he freed from their charges; and he ordered that the revenues of the temples and the contributions in grain and silver given to them each year and likewise the proper share of the gods from the vine-land and the gardens and the other property of the gods are to remain in effect in the country (as they were) in his father's reign; and he ordered also, with regard to the priests, that they should pay no more for the consecration-tax than they were assessed during the reign of his father up until the first year (of his own reign); and he relieved those from the sacred tribes of the annual voyage down to Alexandria; and he directed that impressment into the navy is not to be practiced, and of the tax on byssus-cloth paid in the temples to the royal treasury he removed two-thirds, and all things that had been neglected in former times he restored to their proper arrangement, having a care that the customary (rites) might be performed for the gods according to what is proper; and likewise he dispensed justice to all, just as Hermes the Great and Great; and he ordered that those of the warrior class[409] who came back and those who returned of the others who held disloyal views in the time of troubles are to remain in occupation of their own possessions; and he provided that cavalry and infantry forces and ships should be sent out against those who attacked Egypt[410] by sea and land, submitting to great expenses in silver and grain in order that the temples and all those in them might be in safety; and going to Lykonpolis[411] in the Busirite (nome), which had been occupied and fortified against a siege with an abundant collection of arms and with all other provisions — for long standing was the disloyalty of the impious men gathered there, who had wrought much evil against the temples and those dwelling in Egypt — and encamping over against it, he surrounded it with mounds and trenches and remarkable fortifications, and, when the Nile made a great rise in the eighth year and, as it was wont to inundate the plains, he held it back by damming up in many places the outlets of the streams, spending no small amount of money on these and placing cavalry and foot-soldiers to guard them, (and) in a short time he took the city by storm and destroyed all the impious men in it, just as [Herm]es and Horus, son of Isis and Osiris, subdued the former rebels in the same regions; and all those who led the rebels in his father's reign and troubled the country and did wrong to the temples, arriving in Memphis and avenging his father and his own throne he punished fittingly at the time when he came for the performance of the proper rites for the assumption of the throne. And he remitted what was owing in the temples to the royal treasury up until the eighth year, no small amount of grain and silver; and likewise (he remitted) the prices of the byssus-cloth not delivered to the royal treasury, and of that delivered (he remitted) up until the same time the cost of having it inspected; and he freed the temples from the artaba assessed on (each) aroura of sacred land, and from the jar (of wine assessed on each) aroura of vine-land; and he gave many gifts to Apis and Mnevis and the other sacred beasts in Egypt,[412] in every respect taking much more thought than previous reigns for what belongs to them, giving for their burials what was proper lavishly and splendidly, and (giving) what was regularly paid to their individual temples with sacrifices and festivals and the other customary observances; and he has maintained the honors of the temples of Egypt in the country according to the laws, and he fitted out the temple of Apis with rich works, providing for it no small amount of gold and [silver] and precious stones; and he established temples and shrines and altars and also restored those requiring repair, having the mind of a beneficent god in matters pertaining [to the] divine; and inquiring as to the most honored of the temples he renewed them in his reign, as is fitting; in return for which the gods have given him health, victory, power and [all] other good things, his kingdom remaining to him and his children for all time; with good for-

tune, resolved by the priests of all the temples in the country: greatly to increase [all] the existing honors of the Ever-Living King Ptolemy, Beloved of
Ptah, God Manifest (and) Gracious, and likewise those of his parents, the
Father-Loving Gods, and those of his grandparents the Benefactor Gods,
[and those] of the Brother-and-Sister Gods, and those of the Savior Gods;
and to set up in each temple in the most conspicuous [place] an image of the
Ever-Living King Ptolemy God Manifest (and) Gracious, which shall be
called (that) of "Ptolemy the Avenger of Egypt," beside which shall stand
the principal god of the temple, giving him the armor of victory, which shall
be fashioned in the manner [of the Egyptians]; and for the priests to pay
homage to the images thrice daily and to put on them the sacred adornment
and to perform the other rites just as for the other gods at [the] festivals [in
the country]; and to establish for King Ptolemy, God Manifest (and) Gracious (born) of King Ptolemy and Queen Arsinoe, the Father-Loving Gods,
a statue and a golden shrine[413] [in each of the] temples and to set them up in
the inner sanctuaries with other shrines, and for the [shrine] of the God
Manifest (and) Gracious to join in the procession at the great festivals, at
which occur the processions of the shriners; and, in order that it may be
easily distinguished now and for all time to come, for there to be set upon
the shrine the ten golden royal crowns of the king to which shall be affixed
as asp, [just as with all] the asp-shaped royal crowns that are upon the other
shrines; but in the midst of them shall be the royal crown called Pschent,
wearing which he entered the [temple] in Memphis in order to perform [in
it] the rites for the assumption of the throne; and to place upon the square
area around the crowns, by the aforementioned crown [two] golden amulets
[on which it shall be inscribed] that it is (the shrine) of the king who made
manifest the upper country and the lower; and whereas they have reckoned
the 30th of Mesore, on which is held the birthday celebration of the king,
and likewise [the 17th of Phaophi], on which he received the throne from
his father, as his name-days in the temples, which (days) are the beginnings
of many good things for all, (resolved) to hold on these days feasts [and
festivals in the] temples of Egypt each month, and to perform in (the
temples) sacrifices and libations and the other rites, just also as at the other
festivals, and the offerings that occur————(to or by) those in service in the
temples; and to hold a feast and festival in honor of the Ever-Living and
Beloved of Ptah King Ptolemy, God Manifest (and) Gracious, each year [in
the temples in the] country for five days from the first of Thoth, in which
they shall wear garlands as they perform sacrifices and libations and the
other things that are proper; and for [the priests of the other gods] to be
designated also priests of the God Manifest (and) Gracious in addition to
the other names of the gods of whom they are the priests, and (for them) to
enter in all their documents and (for there to be engraved in addition) on the
rings they wear his priesthood; and for it to be permitted to the rest, private
individuals, to celebrate the feast and to build the aforementioned shrine
and to have it with them as they perform [the rites at the monthly feasts and

at the] yearly (ones), in order that it may be well known that those in Egypt magnify and honor the God Manifest (and) Gracious, (the) king, just as is [their] law; [and to inscribe this decree on stelae] of hard stone in sacred and native[414] and Greek characters, and to set (them) up in each of the first- and second- [and third-rank temples by the image of the Ever-Living king].

138. ROYAL LETTER GUARANTEEING TEMPLE REVENUES

P.Teb. I 6[415]   139[416]

This letter of the sovereigns (Ptolemy VIII Euergetes II and his queens) to the royal administration orders the latter to secure to the temples of the royal cult their proper revenues, which the priests had (in a letter of which the contents are summarized in the royal decree) complained were being infringed in various ways.

[King Ptolemy and] Queen Cleopatra the sister and Queen [Cleopatra the wife to the] *strategoi* and the garrison commanders and the [superintendents of police] and chiefs of police and *epimeletai* [and *oikonomoi* and *basilikoi*] *grammateis* and the other [royal functionaries], greeting. [The priests of. . .][417] and of the Brother-and-Sister Gods and [the Benefactor Gods and the] Father-Loving [Gods] and the Manifest Gods [and the God Eupator and the] Mother-Loving [Gods] and the Benefactor Gods have written to us [concerning the sacred land. . .] with that [which has been dedicated] by the cleruchs, and the [profits from the] honorable offices and posts as prophet or [scribe and all the religious duties] purchased for the temple [and. . .] from properties and [the sums paid] in accordance with the decrees [for. . .] and the several associations and the sacred slaves from trades and manufactures and salaries, and the sums collected by men and women at Alexandria and in the country for treasuries and bowls and cups, and the proceeds of the so-called *aphrodisia*[418] and their revenues in general for. . .are registered, (stating that) certain persons who lease lands and other properties for a long period, and some who even take forcible possession without any contracts, fail to pay the rents due, and do not contribute the full amount of the profits of the [honorable offices] or posts as prophet or scribe, while others steal the sums paid and collected, and setting up *aphrodisia* without the authorization of the priests receive. . .for the sake of collecting the dues to the goddess, and other try to mix themselves up with the revenues and lay hands upon them and manage the temple contrary to custom. In accordance therefore with our previous ordinances concerning the dues which belong to the temples, so long as the aforesaid revenues of the goddess remain [let them be (?)] undisturbed, and permit no one under any circumstances to exact payment of any of the above-mentioned revenues or to drive away by force the agents of the priests engaged in collecting them; and compel those who disobey to pay all the sums regularly, in order that the priests may obtain all their receipts in full, and may be able without hindrance to pay the customary offerings to the gods on behalf of us and our children. Farewell. [Year] 31, Panemos 10 (?).

139. BURIAL PREPARATIONS FOR SACRED COW

PSI IV 328[419]   257

The priests of Hathor at Aphroditopolis (named after the goddess, who was identified with Aphrodite) write to Apollonios asking that myrrh be provided for the burial of the new Hesis cow (who was an assimilation of Hathor and Isis), who could not be installed until preparations for her burial were complete.

The priests of Aphrodite to Apollonios [the *dioiketes*] greeting. In accordance with what the king has written to you, to give one hundred talents of myrrh for the burial of [the Hesis], please order this [to be given]. For you know that the Hesis is not brought up to the nome unless we have in readiness everything required for the burial, because [the embalming is done (?)] on the day (of her death). Know that the Hesis is Isis, and may she give you favor in the eyes of the king. Farewell. Year 28, Hathyr 15.

140. SALE OF PRIESTLY RIGHTS

PSI IX 1022   106

This document belongs to an archive found in a house near the Ptolemaic temple of Deir el-Medina, on the west bank at Thebes. The owner of a temple of Hathor ("Aphrodite") sells the rights to the priestly emoluments (notably shares in sacrifices) in this temple on three days of purification at a rate of two copper talents a day, a significant sum which shows the cash value of priesthoods quite clearly.

(Summary) Year 11 which is also year 8,[420] Pharmouthi 21. Pikos son of Psemminis sold three days of the Aphrodisieion belonging to him for 6 copper talents.

In the reign of Cleopatra and King Ptolemy her son, surnamed Alexander, the Mother-Loving Savior Gods, year 11 which is also 8, Pharmouthi 21, the priest of Alexander and the Savior Gods and the Brother-and-Sister Gods and the Benefactor Gods and the Mother-Loving Gods[421] and the Manifest Gods and the Mother-Loving Gods and the God Eupator and the

Benefactor Gods, the athlophore of Berenike Euergetis and the canephore of Arsinoe Philadelphos and the goddess Arsinoe Eupator[422] being those in office in Alexandria, and in Ptolemais of the Thebaid the priest and priestess of Ptolemy Soter being those in office, before Apollonios who is in charge of the office of *agoranomos* for the Memnoneia of the Pathyrite (nome) of the Thebaid:

Pikos son of Psemminis, about 25 years old, middle height, with honey-colored broken skin, long-headed, straight-nosed, with a scar on his left brow, has sold the perquisites from three days of purification and their emoluments and services and everything pertaining to them and falling due to them in each year and the portion coming to their credit from the epagomenal days and everything that pertains to these in the temple, the sanctuary of Aphrodite belonging to him, called Hathyr, among the graves in the area of the Memnoneia;

And Totoes son of Zmanres, one of the shrine-bearers from the Memnoneia, about 35 years old, honey-colored, smooth-skinned, round-faced, straight-nosed, has bought them for 6 talents of copper money.

The broker and guarantor of the contents of this sale is Pikos the seller, whom Totoes the buyer accepted.

141. GRAVE ROBBERS

UPZ II 187   127/6

Funerary cults, from early times an important part of Egyptian life, occupied a considerable part of the west bank at Thebes. The *choachytai*, a family corporation of libation-pourers and generally priests of the dead, managed the cult at many tombs (cf. no. 110); here one of them complains about the damage to one tomb's occupants when robbers opened it and left it open.

To Di [. . ., one of the friends] and hipparch over men and chief of police of the Theban Nome, from Osoroeris son of Horos, *choachytes* from the Memnoneia. I report that in the 48th year when Lochos the kinsman[423] came to Diospolis Magna some men went to one of the tombs belonging to me in the [Theban] Nome and opened it and unwrapped one of the bodies placed in it and likewise carried off the furnishings which I had deposited there, worth 10 talents of copper. And because the door was left open, it has happened that the unburied bodies were ruined by being devoured by wolves. Since I suspect Poeris also called Pkales, son of Sonathyr (?) and Phagion his brother, I ask that you bring them before you and that you administer the suitable punishment on the basis of your investigation. Farewell.

142-144. PTOLEMAIOS THE *KATOCHOS* OF THE SERAPEUM AT MEMPHIS

The largest archive (104 documents) of Ptolemaic papyri found before 1880 came from the great sanctuary of Sarapis at Memphis and centers around the persons of certain men and women called *katochoi*, of whom Ptolemaios son of Glaukias, the eldest of four sons of a Macedonian military settler who died in an Egyptian rebellion in 164, is the central figure. Ptolemaios, born perhaps around 200, began in 172/1 a period of some twenty years spent entirely within the precinct of the sanctuary in a state called in *katoche*. Various other persons in this state figure in the archive as well, staying in the Serapeum for various lengths of time ranging from a few months upward. The meaning of *katoche* has been argued at length by many scholars. It certainly imposed on the person affected an obligation to remain physically within the Serapeum (it is in fact a distinctive characteristic of the Hellenistic cult of Sarapis). It appears that the obligation was laid on the person by the god (in a dream, typically) and could be removed only by another such divine command. It is not to be confused with asylum, an escape from whatever external problems faced the person. Ptolemaios certainly continued to take an active hand in problems of persons not in the Serapeum, particularly his family. (For another document from this archive see also no. 115.) The most comprehensive study of the question is L. Delekat, *Katoche, Hierodulie und Adoptionsfreilassung* (München 1964).

142. PETITION ABOUT PATERNAL HOUSE

UPZ I 10   160

This petition makes graphically clear the strength of the divine command that held Ptolemaios in the Serapeum, unable to go to his home — no great distance away — and prevent his patrimony from being dissipated, or to protect in person his younger brother, Apollonios.

To King Ptolemy and Queen Cleopatra his sister, the Mother-Loving Gods, greeting from Ptolemaios son of Glaukias, Macedonian, one of those in *katoche* in the great Serapeum at Memphis, now in the thirteenth year there. A house that belonged to my father in the village of Psichis of the Herakleopolite (nome) and now belongs to me was demolished and the goods in it (valued at 20 copper talents) carried off by my neighbors Hesperos and Ataios, his son, and his brother Polemon. The aforesaid, not yet satisfied with what they had done, have built around the court that belonged to it and the open space around the house,[424] using it as their own, scorning me because I cannot come out of the sanctuary and go to the place to bring them to account. Since, O great king and queen, I cannot for the present bring them to account for the goods carried off by them, nor about their building on what was left to me by my father, nor about their using it in any

234

way they wish, I beg you to send my petition to Kydias the *strategos* of the nome so that he may summon the aforementioned men and order the afore-said to refrain from their forcible encroachment on the aforesaid land, and to hand it over to my representatives,[425] and to treat them harshly for the violence they have done, so that I may have shared in your protection for my life.[426] Farewell.

143. PETITION ON BEHALF OF HIS BROTHER

UPZ I 14[427]   158-157

Since Ptolemaios was unable to earn a living for himself while he was in the sanc-tuary, he asked the king to have his younger brother Apollonios enrolled in the Memphite garrison, in the expectation that his pay could support both of them. The petition translated here is followed by a series of official communications imple-menting the king's order (to grant the request but report to him what the cost would be). The papyrus seems to have been Apollonios' own record of the documents and actions relevant to his petition; they are copied with his usual slovenliness. The chronology of the events is set out in detail by Wilcken, running from early October 158 to the end of February 157, when the long circuits of official correspondence finally completed their handling of the matter.

To King Ptolemy and Queen Cleopatra the sister, Mother-Loving Gods, greeting from Ptolemaios son of Glaukias, Macedonian of the Epigone, of the Herakleopolite (nome). As my aforesaid father Glaukias, who belonged to the cleruchs called kinsmen in the Herakleopolite (nome),[428] departed this life at the time of the disturbances[429] and has left behind him both me and my younger brother Apollonios, and as it has happened that I have been in *katoche* in the great Serapeum by Memphis for 15 years and I require, see-ing that I am childless, to procure for my said brother a military post, which will enable me too, who am in *katoche*, to live here decently and receive suc-cor, I beseech you, the most great Mother-Loving Gods, to take note of the above-mentioned years and, inasmuch as I have no means of gaining the necessities of life except by seeking refuge with you, the most great gods and protectors, and obtaining the said military post for my brother, to let me too partake, if it seems good to you, of the pious protection which you afford to all men in such cases and to let an order be written to the proper authorities to enroll my above-named brother in the company of Dexilaos which is garrisoned in Memphis and assign him the same pay as his fellows receive in grain and money, so that being thus decently circumstanced I may be able to perform sacrifices on behalf of you and your children, to the end that you may be lords of every land on which the sun looks down for all time. If this is done, I shall have my livelihood secured by your help in perpetuity. Farewell. (Subscription) Let it be done, but report how much it will cost.

144. LETTER FROM WIFE TO HUSBAND

UPZ I 59[430]   168

Persons claiming a divine command to do something that inconveniences themselves or others have in all eras been looked upon with suspicion by many close to them, and the Hellenistic period was no exception. Hephaistion, a soldier recently returned from the wars, was commanded by Sarapis to remain in the sanctuary at Memphis, like Ptolemaios, and his wife, who had looked to his return and support, is angry. A closely similar letter to this one, from Hephaistion's brother, was written the same day and expresses the same irritation. Isias' opinion of the divine command is well summarized in her implicit remark at the end that such things are not very pressing business.

Isias to her brother[431] Hephaistion [greeting]. If you are well and other things are going right, it would accord with the prayer which I make continually to the gods. I myself and the child and all the household are in good health and think of you always. When I received your letter from Horos, in which you announce that you are in *katoche* in the Serapeum at Memphis, for the news that you are well I straightway thanked the gods, but about your not coming home, when all the others who had been secluded there have come, I am ill-pleased, because after having piloted myself and your child through such bad times and been driven to every extremity owing to the price of wheat, I thought that now at least, with you at home, I should enjoy some respite, whereas you have not even thought of coming home nor given any regard to our circumstances, remembering how I was in want of everything while you were still here, not to mention this long lapse of time and these critical days, during which you have sent us nothing. As, moreover, Horos who delivered the letter has brought news of your having been released from detention,[432] I am thoroughly ill-pleased. Notwithstanding, as your mother also is annoyed, for her sake as well as for mine please return to the city, if nothing more pressing holds you back. You will do me a favor by taking care of your bodily health. Farewell. Year 2, Epeiph 30. (Address) To Hephaistion.

236

145. TRANSPORT OF A BODY

SB I 5216 (*Sel. Pap.* 104)   first century

The chief physician, evidently in Alexandria, writes to the priests of the vestment-keepers in a temple in the Fayum, ordering them to deliver up a body currently in their keeping and to accompany it on the first stage of its journey back to Alexandria.

Athenagoras the chief physician to the priests of the *stolistai*[433] in the Labyrinth[434] and to the *stolistai*, greeting. Since Herakleides, my subordinate over your district, has died and is in your cemetery, I have sent Nikias and Krokos for him. You will do well to release the body without having charged anything, and you will accompany them as far as Ptolemais. The vestment-keepers in Alexandria have also written to you about him. Take care of yourselves, that you may be well. Farewell. Year 14, Hathyr 25. (Address) to the priests of the *stolistai* and to the *stolistai*.

146. ANTISEMITES IN MEMPHIS

SB VI 9564[435]   early first century

This badly written and damaged letter is not without difficulties of interpretation, but Rémondon has adequately established the sense of it (*Chronique d'Egypte* 35 [1960] 244-61). The writer, Herakles, informs his correspondent Ptolemaios the *dioiketes*, that he has asked a third person (Iap...) to inquire after the problems facing a (Jewish) priest of Tebtunis; Ptolemaios is asked to help this priest escape trouble and in particular to give him the same lodging that was given to a certain Artemidoros, in order to protect the priest from the antisemitism of the populace around him — at Memphis, it seems. This is the earliest testimony of antisemitism in the *chora* of Ptolemaic Egypt, and it is a vehement one.

Herakles to Ptolemaios the *dioiketes*, hearty greetings and good health. I asked Iap...in Memphis on behalf of the priest in Tebtunis to write to him a letter so that I may know what his situation is. I ask you to see how he can escape traps and to lead him by the hand: when he has need of anything giving it to him as you do for Artemidoros and in particular do me the favor of furnishing the priest with the same lodging — for you know that they are nauseated by Jews. Embrace...ibas, Epimenes, Tryphonas,..., and take care [of yourself].

NOTES

1. The peace treaty concluded between Philip II of Macedon and the Greeks in 338/7 after his victory at Chaeronea (Wickersham-Verbrugghe, *The Fourth Century*, 74) and renewed by Alexander in 336/5.

2. The council of the Corinthian League, instituted by Philip and continued by Alexander, to which all member states sent delegates, *synhedroi*.

3. Curtius 4.8.12-13 suggests that early in 331 Alexander agreed to a Chian request for the withdrawal of the garrison.

4. I.e., houses beyond the one allowed by the *diagramma*; these would have to be given up by the returning exile.

5. The precise meaning of the text at this point is particularly unclear; for this version cf. Tod, *GHI* II, pp. 298, 300.

6. It seems most likely that the reference here is to a panel of judges brought in from another city, probably Mantinea (note the time limit and the mention of Mantinea a few lines later; cf. also Tod, *GHI* II, p. 301), but the reference might possibly be to a Tegean court which dealt with suits betweeen citizens and foreigners. Cf. n. 33.

7. Athena Alea.

8. Antigonus met with Cassander at the Hellespont in 313/2: Diod. 19.75.6.

9. Antigonus was 71 at the time.

10. Polyperchon, one of the oldest of Alexander's generals, had succeeded Antipater as regent of Greece in 319, much to the dismay of Antipater's son Cassander. Antigonus came to terms with him in 315 and named him *strategos* of the Peloponnesus (Diod. 19.57.5; 60.1; 61.1). Polyperchon refused to desert Antigonus for Cassander, also in 315 (Diod. 19.63.3, cf. 64.1), but when Antigonus' man Telesphoros arrived in 313 with instructions to free the cities, Polyperchon refused to vacate Sikyon and Corinth (Diod. 19.74.2).

11. Both Ptolemy and Antigonus' son Demetrius had married daughters of Antipater.

12. "It is unnecessary to point out that the oath asked of the Greeks would require them to support Antigonus in a new war if he could claim the treaty had been violated." (*RC*, p. 10).

13. Antigonus' younger son.

14. Both Teos and Lebedos were members of the Ionian League, and as such both sent *theoroi* to the cult celebrations of the League at the Panionion. This provision aims at coping with the situation that would arise when Lebedos ceased to exist and could thus not send a *theoros* in its own name.

15. The roofs would normally be made of baked tiles, the walls of less expensive unbaked brick. (It is not easy to see what else the translation of the text could be in this section, but the relation between the requirement to build in three years and the provision of roofs over four years is a matter for curiosity.)

16. Cf. nos. 9, n. 33; 60 with n. 187.

17. The laws of Kos went back ultimately to the seventh-century lawgiver Charondas of Katane (cf. Aristotle, *Politics* 2.12; Herondas, *Mim.* 2.48).

18. For an analogous, but more complicated, grain fund cf. no. 63.

19. Territory directly subject to Antigonus and paying him tribute in grain. He could of course sell as much of the grain as he did not himself require and would no doubt be anxious to do so.

238

20. On this policy of Antigonus, cf. no. 6: he clearly does not feel the enforced synoecism to be at odds with it.
21. In order to obtain the money needed immediately, the 600 wealthiest citizens of Teos are required to advance one-quarter of the amount. Repayment (one year later) is guaranteed them from the city's revenues.
22. The assumption that something is wrong with the text seems inevitable; expected here would be "when this response is read" (as above), or such. The cities' law should of course cease to function only after the formal adoption of those imported from Kos. Cf. *RC*, p. 32.
23. The council of the League, composed of the representatives (*synhedroi*) sent by the member states.
24. A board of presidents of the *synhedrion*; on their functions and selection, see particularly Fragment 3.
25. I.e., the war against Cassander.
26. The Olympic, Pythian, Isthmian, and Nemean games.
27. The *synhedroi* are thus to be fully-empowered representatives, not delegates.
28. The *prohedroi* during the "common war" are not, evidently, to be thus accountable.
29. A fine of only two drachmas seems excessively small.
30. "The common war" seems best taken as referring to a war undertaken by the common decision of the citizenry, the results of which war affected all alike. "Those who have been chosen to supervise the common war" are a board of officials elected to see to the execution of all measures enacted to deal with damages and problems resulting from the war.
31. If, for example, someone has borrowed 1000 drachmas on security of a landed estate clearly worth more than that amount, he might go on to contract an additional loan (or loans) on security of the value of the estate over 1000 drachmas.
32. If, for example, the guarantor had pledged himself for one-quarter of the debt, then he would be liable for one-quarter of the excess of the amount owed over the value of the property.
33. Most likely a panel of judges brought in from a friendly city to aid in the settlement of these disputes. The invocation of judges from elsewhere was a widespread phenomenon in the Hellenistic period (cf. Tarn and Griffith, *Hellenistic Civilization*[3] 88-9; M.N. Tod, *International Arbitration amongst the Greeks* [Oxford 1913]).
34. These two provisions have to do with loans contracted during the war, the preceding ones with loans contracted prior to it. The war apparently began in the month Posideon in the year for which Demagoras was *prytanis* and (cf. the end of the inscription) ended two years later, during the prytany of Apollas. The year of Danaos, mentioned near the end, is likely the first prytany-year after the end of the war.
35. The city more usually known as Ephesos; it was renamed by Lysimachus after his third wife, Arsinoe, daughter of Ptolemy I and later wife of Ptolemy II.
36. The (non-Greek) inhabitants of the lower Maeander valley.
37. On the text here cf. Habicht, *Gottmenschentum*[2] 39 n. 5. The alternative is "[saved the] city by land": so *RC* 44, where this is taken as alluding to Demetrius' naval superiority.
38. This refers specifically to a cult statue; cf. the provision about an altar just below. For the text in this section of the decree, see L. Robert, *Etudes anatoliennes* (Paris 1937) 183-4.
39. Lysimachus does not mention the Pedieis. The soldiers (if the restoration is indeed correct) may be taken to be those of Demetrius in 287/6 (cf. *RC*, p. 43).
40. This refers to a now lost section of the Prienean decree.
41. The king of the Cimmerians who descended upon Asia Minor in the seventh century.
42. The conflict was renewed in the sixth century while Bias was tyrant of Priene. After the first serious battle, in which 1000 Samians were killed, the six-years' truce was signed. The Samian attack referred to here took place in the seventh year.
43. The precise temporal reference is not clear, if indeed it was intended to be; between Bias and Lysimachus three centuries elapsed of which nothing is said by the Prieneans. What the Samians had to say does not survive.
44. 299/8; Isaios, mentioned below, was archon in 284/3.
45. Summer, 301. Along with the forces of Lysimachus at Ipsos were of course those of Seleucus.

46. In 287, with the help of a Ptolemaic fleet. Since early 294 Athens had been under the control of Demetrius, who had returned to Greece after the death of Cassander in 298 or 297.

47. The area of northern Syria, including the cities Antioch-by-Daphne, Seleukia, Apamea, and Laodikeia.

48. A reference to the peace concluded between Antiochus and Antigonus Gonatas in 279 or 278; or possibly to that concluded after the defeat of the Gauls, in 275/4; or perhaps indeed, to both.

49. This indicates that there already existed a cult of Antiochus at Ilion.

50. This issue, treated in all three letters of Antiochus, arises because there were only two categories of land (excluding perhaps some temple land), crown land and city land. Land that passed from the king must needs become part of the territory of some city or another. As an element of the original gift (10) Antiochus gave Aristodikides the choice between Skepsis and Ilion. This was then (11, 12) extended to any allied city, but Aristodikides chose to have his new land attached to the territory of Ilion.

51. It seems extraordinary that Antiochus should not know this. Evidently only inspection on the spot could answer the question.

52. Either a mistake (the figure earlier in the text was 2000) or an act of generosity, perhaps as compensation for Petra. If the figure is correct, the land given to Aristodikides in all these presentations amounted to 6000 *plethra* (the 2000 of 10, the 2000 of 11, which seem to recur in 12, first as 2000 and then as 2500, and the 1500 of 12) or, perhaps, 8000 (if the 2000 of 11 are not the same as the 2000/2500 of 12).

53. Arsinoe (Philadelphos), daughter of Ptolemy I and sister of Ptolemy II, was also the second wife of the latter, the first having been Arsinoe, daughter of Lysimachus.

54. Areus, son of Acrotatus, king of Sparta from 309 to 265/4. He died in battle against Antigonus at the Isthmus in the first year of the war.

55. I.e., from the council of the states in the Spartan alliance; cf. further on in the inscription.

56. Stratonice was the daughter of Demetrius Poliorcetes. She had been married to Seleucus I before he gave her in marriage to his son Antiochus.

57. Or, "from among the synhedroi".

58. This conventional reference need to refer to no more than Antiochus' father, but it might be taken to include Antigonus as well.

59. The chief rite in the League cult of Alexander.

60. The name of Antiochus (son of Antiochus I and co-regent with his father and soon to become Antiochus II) was mistakenly omitted here.

61. See *Milet* I 3.122-126, under the year 279/8.

62. Cf. no. 14.

63. This individual is probably to be identified with the "son Ptolemy" who appears in papyri as co-ruler with Ptolemy II between 267 and 259, and with the son of Ptolemy who revolted from his father at Ephesos in 259 (?) (Athenaeus 593; Trogus, *Prologues* 26).

64. Kallikrates son of Boiskos of Samos was active in the Aegean in Ptolemy's service in the 270's and 260's.

65. Ptolemy I Soter.

66. The reference is to the military year of ten months for which the mercenaries were engaged.

67. The Seleucid era was used by Eumenes; year 44 = 269/8; the freedom from taxes was granted originally by Philetairos.

68. Soldiers awarded a garland of poplar.

69. This is likely Eumenes' cousin, son of his father's brother. It has been suggested that he was taken prisoner by the soldiers and a promise exacted from him on oath.

70. The translation is in the main that of *Sel.Pap.* 93.

71. The most northern of the major port cities of the Ptolemaic province of Syria and Phoenicia.

72. May, 253.

73. The royal peasants were attached to the land. When the property became privately owned and attached to a city, their position would be that of non-citizen residents of the city.

74. December, 253.
75. March, 252.
76. October, 254.
77. Ptolemy II Philadelphos and Arsinoe, his wife and (half-)sister.
78. Ptolemy I Soter and Berenike.
79. The line is counted as descended from Herakles, son of Zeus, through Hyllos. The latter was the son of Herakles and Deianeira, the daughter of Dionysos and Althaia.
80. This refers primarily to Cyrene.
81. I.e., Coele-Syria.
82. The southern shore of Asia Minor, with the exception of Pamphylia and Cilicia, was under Ptolemaic control.
83. Cf. *Syll.*³ 390 on Ptolemaic control of the Aegean islands.
84. See the passage of Jerome quoted above.
85. Cf. Polybius 5.34 for Pamphylia under Ptolemaic control early in the reign of Ptolemy IV Philopator.
86. Cf. Polybius 5.35 for Ephesos (and Samos) in the reign of Philopator; also 5.34.
87. Cf. Polybius 5.34.
88. The Seleucids employed Indian elephants. On the Ptolemaic elephant-corps cf. no. 101.
89. On the eastern expedition, cf. the passage of Jerome quoted above. According to Justin (27.1), Ptolemy, "unless he had been recalled to Egypt by a domestic rebellion, would have taken over the entire kingdom of Seleucus." Cf. Polyaenus 8.50 for the statement that Ptolemy succeeded by a ruse in gaining power from the Tauros to India without a fight, and Jerome (*loc.cit.*) for the report that Ptolemy handed over the provinces across the Euphrates to Xanthippos to govern.
90. Cf. Jerome (quoted above) and the Canopus decree of 239/8 (no. 136). It may be noted that the first two Ptolemies are also credited in Egyptian inscriptions with the same accomplishment.
91. For discussion see M. Holleaux, *Etudes d'épigraphie et d'histoire grecques* III 281-310, with bibliographical additions by L. Robert; subsequent discussions add little. The best text is *W.Chr.* 1, but a number of the somewhat conjectural restorations of Holleaux, especially in column III, have been translated in brackets as representing in all probability the correct sense. Numerous problems exist in the text but cannot be discussed here; some have been decided without explanation, others avoided as too uncertain.
92. Representing the "legitimate" Seleucid government and Laodike.
93. A harbor at the mouth of the Orontes river.
94. On the phenomenon of private altars and offerings in conjunction with civic cults (as in no. 16) see the remarks of L. Robert in *Essays Welles* (New Haven 1966) 175-211.
95. It was in response to an oracle of Apollo that a temple was dedicated to Aphrodite Stratonikis: cf. Tacitus, *Annals* 3.63.
96. The Smyrnaeans had apparently been driven from their city and forced to settle elsewhere. This is, curiously, not among the troubles they refer to in no. 29.
97. During Seleucus' reign the Pythian games were held in 246, 242, 238, 234, 230, and 226 (he may have been dead by this time in 226, however). The ones mentioned here seem best taken as being those of 242 (cf. no. 29).
98. Antiochus I Soter.
99. The daughter of Demetrius Poliorcetes, married first to Seleucus I and then to his son, Antiochus (I).
100. I.e., have cults at Smyrna.
101. Cf. no. 28.
102. The word applies to military settlers. Some of them were resident in Magnesia itself and some were evidently encamped nearby. It may be that a disagreement had arisen between the two groups; just below they are seen each to have sent their own envoys to Smyrna.
103. The lists from which jurors, etc. were selected by lot.
104. Literally, "equality before the law," often a synonym for democracy.
105. A fortress near Magnesia.
106. Antiochus I; the designation is indicative of cultic honors.

107. A minister, or governor, of Antiochus I, perhaps identical with the brother of Seleucus' wife Laodike who supported Antiochus Hierax against Seleucus in the War of the Brothers.

108. The original one plus the two granted by Antiochus I.

109. A special favor, as this would be larger than an infantryman's.

110. The stele commemorating the admission of Orchomenos into the League. Cf. Polybius 2.41.12; also 23.18.1 for reference to another such stele.

111. In all likelihood Nearchos was a tyrant of Orchomenos who abdicated peacefully when Orchomenos joined the League. Cf. Polybius 2.41-44.

112. "Methydrion was one of those towns which ceased to be independent when Megalopolis was founded and instead came to form part of the territory of Megalopolis. A short time, however, before Orchomenos joined the Achaean League, the Methydrians attempted to regain their former autonomy; when the venture was initially successful, they borrowed money required for the defense of the city, giving the golden statue of Victory as security. A short while later, when the Megalopolitans had regained Methydrion, the leaders of the revolt fled to Orchomenos, which was not yet an Achaean city [as was Megalopolis from ca. 235], and there divided up among themselves the borrowed money. When the Orchomenians themselves became Achaeans, they were bound to assist the Megalopolitans in regaining their own property." (Dittenberger).

113. These were involved in the negotiations that resulted in the peace of Naupaktos in August, 217 (see Chr. Habicht in *Ancient Macedonia* [Thessaloniki 1970] 277-8).

114. The reference is to the fighting in Thessaly near the end of the Social War (summer, 217: cf. Polybius 5.99-100).

115. About September, 217. For the dating (year 5 and not year 2) and the year (217) see Habicht, *op.cit.*, 273-9.

116. Philip's information on Rome is not altogether exact. Freed slaves did obtain citizenship but could not themselves hold magistracies (for the text here, cf. Habicht, *op.cit.* 273 n. 1), and seventy colonies is, by any method of reckoning, excessive.

117. Above all at Messene; cf. Polybius 7.10 ff. At precisely this time Philip's negotiations with Hannibal were coming to a conclusion (cf. Livy 23.33-34, 38-39; Polybius 7.9 for the treaty itself).

118. About August, 215.

119. L. Quinctius Flamininus. He served under his brother Titus as legate in charge of the fleet from 198 to 194.

120. Lampsakos shared in the religious federation centered upon the temple of Athena Ilias at Ilion and was thus counted as "related" to Ilion; legend had it that the Romans were descended from the Trojans; thus the Lampsakenes were related to the Romans.

121. Both Lampsakos and Massilia were originally colonies of Phokaia; having the same mother-city they were brothers.

122. I.e., quaestor.

123. Availing themselves of the chance to make use of the close ties of Massilia and Asia Minor (where the Tolostoagii lived), the envoys procured this letter of reference, probably with the aim of facilitating or improving Lampsakene trade with this Gallic tribe.

124. For the text here and on the Gauls in this inscription generally, see M. Holleaux, *Etudes d'épigraphie et d'histoire grecques* V, 141-155.

125. The reference is to the treaty of peace between Rome and Philip V, the main terms of which were drawn up by the senate before the dispatch of the ten senatorial commissioners to Greece in 196 (see Polybius 18.44 and cf. Livy 33.30). On the notion of being included in a treaty compare the parties "written on" (*adscripti*) to the Peace of Phoinike in 205 (Livy 29.12).

126. T. Quinctius Flamininus (consul 198), commander of the Roman forces in Greece from 198 to 194. He is called consul here (*strategos hypatos*), but was, strictly, proconsul at the time (cf. no. 34).

127. For the appointment of the ten see Polybius 18.42 and Livy 33.24.

128. Presumably the kings of Asia Minor, including Eumenes of Pergamon, Prusias of Bithynia and especially no doubt, Antiochus.

129. The usual Greek term for consul. It must be being used in an extended sense here to include proconsul since the letter is certainly after 198, the year of Flamininus' consulship. From 197 to 194 Flamininus held a proconsular command in Greece. Cf. no. 33 and n. 126.

130. This seems a clear reference to the Aetolians, who were critical of the Roman settlement of Greece from the start (cf. esp. Polybius 18.45; the word used of the Aetolians there is the same as appears here (*katalalein*)).

131. M. Valerius M.f. Messalla, praetor 193.

132. Menippos and Hegesianax were the ambassadors sent by Antiochus to Rome in the winter of 194/3; see esp. Livy 34.57-59.

133. The Herakleotai have performed a *deditio in fidem* to the Roman commander, as apparently have other Greek cities in the area. This involved total surrender of the city and all that was in it for the Romans to do with as they liked. The import of the gesture was not always understood by the Greeks: see Polybius 20.9-10 and cf. 36.4.

134. The reference in the letter to the siege of Same, which began in October, 189 and lasted for four months (cf. M. Holleaux, *Etudes* V, 249-86), means that only the consuls of 189 or 188 can be at issue here. As neither of the consuls of 189 was in Rome at the time, and as the name of the other consul of 188 (M. Valerius M.f. Messalla) is too long for the gap on the stone, the name of C. Livius M.f. Salinator must be restored here. The consuls of 188 entered office on the Ides of March, A.U.C. 566, which fell on 21 November 189 B.C. (*Phoenix* 27 [1973] 348). The letter was thus written between that date and the arrival at Rome of the news of the fall of Same (late January/early February, 188).

135. M. Fulvius M.f. Nobilior, consul 189.

136. A large number of Aetolian citizens (mostly from nearby Locris, as well as from Aetolia itself) had come to own houses and property in Delphian territory (cf. *RDGE* 37). After their liberation from the control of the Aetolian League, the Delphians wished them to leave and succeeded in obtaining Rome's support in evicting them.

137. 9 October by the Roman calendar, in fact 30 June 170 B.C. (*Phoenix* 27 [1973] 348-9).

138. Probably M'. Acilius Glabrio (son of the consul who fought against Antiochus in 191) and T. Numisius Tarquiniensis (ambassador to Antiochus and Ptolemy in 169 and member of the senatorial commission to settle the affairs of Macedon in 167).

139. 14 October by the Roman calendar, in fact 5 July 170 B.C. (cf. n. 137).

140. Probably P. Mucius Scaevola (consul 179; his brother served under Licinius Crassus in Greece in 171), M. Claudius Marcellus (ambassador to the Aetolians in 173 and likely the consul of 183), and M'. Sergius, who in 164 served on an embassy to Greece and Asia Minor. It seems likely (*RDGE*, p. 29) that these three, along with the two named earlier (n.138) comprised the group of five selected to help the Thisbeans prepare their case for the Senate.

141. The provision applies to those who had been driven into exile for their support of Rome and not to all who were, or claimed to be, pro-Romans.

142. A. Hostilius Mancinus, consul 170.

143. The details of this are obscure, but it appears that an attempt was made to bribe Lucretius. That the Senate takes it seriously may suggest it had been successful. In fact, Lucretius never appeared before the Senate. His conduct of the war was attacked by tribunes in 170 — he was said to have exhibited excessive cruelty and greed — and when he failed to appear in Rome he was condemned *in absentia* by all 35 tribes and fined 1,000,000 *asses* (see on this Livy 43.4, 7-8).

144. The details of this altercation are even more obscure, but the man Pandosinus is known to have been involved in other foreign enterprises in the period.

145. Eumenes' mother Apollonis was the daughter of a Kyzikene, and Miletos was the mother-city of Kyzikos.

146. Apollo (the) Founder (of Cyrene).

147. The text used here is that of *C.Ord.Ptol.* 53, where the evidence of unpublished partial copies (53 *bis-ter*) is brought to bear, and where a large and recent bibliography may be found. The translation of the original editors has however been used as the basis for this one.

148. The *apomoira*, a tax of a sixth on produce of these types of land, was allocated by the Revenue Laws to Arsinoe Philadelphos (no. 95); it is not certain what part if any was directly paid to the temples before 118, and the effect of this provision is thus not entirely clear. It

evidently constituted a significant royal concession.

149. The famous sacred bulls of Memphis who in succession incarnated the god Apis and who were buried in an elaborate funerary complex there.

150. This, the only death penalty specified in the document, suggests the importance attached by the sovereigns to this measure.

151. This clause avoids claims by those who have returned home to find their belongings confiscated and sold.

152. Who had apparently been one of the chief sources of rebellion against Euergetes.

153. The "taxpayers" in question here and elsewhere in this papyrus are evidently the workers in royal monopolies.

154. It is interesting to see which of the Egyptians are included in this privileged class, notably workers in the essential industries.

155. This is certainly a major innovation and one surely of great importance to the Egyptian subjects of the Ptolemies; the Greek judges are ordered to end and reverse their practice of concentrating judicial matters in their hands.

156. Byssus is a type of flax for linen.

157. Of the four consular Fabii Maximi available (the consuls of 145, 142, 121, and 116) only the last (Eburnus) is not known to have held a proconsular command in Spain or Gaul. He is thus the most likely to be the proconsular governor of Macedonia at issue here.

158. I.e., the *praetor peregrinus*.

159. The spelling of the name varied in antiquity; this form is the less common.

160. The Crimean Bosporus.

161. The phrase is the same in both places. Unless the first refers to early, the second to late, spring, these must be the events of two successive years.

162. This letter is extant, *P.Lond.* 465 (*SB* 6300), and repeats much of the phraeology of *P.Bour.* 10.

163. If the emendation of Schmidt in *BL* II is correct.

164. The proclamation is evidently intended by this "amnesty" to persuade fearful defaulters to clear their record at no cost.

165. Household slaves, that is.

166. The Crown thus reserves the right, denied to individuals, of enslaving its defaulting debtors.

167. Translations mainly those of *CPJud.* 4-5, using Tcherikover's additional restorations. Cf. this edition also for a bibliography.

168. *PSI* IV 325 is a duplicate addressed to another official.

169. A royal financial official outside Egypt, later active in Caria. *PSI* IV 325 is addressed to Hikesios, another such official.

170. This translation is based on that of Edgar in *Annales Service Antiq.* 22 (1922) 218, where a lengthy discussion is to be found.

171. Apollodotos and Hikesios were royal financial officials outside Egypt, perhaps *oikonomoi*.

172. A political opponent of Apollonios, perhaps *dioiketes* and eponymous priest in the next reign after the death and disgrace of Apollonios.

173. A Halikarnassian city official mentioned also in no. 99.

174. Translations based on those of Edgar, *Annales Service Antiq.* 20 (1920) 33-5, where there is an extensive discussion.

175. Sacred ambassador from his city, in this case to the great Ptolemaia of 248.

176. This should be 840.

177. This passage, like others in this text enclosed in parentheses, was bracketed for deletion by the author on second thoughts.

178. These are royal officials.

179. It is not clear if Zenon himself is to write to the officials, royal and civic, in Kalynda, as seems on the face of it to be the meaning, or if he is to get Apollonios to do these things (which he in fact apparently tried to do).

180. A brother of Zenon.

181. Not the *dioiketes*, but evidently another Carian friend.

182. Also in *Sel.Pap*. 416; cf. *BL* III 240 for Ad. Wilhelm's restorations to the text.
183. A crocodile god of the Fayum.
184. See no. 145 on this "sight".
185. An *ad hoc* committee chosen to deal with the arrangements for this loan.
186. Not only is everything owned by all the citizens of Arkesine pledged as security for Praxikles but also everything owned by the metics (resident aliens) as well. This may be related to the provision about overseas property, as Tarn suggests (*op.cit*. 110): "For metics were often traders and ship-owners; and the right given to Praxicles to seize metics' property as well as citizens' property really means the right to seize any ship belonging to any inhabitant of Arcesine without enquiring as to the owner's status. If he insisted on this right, he must have thought that his security over property in Arcesine itself might become valueless; and only one thing could make it valueless, a revolution and cancellation of debts." At issue, however, may be Arkesinean holdings on the small islands nearby.
187. *Symbola* were conventions between individual Greek cities that could provide for judicial procedures in cases involving citizens of both places, for regulation of commerical transactions and the like (cf. P. Gauthier, *Symbola* [Nancy 1972]). The *symbolon* here at issue provided for arbitration of (at least certain kinds of) court cases before another city (the "umpire city" of the inscription).
188. On the serious grain shortage at Athens in the early 320's compare Demosthenes 34.39; 42.20, 31; and no. 3.
189. This occurred during the archonship of Aristophon, 330/29; cf. text at note 191.
190. This took place in the archonship of Euthykritos, 328/7; cf. text at note 193.
191. 330/29.
192. The tyrant of Herakleia, on the northern coast of Asia Minor, about 150 miles east of Byzantium.
193. 328/7.
194. This particularly fertile area was on the mainland of Asia Minor, directly to the east of Samos. As it was temple land under Samian control, the money paid for grain would not in fact be altogether lost to the city (cf. Hands, *op.cit*. 95).
195. I.e., deprived of civic rights.
196. The supervison of the gymnasium involved not only looking after the training of the youths of the city but also the provision of the oil used for the athletic part of the program. It was thus a financial burden, and this presumably explains the difficulty encountered by the gymnasiarch, whose responsibility this was.
197. Ptolemy III Euergetes and Berenike.
198. On the mechanics involved in these operations, cf. in general no. 63, where the procedure is, by contrast, a permanent one.
199. It may be noted that in none of these three cases does Boulagoras permanently part with money. He rather allows the city to use his capital for a time. The same is true in the case of the *theoria* to Alexandria.
200. It is clear from what follows that the oldest group is quite close to the military age.
201. These two instructors were presumably already on hand to teach the ephebes. Since their appointment is not provided for in the present decree, the approval of the *demos* must be obtained before they can be paid out of the proceeds of Polythroos' gift.
202. This evidently refers to a regulation according to which it was not possible to challenge accounts after a certain period of time had elapsed.
203. For this governor of the Hellespontine satrapy, cf. no. 18. (It is, however, not impossible that this is another Meleager and that the kings at issue are Antiochus III and his son, the future Seleucus IV).
204. Seleucus was the elder son of Antiochus I and was associated with his father as king from 275 to 268/7 (cf. *Chiron* 5[1975] 61) at least. From 266 on the co-regent was the king's younger son, Antiochus (the future Antiochus II) who succeeded to the position after the death of his brother (for suspicion of treachery?).
205. On Menches, whose papers figure elsewhere in this collection, see the study of G.M. Harper, *Aegyptus* 14 (1934) 14-32, and on his village, D.J. Crawford, *Kerkeosiris* (Cambridge 1971).

206. Edible seeds of various leguminous plants.

207. Unproductive land was largely a result of the disorganization of the civil administration in charge of irrigation, by the wars of the second century, particularly the civil wars.

208. The reading is uncertain in both copies, and the date is thus not determined without doubt; the reign is that of Euergetes I and Klitarchos is elsewhere known in the 220's.

209. This transaction is somewhat obscure, since there is no mention of charges for official correspondence and no evidence that the system handled anything else.

210. Translation essentially that of *Sel.Pap.* 233.

211. Which was held by continuing leases rather than ownership.

212. Copper money was accepted but only at less than face value, a discount of almost 11 per cent when the transportation charge is included.

213. We do not follow the editor's assumption that the financial year was in use here (and the date thus 250), since it is generally agreed that in the reign of Ptolemy II the regnal year was in use in ordinary correspondence; there is no evidence here that this is not the case. (*P.Mich.* I, p. 55, to which the editor refers, indicates only Edgar's opinion that in the *next* reign the financial year was more widely used. Cf. also Samuel, *Ptolemaic Chronology* [München 1962] 77).

214. The name is for some reason erased.

215. The letter is much corrected and is certainly a first draft.

216. Philadelphos died during his 39th year, 247/6.

217. I.e., to incur the penalties provided by this proclamation, whether it be a general one or the announcement referred to above.

218. In reality no doubt a *hypodioiketes* under Apollonios, but the circumscription of his authority is uncertain.

219. The tax was paid in money, and all receipts were doubtless frozen until taxes were settled.

220. Reekmans, cf. *BL* III, 251 (Préaux thinks early second century).

221. Cf. *PSI* V 531.

222. The "Greek quarter".

223. The cubit being ca. 21 inches, so that the house and bakery would be each 36'9" x 22'9", their courtyards 22'9" x 7'.

224. In all probability this term here refers to the grant of the proceeds of a tax as a concession to an individual (as in no. 118). The banker is the same as in no. 69.

225. Cf. *BL* III, 84; this is an Oxyrhynchite document (Launey).

226. A note on the reverse in a different hand, seemingly irrelevant to this document, says "to build the theater".

227. We do not know why the loss was not simply covered by sureties.

228. Not the same as the addressee of this letter; perhaps an *oikonomos*.

229. Translation from *Sel.Pap.* 409, whose interpretation is adopted.

230. From their home cities.

231. The constant emphasis in Ptolemaic bureaucracy on the checking of one official by another is clearly shown here.

232. See below, no. 87.

233. To the river from the parts of the nome more distant from it.

234. Weaving was, like oilmaking (see no. 95) a royal monopoly, in which the crown purchased the raw materials at a set rate and apportioned them to royal workshops for manufacture, the whole being underwritten by contractors.

235. Paid by the head; hence the importance of an accurate census.

236. Emendations of M. David, B. van Groningen and E.P. Wegener have been incorporated into this paragraph and the next; cf. *BL* III, 244.

237. Wood is very scarce in Egypt, which lacks forests of trees usable for building material and which has for thousands of years imported its lumber.

238. Cf. no. 103 below for sanctions about deserters from the military as early as the middle of the third century.

239. Cf. *BL* I.

240. The plan and directions on it are in the papyrus, but the dimensions are editorial additions.

246

241. This total is not quite accurate: 1 tal. 3828, 3 1/3 ob. is the right amount.
242. Labor would be much cheaper in the off-season.
243. It is not clear what the reference is, whether to the cost of the work just mentioned or to another figure like that for damage (if that is correct) above.
244. Apollonios, no doubt.
245. The author is evidently Diodoros, known elsewhere to have been Apollonios' director of construction on this project during these years.
246. The bureau of the *basilikos grammateus*, which kept the official records, took part in the making of the schedule. It is not certain whether the *basilikos grammateus* himself or one of his subordinates (*topogrammateus, komogrammateus*) is here meant.
247. Of the Oxyrhynchite Nome, showing again the flexibility of the area to which a nomarch might be assigned.
248. This holding had probably been reclaimed by the crown but was still known by the name of its former cleruch.
249. An estate analogous to that of the *dioiketes* Apollonios.
250. *Arakos*: a leguminous crop used as fodder.
251. A blank is left here for an unknown reason.
252. No doubt the superintendent of revenues.
253. The procrastination appears equally to be on the part of the petitioner; if his case was so clear, why did he wait so long to appeal?
254. Cols. I-III only; cf. the corrections in *BL* I. We have followed Wilcken's changes of interpretation (*W.Chr.* 331) in several places, but rejected P. Kool's restoration in line 27 (*BL* III, 240)
255. What follows is still of doubtful interpretation on some points, as the writing is very ungrammatical.
256. Cf. *BL* II.2, 76 for correction of the priest's name.
257. The three children of Ptolemy V and Cleopatra, associated as sovereigns in the aftermath of Antiochus IV's invasion of Egypt.
258. Many documents of the later Ptolemaic period omit the names of these functionaries through ignorance or laziness; the purpose of retaining their titles is thus removed.
259. The Macedonian and Egyptian calendars were systematically equated to one another from the reign of Epiphanes; see A.E. Samuel, *Ptol. Chronology*, 129 ff.
260. The remaining clauses, preserved only in the second copy and only fragmentarily there, contain provisions for penalties, for failure to transplant; Apollonios' payment of some exaction for the wine press; the disposition of any "raisin" wine; disposition of any timber; the right of the lessor to install his own guard at the lessee's expense; loan of a shovel from lessor to lessee; etc.
261. That is, in the schedule of crops, cf. no. 87.
262. Translation also in *Sel.Pap.* 276, some of whose wording has been adopted.
263. Apollodoros is involved not in manufacture but rather the retail distribution and the tax on it.
264. A hippopotamus goddess.
265. On the date and persons see *Ancient Society* 3 (1972) 111-9; 10 (1979) 159-65.
266. Imouthes apparently succeeded his father in the position of *basilikos grammateus* not long afterward; despite the foreign rule, the long-standing Egyptian practice of appointing sons to be their father's "staff of old age" and thus successors apparently continued.
267. Cf. the valuable introduction to *W.Chr.* 309 and the translation as *Sel.Pap.* 223, from which some phraseology is taken.
268. This unexplained reference reinforces the theory that some kind of abnormal forced sale was intended, requiring perhaps an armed guard for the myrrh (or the collector).
269. Translation in *Sel.Pap.* 410.
270. The royal treasurer in Halikarnassos.
271. A royal tax on the Halikarnassians for medical service. Xanthippos can either repay all of it to Apollodotos or, as Apollodotos would prefer, split the repayment so that 2000 dr. would be credited to Apollodotos' (and thus the Halikarnassians') account in Alexandria and thus saving Apollodotos the trouble of sending it.

247

272. A contribution, generally involuntary, by the city to the king on some special occasion.
273. Cf. the text and introduction in *W.Chr.* 451
274. A town in the Apollonopolite Nome.
275. The note of Antipatros, evidently.
276. Perhaps a village *epistates*, but possibly another official connected with quartering.
277. The ordinance (see *C.Ord.Ptol.* 5-10) ordering that lodgers are to occupy not more than a half of the house, owners the other half.
278. Lines 85-105, 109-122, 141-153, and 235-245 are translated here, the remainder being too fragmentary for connected translation. The text and translation of the first two sections are from the article by Bagnall cited below.
279. These sailors were in all probability neither slaves nor demonstrably convicts; the branding of persons is not otherwise attested in Ptolemaic Egypt. The principle embodied in this passage is that if an official causes the loss of a man to the Crown, he must be personally liable for it, just as with money. The passage probably reflects problems with the fleet in the aftermath of the Third Syrian War (246-241).
280. Insecure conditions have evidently made night travel very hazardous, and these provisions allow it only under special circumstances.
281. The internal trade of Egypt was tightly regulated, and private movement of most items was either prohibited or heavily taxed. These officials are probably members of the central administration in Alexandria, and the exemptions they granted were no doubt few in number. Zenon appears to have held one of them.
282. This section is heavily restored (by Turner) and frankly conjectural. *Individual sections are not bracketed.*
283. No subsequent complete edition exists; sources for texts and translations of some individual sections are indicated severally below. For textual emendations see *BL* II.2 and III, but these mostly affect untranslated portions (largely Column XI) and most restorations are uncertain.
284. See nos. 53, 85, 95, 103, 108, 118, and 138.
285. On Ptolemaic Alexandria generally, see P.M. Fraser, *Ptolemaic Alexandria* (Oxford 1972).
286. Such as the present papyrus.
287. That is, convictions for perjury do not automatically invalidate the original decision based on perjured evidence if the perjury took place on both sides.
288. These witnesses could not be tried themselves, not being in Alexandria; thus any penalties for perjury could be exacted only from the Alexandrian party who had called them.
289. The word used (*asty*) designates the densely built and walled urban center; *polis* generally includes the entire territory of the city, inside or outside the walls.
290. Lines 103-107 are omitted as too fragmentary.
291. Beyond what he had deposited at the start as a pledge, which was forfeited to the winner.
292. Translation of the seven paragraphs following is from *Sel.Pap.* 201.
293. Primarily on military service, that is.
294. Such action would suggest that they were not helpless dependants and that they could handle lawsuits in the absence of the head of the family.
295. Money deposited against a possibly unfavorable outcome, in which case it would be forfeited to the winner.
296. Translation of this paragraph is from *Sel.Pap.* 207; the most recent text, with extensive bibliography, is *C.Ord.Ptol.* 24.
297. Next five paragraphs translated in *Sel.Pap.* 202.
298. A common practice in some Greek cities.
299. This is not a restored lacuna but Schubart's supplement to replace what he believed the copiest omitted.
300. The points about which the witness must give information.
301. Lines 234-259, which follow here and deal with the law governing sales, are incomplete, and the many — often conflicting — restorations that have been offered do not have sufficient certitude to justify presenting them here.

302. He did this presumably in order to avoid actually making a written contract specifying such usurious interest; the maximum legal interest at the time was apparently 24 per cent per annum.

303. From 267-259 a son of Ptolemy II ruled as co-regent with his father, until he revolted in Asia Minor in one of the less well-documented but most discussed episodes of Hellenistic history; cf. no. 21.

304. A prominent military commander, probably at this time actually on duty in the Aegean in the Chremonidean War. His son Pelops served as governor of Cyprus.

305. The editors note that this contract signed in the Oxyrhynchite Nome nonetheless refers to a case to be tried in the neighboring Herakleopolite Nome.

306. One would expect 400 (including the interest), as T. Reekmans has pointed out (*BL* III, 84).

307. We follow Edgar's interpretation of lines 3-5 in *P.Mich.*, not that of his first edition (adopted by Lenger) regarding the person who was the surety.

308. Evidently an official in charge of promulgating royal ordinances, who had held that office for more than 30 years; see *C.Ord.Ptol.* 27 with discussion of the juristic questions involved here and a bibliography.

309. The editor suggests on the basis of the phraseology of the generalized application of the rule in this text that a line has been dropped by the copiest and the bracketed reading is probably the true one; Lenger and most others follow this interpretation.

310. Also *M.Chr.* 42.

311. The *basilikos grammateus*.

312. The nome capital, about 14 miles from Kerkeosiris; since Menches dates the report on the same day as the announcement to Heras, he may have handed the report in to the *basilikos grammateus* in Ptolemais Euergetis; or this (his copy) may be backdated.

313. Thebes, "the great city of Amun".

314. I.e., Mut.

315. I.e., Epet.

316. As we shall see below, this applied only to the *taricheutai*, not to the *choachytai*.

317. See below, where the defendants argue (successfully) that this has nothing to do with their case.

318. That is, a document of his having deposited the purchase price into the bank.

319. That is, if Hermias was to force every detail of court procedure and proof on his opponents, he would be subject to similar demands before the *laokritai*.

320. Action before the *chrematistai* is apparently meant.

321. See no. 45 for this amnesty, which was evidently extended several months beyond its original cut-off date.

322. See *UPZ* II 161 for this, the earlier victory by Horos et al.

323. Here we have the summing up by the *epistates* preparatory to sentencing.

324. *Xenikon praktor* ("collector of foreign things") was an official who executed court judgments; it is usually thought that his competence extended over cases where the parties to a dispute lived in different jurisdictions; Cl. Préaux, *Chronique d'Egypte* 30 (1955) 107-11, argues that they collected in cases not under the law of any Greek city.

325. The trousseau is thus worth 1 talent, 4100 dr.

326. It seems that the date was first written as year 31, but the writer realized that it was now year 32 and changed it; the Macedonian year changed at sundown on Pharmouthi 1.

327. Cf. *BL* II, 2.

328. Textual corrections from *BL* III, 45 by Welles are incorporated here; the editors' reading in line 16 is preferred to that of Préaux cited in the *BL*.

329. In *katoche*, like Ptolemaios (see nos. 142-144).

330. This petition is extant (*UPZ* I 7). with the instructions of the *strategos* to Menedemos to see that Ptolemaios got justice. The remark here apparently means that there was no one to perform the errands from one bureaucrat to another that fell upon a petitioner, and that the instructions thus went unexecuted.

331. Demotic, that is.

332. A medical specialty attested in this form only here.

333. Translation is that of *Sel.Pap.* 269.

334. An Aetolian mercenary who rose to high rank in the confused years of the minority of Ptolemy V; he receives a concession of a tax here as a source of income.

335. Presumably the price would be lower to compensate the buyer for this added expense.

336. See Pringsheim's discussion of this term and procedure as well as the editor's discussion. The procedure involved the prolongation of the auction process.

337. See n. 324.

338. The sense of this passage is uncertain. We follow the interpretation of Edgar and Hunt in *Sel.Pap.* II, p. 41 here and in line 27, in preference to that of E. Schönbauer in *Archiv für Papyrusforschung* 10 (1932) 185. On the interpretation adopted, the penultimate paragraph involves a tax on the contract of pledging the person, the last paragraph a further tax on the eventual execution of the pledge.

339. Only Column I is translated, since all of Column II is damaged and much is heavily restored. Text also as *M.Chr.* 370, but cf. *BL* I, 203.

340. That is, where a royal ordinance has superseded the city law.

341. This passage probably allowed such actions only with court order.

342. Translation as in *CPJud.* 1; also *Sel.Pap.* 31. Two copies are written on the papyrus, and restorations are bracketed here only when neither copy has the words in question.

343. The names were probably unknown this early in the year in Syria.

344. Or Babylonian, less likely.

345. *Sel.Pap.* 234.

346. The native name of Hierapolis.

347. These letters were symbols of consecration to the gods of Hierapolis, Hadad and Atargatis, and probably were the first letters of those divinities' names in Aramaic.

348. This and the next provision refer to special cases of the preceding ("whoever brings back...") rather than to different situations where the slave is not returned.

349. Translation in *Sel.Pap.* 1; cf. *BL* V, 27. Discussion by H.J. Wolff, *Written and Unwritten Marriages*, 10-21.

350. *Sel.Pap.* 82.

351. Cf. *BL* II.2, 53 and III, 50. Translation partly based on *Sel.Pap.* 268.

352. A bawdy comedian.

353. The epithet of a cult of Arsinoe Philadelphos, probably located on the sea-shore ("of the headland").

354. An epiphany of Apollo had evidently preceded that of his sister.

355. The Pythian games were held in 222, the Olympic in 220.

356. This suggests that the kings accepted the games but that the leagues and cities accepted more; cf. no. 128.

357. About Theordorus nothing further is known, and his appearance here is odd, as Amynander is king of Athamania from as early as 220; cf. no. 130 n. 372.

358. Among the sons of Hellen (whence "Hellenes") was Athamas (whence "Athamanians").

359. These are public officials of the city of Delos.

360. Philip V of Macedon, who is named elsewhere in these accounts. Telesarchides' (second) archonship was in 181. This jar reappears in B (expenditures).

361. King of Numidia and long-time ally of Rome; he frequently sent shipments of grain to Delos.

362. Eumenes II of Pergamon.

363. Daughter of Demetrius Poliorcetes, wife of Seleucus I then Antiochus I. Her offerings appear also in the inventory for 250.

364. This dedication, one of many from Echenike, was made in 250.

365. The famous Spartan admiral. Another Spartan admiral, Pharax (active from the 390's) appears below.

366. Ptolemy I.

367. Demetrius Poliorcetes. His father Antigonus appears below.

368. A naval commander in the service of Ptolemy I (cf. Diodorus 19.62, 64); the dedication was made prior to 280.

369. King of the Sidonians; the dedication dates from before 280.

370. This dedication also pre-dates 280. Iomilkos was a Carthaginian; he is elsewhere designated as "king".

371. King of Salamis (Cyprus), predecessor of Nikokreon. the dedication was there in 280.

372. Daughter of Theodoros King of Athamania; cf. no. 129.

373. A Theban flutist active in the 280's. The crown, dedicated by 280, is likely a prize he won.

374. In Antiochus' letter he appears as a relation of the king. He is to be identified with the Ptolemy of Telmessos of Livy 37.56.4 and seen as the grandson of the Ptolemy son of Lysimachus who received Telmessos from Ptolemy III in 240/39 (*OGIS* 55) or even earlier. Descent from Lysimachus would make him a relative of Seleucids and Ptolemies alike.

375. 9 May 193 B.C.

376. Seleucus III, who ruled from 226 to 223.

377. Daphne was held in special regard by the Seleucids, who claimed descent from Apollo.

378. 12 October 189 B.C.

379. Republished in *C.Ord.Ptol.* 29 with extensive bibliography. The translation of *Sel.Pap.* II 208 is used.

380. The date is based on the fact that this decree is written on the back of a document of 215/4.

381. See Lenger's summary of viewpoints (n. 379).

382. Nock comments that Zeus Hypsistos or the Theos Hypsistos (highest god) are usefully vague terms, which appear alike in Macedonian and Semitic situations; exactly what is meant here is not certain, but is clearly not a Jewish cult.

383. The contrast to Greek associations, typically made for permanence, endowed with a multiplicity of officers and other institutions, often owners of property and communal buildings, is very striking.

384. Zenon had a brother of this name, but he is known to have been at large and active in the year preceding the date of the letter; this is therefore a different person, probably a Carian friend.

385. Ptolemy III Euergetes ("Benefactor") and Berenike, daughter of Magas of Cyrene.

386. The canephore ("basket-bearer") was the priestess of the deified wife of Ptolemy II Philadelphos, a Greek like the other official priests.

387. 7 March 238 B.C.

388. Interpreters of the sacred writings associated with various divinities.

389. The formula is that of a standard Greek decree. Here, however, the "proposer" is everyone at the meeting.

390. Mnevis was the sacred bull associated with Heliopolis, analogous to the more famous Apis bull at Memphis. For other sacred beasts cf. Diodorus 1.84.

391. Cf. no. 26.

392. Ptolemy I Soter and his wife Berenike.

393. I.e., Sirius; at this time it rose at Alexandria about 24 July.

394. The tenth month of the Egyptian calendar which was at this time some two to three weeks ahead of the seasonal year.

395. The Egyptian year had twelve months of 30 days each, plus five additional days at the end. Every four years it would move one day ahead in relation to the seasonal (solar) year, since over the four year period it provided 1,460 days instead of the required 1,461.

396. The needed "leap-year" was thus provided for, but the provision fell before long into disuse.

397. The word is the same as that for queen.

398. I.e., hieroglyphics.

399. I.e., Demotic Egyptian writing.

400. Ptolemy V was twelve years old at the time.

401. The 30-years feast is the Egyptian Heb-Sed festival celebrated by Pharaohs (from at least the Old Kingdom) after 30 years of rule, more frequently thereafter.

402. I.e., Re.

403. I.e., Amun.

404. Ptolemy V Epiphanes Eucharistos.
405. For the canephore of Arsinoe, cf. n. 386.
406. 27 March 196.
407. Cf. n. 388.
408. Cf. n. 389.
409. The Egyptian *machimoi*. Having seen little military service under the first three Ptolemies,many of them fought in Ptolemy IV's war against Antiochus III and distinguished themselves in Ptolemy's victory at Raphia in 217. Thereafter rebelliousness among them was not uncommon; cf. Polybius 5.107.
410. The reference is to the attacks of Antiochus III and Philip V on Ptolemaic possessions in 202 (?)-197.
411. On the siege of Lykonpolis, cf. Polybius 22.17.
412. Cf. n. 390.
413. A portable shrine.
414. Cf. notes 398, 399.
415. *C.Ord.Ptol.* 47, with bibliography. Only lines 12 ff. are given here, the cover letter to this circular letter being too badly damaged to be restored.
416. Lenger, p. 112, hesitates to accept the necessity of assuming the first system of assimilation of the Greek and Egyptian calendars, to equate Panemos in this text with Tybi and hence date the papyrus in February, 139. But Samuel, *Ptolemaic Chronology*, 129-38, shows clearly that only this method of equation was in use at the time, and the February date is thus necessary.
417. The country-wide distribution and application of this order seem to suggest that the notion of the editors and of Lenger that a place name (location of a particular cult) is lost in some part of this lacuna is incorrect, but no satisfactory restoration has been proposed.
418. These are apparently brothels run by the temples, and to the operation of which they claimed to have monopolistic rights of some sort (they protest below against unauthorized establishments of this kind).
419. Various corrections are incorporated into the edition as *Sel.Pap.* 411, from which this translation is adapted.
420. Cleopatra III reckoned her regnal years from an earlier date than did Alexander.
421. A mistake for "the Father-Loving Gods".
422. A mistake for "priestess of Arsinoe Philopator".
423. The governor of the Thebaid under Euergetes II.
424. Another draft of the same petition, *UPZ* I 11, gives the date of September 161 for this activity.
425. In *UPZ* 11 it is specified: to Apollonios my younger brother, who is also to receive the value of the goods seized.
426. A less dramatic version of the farewell than in the other draft ("so that I may not perish of hunger").
427. Lines 5-35 only, as in *Sel.Pap.* 272.
428. A particular group of settlers, so designated by the king. The significance is not clear.
429. The Egyptian revolt of 164 (Dionysios), probably, or else the dynastic strife of the time.
430. *Sel.Pap.* 97.
431. Wilcken considered that this is to be taken literally, and that Isias was both wife and sister of Hephaistion. For a contrary view (right, we believe) see J. Modrzejewski, *Journal of Juristic Papyrology* 9-10 (1955-56) 346-7.
432. Hephaistion had not left the Serapeum, or the papyrus would not have been found there. It is possible that Horos did not understand the *katoche* and gave misleading information to Isias. Then again, Hephaistion may have been avoiding a return home.
433. Vestment-keepers to a god's cult.
434. A large construction in the Fayum near the metropolis of the nome and adjacent to the pyramid of its builder, Ammenemes III of the Twelfth Dynasty; it probably embodied a mortuary temple for its builder and various shrines of the gods. See recent articles by A.B. Lloyd, *Journal of Egyptian Archaeology* 56 (1970) 81-100 and K. Michaelowski in the same journal 54

(1968) 219-22.

435. This text, based on the article by Rémondon cited in the introduction, is preferable to that in *CPJud*. 141.

APPENDIX I
PTOLEMAIC ADMINISTRATION

The essential basis of the administration of Egypt in all of antiquity was the nome, the administrative district. The entire country was divided into these nomes, whose size and number varied from time to time. In early Ptolemaic times the number stood in the low forties, divided almost equally between upper (southern) and lower (northern) Egypt. The nome division was in general of great antiquity and was fundamental to whatever administrative superstructure might be placed over it. We know little of the officials of the nomes in the country before the arrival of Ptolemy I as satrap, but it appears that Alexander and Ptolemy both left the essential structure unchanged. There were three branches of the nome administration, the bureaus of the nomarch, *oikonomos* and *basilikos grammateus*. In the theoretical form of third-century Ptolemaic administration, the nomarch (with his subordinates the toparchs and komarchs at local levels) was in charge of agricultural production; the *oikonomos* and his checking-clerks (*antigrapheis*) supervised finances; and the *basilikos grammateus* (again with subordinate *topogrammateis* and *komogrammateis*) kept the necessary records, especially of the land. Other offices are mostly minor adjuncts to this system, except for the police. All of these officials reported to the *dioiketes* in Alexandria, the chief finance and interior minister of the king.

To this structure, largely traditional except perhaps for the nomarch's position as equal rather than superior to the others, the Ptolemies made one significant addition. It was necessary, in order for the king to maintain an army of Greeks and Macedonians, to provide sustenance for the troops. Rather than keep all of them constantly under arms, which was both expensive and dangerous, the king distributed them throughout the nomes on lots of land (*kleroi*) which were to provide incomes for the soldiers and their families. This practice was not new in Egyptian experience, but it was probably much the largest application of such a scheme. There developed, hence, a military structure in the country with ordinary infantry, cavalry, and their commanders of all ranks. The exact structure of the upper command is not certain, but it seems that what modern scholars call "eponymous commanders" (because the troops were designated "of the men of e.g. Nautas") bore a major responsibility for surveillance and mobilization. A more direct control over the military cleruchs fell to the highest echelon of officers, the *strategoi*. In the earliest times it was their responsibility to look after the interests of their subordinates and to regulate their affairs. The authority of the regular bureaucrats, which was complete over the native population, was proportionately diminished over the soldiers as the latter relied on their military commmanders rather than on the civil authority. The military thus constituted a state within a state.

The development of the position of the *strategos* from these beginnings is one of the most fascinating phenomena of Ptolemaic administration. As the third century went on, the *strategoi* gained more power in nome affairs, often sharing surveillance of matters with the regular nome officials. A curious situation resulted, for the *strategos* seems to have been a direct royal appointee rather than a bureaucrat answerable to the *dioiketes*. For the rest of Ptolemaic rule the power of the *strategos* continued to grow at the expense of that of other chief nome officers, especially the nomarch. It is not hard to see that with the three bureaucrats each heading a department and one equal to another in authority, a lack of one dominant person at the nome level would be felt; the *strategos* filled this gap. As time went on, however, this power was tempered by the fact that as the *strategos* superseded the *dioiketes'* men, he too came under the all-powerful chief minister. It was the Macedonian position that became dominant, but only at the price of assimilating itself to the basic pattern of Egyptian bureaucracy.

Of the central administration in Alexandria that presided over this situation we know rather less. We know that the nome officials reported to the office of the *dioiketes*, where hordes of secretaries must have taken care of central accounting and record-keeping. Beyond this, the king had his court retainers, his chancery, and his military organization. Later development added the office of the *idios logos*, in charge of administering what we might call non-recurring income. This post was at times combined with that of *dioiketes*. The papyri do not tell us all we would like to know about the central record offices, largely because papyri have not been found at Alexandria.

The nature of landholding in the nomes is clear only in its broad outlines. The Greeks did not have precise terminology for the classes of land tenure. The king viewed Egypt as a whole as his property but exercised his rights directly over part of it only, the royal land. This land was cultivated by royal peasants on leases. It seems that a large portion of the land in the Arsinoite Nome (the Fayum) was royal land; we cannot tell the proportions elsewhere. The peasants were not bondsmen who could be granted with the land. They paid a fixed rent each year, determined by the condition of the land after the inundation of the year.

All other land was considered released for other uses by the king — cleruchic plots, temple lands, city land, royal "gifts", and private land. The privileges and obligations of holders of these classes varied widely, and no one system can be described for all. There were few if any blanket exemptions from taxes, and cleruchs paid taxes just as did private owners, perhaps even bearing some unique to them.

The larger part of government revenues from taxes came from taxes in kind: fixed rents and proportionate taxes in grain and other produce. As well as grain lands, vineyards, orchards and other producing lands were subject to taxes. Peasants on royal land paid a rent fixed annually, while some other categories paid a percentage of the total crop; vineyards, for example, paid an *apomoira* of one-sixth (after 259, paid to the cult of Arsinoe Philadelphos). Taxes in money were also numerous. Those exercising trades were subject to a tax at a flat rate. There was a salt-tax; there were taxes like the *ennomion*, pasture-tax, that fell on those using resources belonging to the king. In addition, a variety of taxes were paid to support specific state services, such as police-tax, medical-tax, and dike-tax.

The money taxes were generally collected through a tax-farming system which differed substantially from the Greek methods that were its ancestors. The tax-farmers, wealthy men able to post a large surety-bond, and often operating as a consortium, underwrote a guarantee of the revenues for a year from a specific tax. They bid for the contracts for the taxes at annual auctions. If collections fell short of the sum bid, the farmers were forced to pay the difference, but if there was a surplus, the farmers retained an additional profit, though not always the entire surplus. It was obviously necessary for the tax-farmers to be thoroughly familiar with the district for which they were bidding. The farmers supervised the various stages of tax collection in order to make sure that their position was not jeopardized by official incompetence or malfeasance, but they did not themselves collect the taxes.

The farmers also played a major role in another main source of royal revenues, the monopolies and government industries. Foremost among these was the production of oil from seeds, a business very closely regulated by the state for its own profit. Other monopolies included linen, beer, and a host of less important ones.

It is difficult to speak of the role of judicial proceedings in the governing of Egypt. The bureaucrats enumerated earlier decided many things that would now require a legal decision, but it is probably more accurate to say that this reflects the extent of the administration's powers and grip on the lives of the people than to attribute to these officials "judicial powers" in the modern sense. It is true that many officials, notably the nomarch and *strategos*, heard "cases" of complaints and decided them; petitions to the king were routinely referred to the *strategoi* for action. Modern scholars have often considered this activity judicial, but to make a real distinction between administrative and judicial activities of a bureaucrat is probably to impose a modern conception on the ancient situation.

There was, however, a judicial system independent of these officials. Standing courts, *dikasteria*, are attested in the *metropoleis* of the nomes, for the needs of Greek settlers, as early as 270. The Egyptians operated under their own law where it was not superseded by royal edict and with their own native judges, the *laokritai*. The most distinctive feature of the Ptolemaic judicial system was the court of the *chrematistai*, the royal judges. Each board had three members and a clerk; each was responsible for an administrative area. The format became gradually more systematized as time went on. At the head of it was the *archidikastes*, a prominent official resident in Alexandria. Our evidence for his functions is not extensive, but we can safely conclude that he was the king's deputy charged with overseeing the work of the entire judicial system. By the end of the Ptolemaic dynasty his control over the *chrematistai* and the other courts was explicitly spelled out in his titulature, and it is probable that the function if not the title goes back to the third century.

The nature of the civic administration of Alexandria, where the *archidikastes* had his seat, where the royal palace was located, is still very much of a question because of the paucity of source material. It was a Greek city, with a social organization of tribes and demes, with cultural institutions like the gymnasium. But the government of the city is poorly known. There was no *boule* at the end of the Ptolemaic period, but scholars have often hypothesized the earlier existence of one and the date of its disappearance. The presence of the overwhelming size and power of the royal government must have inhibited the growth of democratic institutions; such vital elements of civic life and business as the port and foreign trade were controlled by the king, not the city.

In contrast, Ptolemais, in the Thebaid, appears to have had at least in form the typical institutions of Greek political life, such as the *boule* and *demos*. This did not hinder royal control, of course, and a royal official might hold a civic office. But in form Ptolemais acted as a Greek city. The same seems to be true for Naukratis, although we know it less well than Ptolemais.

TABLES AND CHARTS

I. Ptolemaic Kings
Ptolemy I Soter	323-283	
Ptolemy II Philadelphos	285-246	
Ptolemy III Euergetes	246-222	
Ptolemy IV Philopator	221-205	
Ptolemy V Epiphanes	204-180	
Ptolemy VI Philometor	180-145	
Ptolemy VII Neos Philopator	145	
Ptolemy VIII Euergetes II	170-116	
Ptolemy IX Soter II	116-80	
Ptolemy X Alexander	114-88	
Ptolemy XI Alexander II	80	
Ptolemy XII Neos Dionysos (Auletes)	80-51	
Ptolemy XIII Dionysos	52-47	ruled with Cleopatra VII (57-30)
Ptolemy XIV Philopator	47-44	

II. Seleucid Kings to 96 B.C.
Seleucus I Nicator	312-281	(312 start of Seleucid era)
Antiochus I Soter	280-261	
Antiochus II Theos	261-247	
Seleucus II Callinicus	246-226	
Seleucus III Ceranus	226-223	
Antiochus III "The Great"	223-187	
Seleucus IV Philopator	187-175	
Antiochus IV Epiphanes	175-163	
Demetrius I Soter	162-150	
Alexander Balas	150-147	(pretender)
Demetrius II Nicator	146-140, 129-126	
Antiochus VI Epiphanes	145-142	(pretender)
Antiochus VII Euergetes (Sidetes)	139-129	
Seleucus V	126-125	
Antiochus VIII Philometor (Grypus)	125-96	
Antiochus IX Philopator (Cyzicenus)	116-95	

III. Antigonid Kings
Antigonus I Monophthalmos	306-301	(took crown in 306)
Demetrius I Poliorcetes	306-283	
Antigonus II Gonatas	283-238	
Demetrius II Aetolicus	239-229	
Antigonus III Doson	229-221	
Philip V	221-179	
Perseus	181-168	

IV. Attalid Rulers

Philetairos	d. 263
Eumenes I	263-241
Attalus I Soter	241-197
Eumenes II	197-159
Attalus II Philadelphos	159-138
Attalus III Philometor	138-133

V. Months

A. Athenian

Hekatombaion	Gamelion
Metageitnion	Anthesterion
Boedromion	Elaphebolion
Pyanepsion	Mounychion
Maimakterion	Thargelion
Poseideon	Skirophorion

B. Delian

Lenaion	Hekatombaion
Hieros (Sacred)	Metageitnion
Galaxion	Bouphonion
Artemision	Apatourion
Thargelion	Aresion
Panemos	Posideon

C. Macedonian

Dystros	Gorpiaios
Xandikos	Hyperberetaios
Artemisios	Dios
Daisios	Apellaios
Panemos	Audnaios
Loios	Peritios

D. Egyptian

Thoth	Phamenoth
Phaophi	Pharmouthi
Hathyr	Pachon
Choiak	Pauni
Tybi	Epeiph
Mecheir	Mesore (with epagomenal days)

VI. Currency

6 obols = 1 drachma
100 drachmas = 1 mina
60 minas = 1 talent

GLOSSARY AND INDEX
OF GREEK TERMS

For all items except a few very common ones, references are given to the texts in which the terms appear; these are cited *by document number*.

agonothetes: official responsible for putting on public games: 13 (Athens), 16 (Ilion), 64 (Samos).

agora: market place: 11 (Priene), 29B (Smyrna), 67 (Pergamon).

agoranomos: in Greek cities a magistrate in charge of supervision of the *agora*. His function in Egypt is mainly that of a notary public: 118, 140.

aisymnetes, -ai: eponymous magistrate at Naxos: 60.

antigrapheus: checking clerk in Ptolemaic administration, particularly of an *oikonomos*: 45, 83, 95.

apomoira: a Ptolemaic tax on produce of vineyards, orchards and similar land, of one-sixth of the net, paid (after legislation of Ptolemy II) to the cult of Arsinoe Philadelphos: 45, 72, 94, 95.

architheoros: head of a *theoria* (q.v.): 17 (Kos), 64 (Samos).

archon: eponymous and chief civil magistrate at Athens; eponymous magistrate at Arkesine (60).

aroura: unit of measure of land surface used in Egypt, about two-thirds of an acre: *passim*.

artaba: Persian unit of dry measurement, used in Egypt, especially for grains; somewhat more than bushel: *passim*.

artaba-tax: a tax on grainland in Ptolemaic Egypt, evidently calculated at the rate of one artaba per aroura.

athlophore: a priestess of Berenike II Euergetis: 94, 140.

basileus, -eis: (literally "king"), title of magistrates at Mytilene (5), Chersonnesos (48).

basilikos grammateus, -oi, -eis: "royal scribe", head of the record-keeping department for the nome in Ptolemaic administration: 77, 80, 86, 91, 93, 95, 100, 110, 138.

boule: the deliberative council of a Greek *polis*: *passim*.

bouleuterion: building where the *boule* met: 65 (Teos).

chiliastys, -yes: division of the citizen body at Samos (63).

choachytes, -ai: Egyptian "libation-pourer", generally a priest of the dead: 110, 141.

choregos: individual responsible for the provision of a chorus for public festivals: 7 (Teos).

choinix: measure of grain or other dry good, a part (varying) of an artaba: *passim*.

chora: the "country", referring variously to the territory surrounding the urban center of a *polis* and belonging to it or to areas not part of any city, especially in Egypt, where the *chora* is all land not part of the territories of Naukratis, Alexandria and Ptolemais: *passim*.

chous: unit of liquid measure, part (varying) of a *metretes*: *passim*.

chrematistes, -ai: member of panel (usually of three) of Greek judges in Egypt: 45, 95, 105, 110, 111, 112.

cleruch: soldier assigned a *kleros* for support and income rather than being paid in money, mainly in Ptolemaic Egypt: 77, 95, 120, 138, 143.

crown-tax: tax collected to provide kings with "crowns" (theoretically, voluntary gifts) of precious metals on special occasions: 45.

damiourgos, -oi: federal magistrate of the Achaean League (30); magistrate at Dyme (46).

daneistes, -ai: (pl.) a loan committee at Arkesine (60 with n. 185); generally, lender.

dekanos, -oi: "chief of ten men", a subordinate officer of police in Ptolemaic Egypt: 91.

demos: the full citizen body of a Greek *polis*, represented by the public assembly open to all citizens: *passim*.

diadochos, -oi: "Successor", used as one of the lower ranks in the Ptolemaic court hierarchy in the second century. Its earlier meaning is not certain: 110.

diagramma: royal edict or set of instructions, usually containing specific directions or schedules rather than general legislation: 4 (Tegea: from Alexander), 7 (Teos: from Antigonus), 95, 103 (both Ptolemaic).

diaitetes, -ai: an arbitrator, found in Alexandria as member of a type of court: 104.

diaskopos, -oi: magistrate (public investigator?) at Mytilene: 5.

dikasterion: court of the *dikastai* (q.v.): 104.

dikastes, -ai: juryman, member of the main civic law court in many Greek cities: 104.

doiketes: royal official in charge of (financial) administration of an area. In the Ptolemaic kingdom he is the chief royal minister, head of practically all departments of the government except the military: 45, 52, 57, 68, 71, 76, 77, 86, 91, 95, 97, 99, 105, 120, 139, 146; in the Seleucid kingdom he is a lower-ranking official: 64 (Samos).

dorea: "gift" estate or concession of varying sorts in the Ptolemaic kingdom: 79.

eisagogeus, -eis: magistrate responsible for bringing cases into court: 9 (Ephesos).

eparourion: a land tax in Ptolemaic Egypt: 45.

ephor: chief magistrate at Sparta (board of five of whom one was eponymous): 19.

Epigone: "descent, offspring", used in Ptolemaic Egypt to refer to descendants of foreign settlers in Egypt, as in "Macedonian of the Epigone": 94, 107, 143.

epimeletes, -ai: supervisor or overseer, a financial official in Ptolemaic Egypt: 78, 138.

epimenios: monthly president of the *boule* or assembly: 16 (Ilion); 29 (Smyrna: *boule*).

epistates: title of magistrate or official, used (1) in Greek cities for the president of the *boule* or assembly: 14 (Miletos), 16 (Ilion), 21 (Miletos), 63 (Samos),; (2) for the subordinate of the *strategos* of a nome in Egypt, active at the village level, and (3) a similar official in later Ptolemaic times at the nome level. Both have law enforcement duties, but there is also an *epistates* of police at the nome level: 80, 89, 96, 98, 103, 110, 117, 123.

epistrategos, -oi: official like *strategos* but of superior rank, found primarily in Ptolemaic times in charge of the Thebaid: 50, 110.

exetastes, -ai: magistrate in charge of auditing public accounts: 29 (Smyrna), 64 (Samos).

friends (of the king): a court title in Egypt: 110.

gerontes: council of elders at Sparta (= *gerousia*): 19.

gymnasiarch: official responsible for maintenance of the gymnasium: 31 (Larisa; one of the eponyms), 64 (Samos), 65 (Teos), 110 (Egypt).

half-artaba tax: a tax on land probably introduced by Ptolemy VIII, of one-half artaba of grain per aroura: 45.

hegemon (over men): military officer of subordinate rank; "over men" indicates a commander of troops on active duty (as opposed to staff officers): 110.

hieronomos, -oi: supervisor of a sancutary: 16 (Ilion).

hieropoios, -oi: official responsible for a sanctuary: 11 (Priene).

hipparch, hipparchy: commander of cavalry, (1) at Athens, of the commanders of the tribal contingents (19: cf. taxiarch); (2) in the Achaean League, the second-highest federal magistrate, next to the *strategos* (30: Orchomenos); (3) in Ptolemaic Egypt: 95, 123 (hipparchy is his command).

hyparch: subordinate governor; official in charge of a (Seleucid) satrapy: 25 (Didyma), 131 (Eriza).

hyparchy: administrative subdivision in Ptolemiac Syria: 53.

intercalary: "extra" month inserted in various calendars at intervals to bring average year length closer to 365 days.

katoche: "detention" in sanctuary of Sarapis (notably at Memphis) by order of the god: 115, 142-144.

katoikic: of or characterizing *katoikoi* (q.v.).

katoikos, -oi: soldier settled on land given him in return for military service; military colonist: 29 (Magnesia).

kinsman (of the king): highest level of the hierarchy of court rank under the Ptolemies: 91, 110, 141.

kleros, -oi: plot of land allotted to someone, particularly to a Ptolemaic soldier: 102.

koinon: usually a league, or confederation of states, as: of the Ionians (10, 20, 41), of the Achaeans (30); also of other groups acting as political units, as of those in Magnesia (29); of the Delphians (39); or of other associations, as of the Pompeistai at Delos (51).

komarch: official of nomarch's (q.v.) bureau at village level, responsible for supervision of agricultural production: 53, 85, 95.

komogrammateus, -eis: "village scribe", head of records for a village under the department of the *basilikos grammateus*: 68, 70, 80, 85, 90, 91, 96, 98, 109, 110.

kriterion: judge's court or tribunal: 104 (Alexandria).

krites: judge: 104 (Alexandria).

kroton: plant that produces seeds from which castor oil is made, or the produce of this plant: 24.

laokritai: native Egyptian judges: 45, 110.

libyarch: Ptolemaic administrator of uncertain competence, probably in charge of desert areas on edge of Nile Valley: 95.

liturgikon: a tax probably paid in lieu of performance of a compulsory service in Ptolemaic Egypt: 45.

machimoi: the native Egyptian warrior class: 137

medimnos, -oi: a dry measure: 3 (Cyrene), 13 (Athens), 23 (Pergamon), 62 (Athens).

metretes, -ai: a unit of liquid measure: 23, 24, 57.

modius: a Roman dry measure, equivalent to a *hekteus* (q.v.): 49 (Nysa).

nauarch: naval commander, admiral; magistrate of the Achaean League: 30 (Orchomenos).

naubion: a cubic measure of earth: 86.

neopoies, -ai: official in charge of a temple building: 9 (Ephesos).

nesiarch: chief magistrate of the League of the Islanders: 61 (Delos).

nomarch: chief administrative officer of a nome for agricultural affairs: 88, 95, 103, 110.

nome: administrative subdivision of Egypt; there were over forty of them under the Ptolemies:*passim.*

nomophylax: "guardian of the laws", official in various Greek cities: 56, 104, 119.

oikonomos: "manager" of royal financial affairs, in Egypt at the nome level: 45, 53, 57, 71, 77, 91, 95, 96, 104, 138; in the Seleucid kingdom: 25 (Didyma).

olyra: a variety of wheat: *passim.*

paidonomos, -oi: magistrate in charge of education: 65 (Teos).

paroikos, -oi: resident alien, or metic (*metoikos*): 16 (Ilion), 17 (Kos).

pentadrachm: five-drachma piece.

peplos: at Athens, the embroidered robe carried in the procession of the Panathenaic festival and presented to Athena: 13.

peridromos, -oi: at Mytilene, magistrate in charge of a circuit court: 5.

phylarch: head of a tribe (*phyle*): 19 (Athens; one of the 12 tribal divisions of the citizenry); 136 (Canopus: of one of the tribes of Egyptian priests).

phrourarch: garrison commander.

plethron, -a: measure of length (100 feet) and area (10,000 square feet): 18 (Ilion).

poletes, -ai: magistrate in charge of letting public contracts: 17 (Kos).

praktor: a collector; various types are known in Ptolemaic administration and cities: 104, 105, 111, 118.

proaisymnetes: eponymous magistrate at Chersonnesos: 48.

probouleuma: at Athens, a preliminary statement on a subject (not necessarily a specific proposal) put before the assembly by the *boule*: 62.

proegoros: public attorney, as a magistracy at Samos: 64.

prohedria: privilege of front seats at public contests, frequently granted as a mark of honor: 13 (Athens).

prohedros, -oi: presiding officer of *boule* and assembly, at Athens (13, 19, 62); of the *synhedrion* (q.v.) of the Hellenic League (8, with n. 24).

prostagma, -ata: royal ordinance, usually setting forth general rules: 53.

prostates, -ai: chief civil magistrate at Kos: 17.

proxenia: status of *proxenos* (q.v.): 1 (Priene).

proxenos, -oi: originally, one who represented the interests of a foreign state in his own, but by the Hellenistic period simply a foreigner recognized as having done a service to a state. Recognition as *proxenos* (grant of *proxenia*) carried with it certain privileges: 7 (Teos), 62

(Athens), 66 (Ilion).

prytaneion: town-hall or magistrates' residence: 13, 19 (Athens), 29 (Smyrna).

prytanis, -eis: magistrate at Priene (1), Chios (2), Mytilene (5), Ephesos (9), Ilion (9), Kalynda (57), Pergamon and Temnos (59); one of the monthly presidents of *boule* and assembly at Miletos (14), Samos (63-64); at Athens, member of the tribe holding the prytany, or presidency of *boule* and assembly for one-twelfth (or one-tenth, depending on the number of tribes in existence) of the civil year: 13, 19, 62.

prytany: see *prytanis*.

satrap: provincial governor, a post in Persian administration taken over by Alexander the Great and the Seleucids: 122 (Ptolemy I as satrap).

schoinion, -a: linear measure, equal to 100 cubits; the side of one aroura: 86.

sitologos, -oi: royal officials in charge of grain revenues and supplies: 45, 85.

stater: Greek coin, of whatever weight, considered to be the standard; used in Hellenistic Egypt and elsewhere as a term for the tetradrachm, or four-drachma piece.

stathmos, -oi: lodging for a Ptolemaic soldier, especially in the house of another person from whom space was involuntarily requisitioned by the Crown.

stephanephoros, -oi: eponymous magistrate at Miletos (14, 21), Magnesia (127), Smyrna (29).

strategos, -oi: "General". City magistrate at Mytilene (5), [Priene (11)], Athens (19), Smyrna (29), Pergamon (59, 67; in 59 specified as royal appointees), Arkesine (60); the chief federal magistrate of the Achaean League (30: Orchomenos); royal officials (1) of Antigonus and Demetrius in Greece (8: Epidauros), (2) of Lysimachus in charge of Ionian cities (10: Miletos); (3) in charge of royal forces of Lysimachus (11: Priene), of Mithridates (48: Chersonnesos); (4) holders of wider supervisory commands, as Cassander of Europe (6, introd.), Polyperchon, of the Peloponnesos (6, n. 10). In Ptolemaic administration, the chief officer of military and later civil administration in a nome of Egypt or a province outside it: 27, 45, 52, 57, 83, 89, 95, 103, 107, 110, 115, 117, 121, 123, 126, 138, 142.

symbolon, -a: a convention, generally judicial or commercial in content, between two cities; see n. 187 (60: Arkesine).

symmnamones: board of magistrates at Chersonnesos (48).

synhedrion: council, frequently of a league or confederation, composed of representatives (*synhedroi*) sent by the member-states, as of the League of Corinth (2: Chios; cf. n. 2); of the Hellenic League of 302 (8: Epidauros); of the Ionian League (20: Klazomenai). Council of the city of Dyme (46).

synhedros, -oi: member of a *synhedrion* (q.v.): 8, 14 (Miletos: an *ad hoc* deliberative group), 16 (Ilion: of the Ilian confederation, cf. n. 120), 19 (of the Peloponnesian League; *ibid.*, the Athenians selected to deliberate with the Peloponnesians), 20, 30 (of the Achaean League), 46 (Miletos: an *ad hoc* deliberative group to consider the disposition of Eudemos' gift).

tagoi: chief magistrates of the Thessalian League: 31 (Larisa); and at Thessalian Chyretiai: 34.

talent: see table of currency.

taricheutes, -ai: embalmer of bodies in Egypt: 110.

taxiarch: at Athens, commander of the contingent (*taxis*) of infantry supplied by each of the tribes (19); commander of a squadron in Hellenistic armies: 108.

teichopoioi: at Miletos, board of magistrates in charge of the maintenance of the city's walls: 10, 14.

technites, -ai: skilled craftsman, applied in many documents to the theatrical artists of Dionysos who acted and performed music in Dionysiac festivals.

theokolos: eponymous priest at Dyme: 46.

theoria: an embassy dispatched on any matter having to do with religion, including groups officially sent to attend or to announce festivals and games. See *theoros*.

theoros, -oi: member of a *theoria* (q.v.): 7 (n. 17, Teos), 17 (Kos), 28 (Delphi), 57 (Kalynda), 64 (Samos), 128 (from Magnesia).

timouchoi: board of magistrates at Teos: 65.

toparch (toparchy): official of nomarch's bureau in charge of a section of a nome; his district: 69, 85, 88, 95.

topogrammateus, -eis: "local scribe" in charge of record-keeping for a district: 68, 91, 110.

trierarch: individual required, owing to his wealth, to fit out a trireme for a city's fleet: 7 (Teos); a naval commander in the Ptolemaic fleet: 99.

CONCORDANCE
Inscriptions

Publication	Bagnall-Derow
Erythrai 31	22
504	20
GHI 186	1
192	2
196	3
201	5
202	4
I. Délos 442	130
IPE I² 352	48
Ilion 32	16
33	17
34	66
Milet I 3 138	14
139	21
Moretti 44	8
OGIS 2	5
5	6
6	6
11	11
12	11
13	12
54	26
56	136
90	137
219	16
220	66
221	18
222	20
223	22
224	131
225	25
228	28
229	29
244	132
257	47
265	59
266	23
267	67
315	42
763	41
Priene 14-15	11

Papyri

INDEX OF PERSONS, PLACES AND SUBJECTS
(References are to page numbers)